T0305122

CONTESTING AVIATION EXPANSION

Depoliticisation, Technologies of Government and Post-Aviation Futures

Steven Griggs and David Howarth

First published in Great Britain in 2023 by

Policy Press, an imprint of
Bristol University Press
University of Bristol
1–9 Old Park Hill
Bristol
BS2 8BB
UK
t: +44 (0)117 374 6645
e: bup-info@bristol.ac.uk

Details of international sales and distribution partners are available at
policy.bristoluniversitypress.co.uk

© Bristol University Press 2023

British Library Cataloguing in Publication Data
A catalogue record for this book is available from the British Library

ISBN 978-1-4473-4428-5 hardcover
ISBN 978-1-4473-4430-8 ePub
ISBN 978-1-4473-4429-2 ePdf

The right of Steven Griggs and David Howarth to be identified as authors of this work has been
asserted by them in accordance with the Copyright, Designs and Patents Act 1988.

All rights reserved: no part of this publication may be reproduced, stored in a retrieval system, or
transmitted in any form or by any means, electronic, mechanical, photocopying, recording, or
otherwise without the prior permission of Bristol University Press.

Every reasonable effort has been made to obtain permission to reproduce copyrighted material. If,
however, anyone knows of an oversight, please contact the publisher.

The statements and opinions contained within this publication are solely those of the authors and
not of the University of Bristol or Bristol University Press. The University of Bristol and Bristol
University Press disclaim responsibility for any injury to persons or property resulting from any
material published in this publication.

Bristol University Press and Policy Press work to counter discrimination on grounds
of gender, race, disability, age and sexuality.

Cover design: Andrew Corbett
Front cover image: 123RF/katatonia
Bristol University Press and Policy Press use environmentally
responsible print partners.
Printed and bound in Great Britain by CPI Group (UK) Ltd, Croydon, CR0 4YY

Contents

List of figures and tables

Figure

Tables

List of abbreviations

AC	Airports Commission
ACC	Airport Consultative Committee
ACI	Airports Council International
AEF	Aviation Environment Federation
ANPS	Airports National Policy Statement
APD	Air Passenger Duty
ASA	Air Service Agreement
ATAG	Air Transport Action Group
ATWP	Air Transport White Paper
AXO	Airport eXpansion Opposition, anti-Southampton airport expansion group
BA	British Airways
BAA	British Airports Authority
CAA	Civil Aviation Authority
CBA	Cost-benefit analysis
CCA	Climate Change Act (2008)
CCC	Climate Change Committee (formerly Committee on Climate Change)
COP	Conference of the Parties
CORSIA	Carbon Offsetting and Reduction Scheme for International Aviation
DCO	Development Consent Order
DETR	Department of the Environment, Transport and the Regions
DfT	Department for Transport
EAC	House of Commons Environmental Audit Committee
ETS	Emissions trading scheme
EU	European Union
FoE	Friends of the Earth
GACC	Gatwick Area Conservation Committee
GALBA	Group for Action on Leeds Bradford Airport
GFC	Global financial crisis
GIC	Government of Singapore Investment Corporation
HACAN	Heathrow Association for the Control of Aircraft Noise
HAL	Heathrow Airport Limited
HCEB	Heathrow Community Engagement Board
HS2	Proposed high-speed rail link from London to the North West
IAG	International Airlines Group
IATA	International Air Transport Association
ICAO	International Civil Aviation Organisation
ICCAN	Independent Commission on Civil Aviation Noise
ICCT	International Council on Clean Transportation

IPC	Infrastructure Planning Commission
IPCC	Intergovernmental Panel on Climate Change
MAG	Manchester Airports Group
MP	Member of Parliament
NNI	Noise and Number Index
NPS	National Policy Statement
OECD	Organisation for Economic Co-operation and Development
PA	Planning Act (2008)
PDT	Poststructuralist Discourse Theory
RAB	Regulated Asset Base
SBAEx	Stop Bristol Airport Expansion
S-CGE	Spatial Computable General Equilibrium model
SERAS	South East and East of England Regional Air Services Study
SHE	Stop Heathrow Expansion
SNP	Scottish National Party
SSE	Stop Stansted Expansion
TC	Transport Committee
UK	United Kingdom
US	United States
USS	Universities Superannuation Scheme
VAT	Value-added Tax
ZAD	Zone to be Defended

Acknowledgements

The writing of this book has been shaped by the thoughts and reflections of a community of scholars, campaigners, practitioners and stakeholders, who have challenged our emerging arguments, exposed new lines of inquiry and helped us to refine our eventual claims and conclusions. Although we accept full responsibility for the statements and recommendations that we advance in this book, we would like to thank all those who invited us to speak at conferences and workshops, and who generously discussed and contributed to our research.

We presented initial ideas and draft chapters of the book at the following workshops: the European Consortium of Political Research (ECPR) General Conference in Bordeaux in September 2013; the Policy & Politics Conference in Bristol in September 2014; the *Journal of Environmental Policy & Planning* workshop at the University of Freiburg in October 2014; the Critical Geographies of Urban Infrastructure Conference at the Bartlett School, University College London in November 2014; the Depoliticisation and Anti-Politics workshop at York University in December 2014; the Research Seminar Series of the Department of People and Organisations at the Open University in February 2015; the Political Studies Association Conference at the University of Sheffield at the end of March 2015; the Groupe de Sociologie Pragmatique et Réflexive at the École des Hautes Études en Sciences Sociales (EHESS) in Paris in May 2015; the Economic and Social Research Council (ESRC) Advanced Training Initiative of the Social Studies of Environment & Sustainability at the University of East Anglia in June 2015; the Comparative Depoliticisation workshop at Sheffield University in June 2015; the workshop on Noise, Planning, and Democratic Governance: the Comparative Politics of Airports and Aviation Expansion at De Montfort University in September 2015, which was sponsored by *Political Quarterly*; the International Conference on Public Controversies and the Environment at the University of Marseilles in June 2016; the workshop on Activist Dilemmas, Environmental Politics and Airport Protests at Nottingham Trent University in June 2016, sponsored by the ESRC; the Comparative Peri-urban Infrastructures workshop at De Montfort University in May 2017; the Politics of Numbers within Technologies of Governance at the University of Essex in April 2019; the DESIRE Conference: New Directions in Discourse Theory, at the Free University of Brussels, Belgium in May 2019; the ECPR workshops in Toulouse in April 2021 (convened online); the Second Politics of Numbers workshop at the University of Essex in May 2021; the Public Administration & Policy Group's Food for Thought seminar series at Wageningen University in February 2022; the workshop Seeing Democracy Like A City: Practices, Movements, State, at the University of Glasgow in June 2022; and the Essex Summer School in July 2022.

We would also like to thank Jonathan Saks, then Deputy Director of Aviation and Maritime Analysis at the Department for Transport, for inviting us to present our research on the power and influence of local campaigns and campaigning in aviation policymaking in April 2018. We have enjoyed many conversations with local campaigners and environmental activists from across the UK and Europe, who have generously given their time to exchange ideas and support our work, notably those campaigning against expansion at Bristol, Gatwick, Heathrow, Manchester and Stansted, and Frankfurt, Munich, Nantes, Paris and Schiphol.

We have thus benefitted immensely from the comments, criticisms and thoughts of many people in a wide range of contexts. In particular, we would like to thank Heidrun Åm, Neil Barnett, Jane Bennett, Jelle Behagel, Peter Bloom, Lucy Budd, Jim Buller, David Carter, Francis Chateauraynaud, William Connolly, Josquin Debaz, Pinar Dönmez, Geoff Dudley, Dan Durrant, Peter Feindt, Alan Finlayson, Frank Fischer, Richard Freeman, Jeff Gazzard, Jason Glynos, Henri Gracineau, Jaap de Groot, Valeria Guarneros-Meza, Stephen Hall, Charlotte Halpern, Graeme Hayes, Steve Ison, Stephen Jeffares, Tim Johnson, Reiner Keller, Geneviève Lebouteux, Tim Marshall, Aysem Mert, Tamara Metze, Aletta Norval, Konstantinos Roussos, Mark Smalley, Florian Sperk, Adam Standring, Jan Starke, John Stewart, Helen Sullivan, Imrat Verhoeven, Hendrik Wagenaar, Rebecca Warren, John Wincott, Matt Wood and Dvora Yanow for either inviting us to present our ideas or to participate in discussions, or often both. We are especially thankful to our graduate students, early career researchers and colleagues in the Department of Government and the Centre for Ideology and Discourse Analysis (CiDA) at the University of Essex, the Department of Politics, People and Place at De Montfort University and the School of Justice, Security and Sustainability at Staffordshire University, for their ongoing support and critical engagement during the course of this study.

We would like to thank the anonymous reviewers of our manuscript for their helpful comments and Emily Watt, Anna Richardson and Freya Trand, our editor and editorial assistants at Bristol University Press, for their continued support and enthusiasm throughout this lengthy project. Our thanks also go to Helen Flitton, our project manager at Newgen Publishing, for her invaluable advice and forbearance in preparing the final manuscript.

Finally, we would like to thank Aletta, James, Madeline, Martha and Ruth for enduring the lows – and occasional highs – in the researching and writing of this book. Their constant support, patience, understanding and intellectual contributions are greatly received and appreciated, making it all worthwhile.

Introduction: Problematising the dilemmas of UK airport expansion – puzzles and research strategies

Perhaps nothing better illustrates our current obsession with air travel than the rise of scenic 'joy flights' for passengers 'missing the excitement of travel' during the COVID-19 pandemic (Choat, 2020).[1] Tickets for one such 7-hour round trip from Sydney on Qantas sold out within 10 minutes, making it one of the airline's fastest selling flights ever. Seat prices on the 10 October flight ranged from £607 economy to £2,750 for business class. Employing 787 Dreamliner aircraft normally used for long-haul international flights, Qantas's Great Southern Land flight promised to fly as low as 1,220 metres over New South Wales, the Northern Territory and Queensland, giving passengers the chance to see Australia's most famous landmarks, including Sydney harbour, Uluru and the Great Barrier Reef. A Qantas advert for the trip promised it would 'reignite the joy of flying', adding that 'from the sky, there are no border restrictions'. In its defence, Qantas pleaded that it was not alone in offering its customers 'flights to nowhere' as airlines strived to generate business in the midst of global restrictions on air travel. Yet, it is still extraordinary that just months after forest fires devastated Australia, and after scientific studies concluded that global warming 'boosts' the hot dry weather likely to cause bush fires by at least 30 per cent, people were still clamouring to take unnecessary pleasure flights (Ghosh, 2020). Ironically, Qantas publicly promoted its commitment to tackling climate change through a 'simple philosophy: measure, reduce, offset and influence'.[2]

That such flights were over-subscribed epitomises how far the consumption of flying has for many become an integral part of their everyday enjoyment and routines. This was not lost on Qantas, whose chief executive was quick to justify the flights as a response to customer demand, pointing out that 'so many of our frequent fliers are used to being on a plane every other week and have been telling us they miss the experience of flying as much as the destinations themselves' (McGregor, 2020). More generally, it is shocking that in some quarters the plane has become an 'acceptable' substitute for the coach or train, even for short domestic trips. In mid-October 2021, 2 weeks before the opening of the United Nations Climate Change Conference in Glasgow, the first team squad of Manchester United Football Club took a 10-minute flight to get to its Premier League match against Leicester City. The club explained away the decision to fly as a 'bid to beat congestion' on the motorway (McCarthy, 2021).

Contesting Aviation Expansion exposes these obsessions and pathologies, as well as the efforts by states and public authorities to sponsor the aviation industry over many decades, often in the face of hostile protests and political campaigning, as well as growing scientific evidence of the impact of flying on rising carbon emissions and climate change. As researchers in the field of aviation policy and politics for more than 25 years, we have become increasingly frustrated at how governments have persistently backed the expansion of the aviation industry, while fuelling the ideological and fantasmatic narratives of 'technological fixes' and 'sustainable aviation' in their efforts to defuse persistent opposition to airport expansion. Our book thus sheds light on the technologies and techniques that have been developed by UK governments and the state in their multifarious practices to *depoliticise* the contradictions and political oppositions thrown up by plans for aviation expansion and/or the desire to create new airport infrastructures.

But our genealogical narratives of these processes also provide the critical resources to enable us to articulate our normative commitments and alternative visions vis-à-vis the continued expansion of aviation. Indeed, we make the case for a radical re-routing of airport and aviation policy along a path of degrowth, which can bring about the just transition and transformation of the aviation industry as a whole. With no viable technological fix in aviation currently available or likely to emerge in the foreseeable future, we cannot continue to indulge our seemingly unquenchable desire for, and acceptance of, 'binge flying', oblivious and disregarding of the cost for local communities, the vast majority of the population who do not fly, not to mention the planet. Moreover, it is important to stress that our alternative imaginary is not plucked out of thin air, but emerges from our genealogical interpretations and deconstructive readings of key episodes in the post-war state sponsorship of aviation in the UK. Bringing together and developing Thomas Princen's 'logic of sufficiency' and the ideals and values of an 'alternative hedonism', which have been elegantly advocated by Kate Soper, articulated within an overarching project of radical democracy, we thus set out a manifesto to disinvest from aviation, which can furnish the conditions to institute a just resolution of the dilemmas of flying in a post-COVID-19 and sustainable world.

Our book also shows that far from a niche topic of marginal interest, the problem of aviation and its attendant infrastructure needs is a *paradigmatic* issue of our time, highlighting a number of salient material, political and symbolic features of contemporary society. The dilemmas surrounding UK airports policy illuminate a cluster of adjacent problems and pressing issues in the present, where the aviation industry functions as a hinge between a host of social practices and a series of intercalated processes in the natural world. Aeromobilities have long been connected to the logics of globalisation and neoliberalism, as airlines and airports are fundamental to the fast mobility of people, global business and the efficient movement of goods in late capitalism (Cwerner et al, 2009). Equally, as sites of neoliberal accumulation strategies, airports have often been at the forefront of the logics of privatisation, deregulation and outsourcing (Vernon, 2021).

But, importantly for our analysis, airports are also an integral component of the increasingly prominent politics and ideology of large infrastructure projects, in which the state (and other powerful actors) is immersed in governing an array of competing social forces and citizens (see Roberts, 2010: 90). Infrastructures are 'built networks', which shape and 'facilitate' our systems of social relations (Larkin, 2013: 328), furnishing the production of carbon-based (or other forms of) energy; giving us the capacity to move things, information and people over large distances; and guaranteeing the availability of healthy drinking water, clean air, adequate supplies of water for irrigation and other goods and services, which are vital to our social well-being, though they are also the harbinger of public bads, such as polluted air and contaminated water (Mitchell, 2014: 438; 2020). In so doing, they structure our practices and interactions with the natural world. As Timothy Mitchell concludes, the building of infrastructure is implicated in 'a politics of nature', in which the planning and provision of its grids and networks must negotiate questions of 'the scarcity, pollution, depletion, fair distribution, and subsequent disposal of available reserves'. Indeed, nature is in many respects 'produced' in and through infrastructures, where 'the spaces, flows, measures, and calculations out of which infrastructures are built create the most common forms in which humans, encounter and measure the reserves of nature – or experience their lack' (Mitchell, 2014: 438).

Increasingly, too, campaigns against airport expansion and other large infrastructure projects serve as vectors for broad struggles against late capitalism. Traditional issues like noise, planning and land use, housing prices and compensation, often misleadingly bracketed as NIMBY concerns, have been accompanied by growing concerns about air pollution and the devastation of biodiversity caused by tourism, as well as the exposure of streams, rivers and wetlands to pollutants discharged in storm water runoff from airports. But it is climate change, and especially aviation's ever-increasing carbon emissions, which has rapidly amplified the policy dilemmas facing the aviation industry and its appetite for more airports and other infrastructures, as well as its reliance on fossil fuels. Eco-politics, concerns about peak oil and the future of fossil fuel companies, and the demands for climate justice have heightened debates about the future development of the aviation industry, prompting the search for solutions, whether in the form of technological fixes and more efficient aircraft, emissions caps and trading, the search for bio-fuels, and other modernising strategies, or more radical approaches and demands to divest from aviation, moving even to its 'phasing out' (Buck, 2021; see also Mitchell, 2011; Princen et al, 2015).

In fact, the current structures and tendencies of the aviation industry and the airports question highlight three sharp contradictions: the tension between the logic of continued economic growth, and the moral and political imperatives of environmental protection; demands for the 'freedom to fly' versus a more sustainable and socially just, post-mobile world; and the antagonisms between, on the one hand, the interests of global tourism, the leisure industry, and 'passenger-consumers' and, on the other hand, the possibilities of new forms of enjoyment and pleasure, which both secure the planet for future generations and procure more rewarding lifestyles. Put differently, it is striking that many citizens often say that they want action on climate change, but governments and industry encourage them to fly, and many passenger-consumers often do.

Such tensions and antagonisms are increasingly experienced in other parts of Western Europe and across the globe. In 2020, Environmental Justice and Stay Grounded mapped over 300 plans for airport expansion where there was evidence of conflict, mostly over land acquisition.[3] Campaigns against expansion have been successful in delaying projects or forcing governments to abandon them. In early 2013, the Italian government cancelled plans to develop Viterbo airport in northern Lazio as the 'third airport of Rome', partly because of sustained citizen protest. The proposed construction of a third runway at Munich airport was halted after a concerted campaign of action, although plans are due to be reviewed in 2028. There have been major protests at Frankfurt against aircraft noise and in Berlin about the flight paths, delays and spiralling costs surrounding the long-overdue Brandenburg Airport. Most spectacularly, in Nantes, an alliance of peasant farmers, local residents, anarchists and environmentalists, successfully prevented the building of a new international airport near the village of Notre-Dame-des-Landes on the outskirts of the French city (Griggs and Howarth, 2020).

Of course, in other contexts, especially in China, India and the Middle East, the building of new airports and runways has proceeded very rapidly as the centre of gravity of global aviation markets has shifted to emerging markets (Bowen, 2013, 2019). But such expansion has also been controversial. In Turkey, the new Istanbul Grand Airport opened in April 2019 and it is planned to have a capacity of 150 million passengers per year when fully operational. However, its construction was dogged by violent disputes, notably as workers went on strike against poor working conditions and health and safety concerns, which earned the construction site of the airport the nickname of 'the cemetery'. Links were also made between the building of the airport and the protests against the plans to destroy Gezi Park – one of the few remaining green spaces in the centre of the European side of Istanbul – which began in May 2013 (Garner-Purkis, 2019). Indeed, in many parts of the world the frequency and scale of protest against airport expansion continues to grow, as governments and citizens find themselves caught on the horns of a dilemma: they must try to balance the interests of business, consumers and tourists against the demands of environmental protection and the needs of local communities. In short, airports and aviation constitute a growing global challenge, whose multiple dimensions and ramifications are becoming increasingly evident.

A growing global challenge: airports and aviation in context

In 2019, approximately 4.5 billion passengers travelled on 46.8 million scheduled flights that were offered by 1,478 commercial airline companies working out of 3,780 airports across the globe – a total of 8.68 trillion passenger kilometres flown in just 12 months. Every day 12.5 million passengers took to the sky, flying on 128,000 flights that shipped $18 billion worth of goods (equivalent over the year to 35 per cent of world trade by value). This mass transit through our skies supported 87.7 million jobs – 11.3 million of them directly in airlines, airport operators, on-airport jobs, civil aerospace and air navigation service providers. Globally, this amounted to an estimated economic impact of $3.5 trillion or 4.1 per cent of global GDP (ATAG, 2020a: 10–12).

The COVID-19 pandemic threw commercial aviation into crisis, with a 60 per cent fall in global passenger numbers in 2020, equivalent to 2.699 billion passengers (ICAO, 2021a). The fall in passengers exposed the fragile economics of many airlines and airports in a sector that has been littered with the high-profile failure of carriers (including the bankruptcy of airlines such as Monarch, Flybe, Wow and Air Berlin). Yet, despite what many industry watchers currently see as the 'loss' of 2 years of growth in passenger demand, it is widely forecast that aviation will return to 2019 levels of activity by the mid-2020s (Eurocontrol, 2021; IATA, 2021). Over the long-term, it is predicted that aviation will experience 3.6 per cent annual growth in revenue passenger kilometres from 2018 to 2050, with passenger numbers in China and India growing between 2019 and 2040 by 1,023 million and 293.5 million respectively (IATA, 2021; ICAO, 2021b). In the past, global passenger numbers have usually bounced back after global economic crises. This was the case, for example, after the oil crisis in 1973 and the global financial crisis (GFC) in 2008. The general direction of travel has thus been upwards, with increases in passenger numbers accelerating in the last 20 years: 310.4 million passengers in 1970; 1.67 billion in 2000; 2.7 billion in 2010; and 4.378 billion in 2019 (ICAO, 2019a; World Bank, 2020).

A return to such patterns of growth will put increasing pressures on governments in their efforts to meet international climate change commitments. Commercial aviation contributes approximately 2.4 per cent of global carbon emissions from fossil fuel use (ICCT, 2019: 1). And this contribution to anthropogenic global warming does not consider military flights and private jets, which accounted respectively for 8 per cent and 4 per cent of aviation fuel use and carbon emissions in 2018 (commercial passenger aviation accounted for 71 per cent and commercial freight for 17 per cent) (Gössling and Humpe, 2020: 3). But flying also contributes to non-CO_2 radiative forcing, releasing nitrogen oxides and producing contrails high in the atmosphere. Its contribution to human global warming thus rises to 3.5 per cent of effective radiative forcing once its non-CO_2 impacts are calculated. In fact, the formation of contrail cirrus and the release of NO_x account for 66 per cent of the effective radiative forcing impacts of aviation (Lee and Forster, 2020).

Even more disturbingly, the contribution of aviation to global warming has accelerated in recent years as passenger numbers have grown, and fuel efficiencies have not kept pace with rising passenger numbers. Nearly 50 per cent of the total historical cumulative emissions of CO_2 from aviation since 1940 were released into the atmosphere in the last 20 years (Lee et al, 2021: 4). This contribution to global warming is expected to triple by 2050, coming to represent potentially 25 per cent of the global carbon budget as other sectors decarbonise (ICCT, 2019: 1), and there is no readily available technological fix of either electric or hydrogen planes or sustainable aviation fuel that can replace kerosene-dependent aircraft engines. Moreover, the production of sustainable aviation fuels will require the putting aside of large areas of agricultural land for aviation, as well as large scale investments in infrastructure. Still, it is estimated that even with targeted policy support, the production of sustainable aviation fuel will meet little more than 5.5 per cent of jet fuel demand in the EU by 2030 (ICCT, 2021). Hence, for the increasing numbers of those that fly, it is likely that aviation will remain a high proportion of their individual emissions – a roundtrip economy domestic flight of 75 minutes from London Stansted to Edinburgh equates to almost half of the maximum amount of CO_2 that can be generated by a single person in a year if we are to stop climate change.[4]

Yet, despite the efforts by governments and the aviation industry to convince us otherwise, it is important to recognise that not everyone flies. In fact, flying reflects and reinforces social inequalities, posing significant challenges of environmental justice. First, 90 per cent of the global population does not fly in any given year. Of those who do fly, between 11 and 26.5 per cent report just one trip per year (Gössling and Humpe, 2020: 7–8). Half of the world's population was responsible for only 10 per cent of all emissions from commercial flights in 2018 (ICCT, 2019: 7). In other words, flying is at best a very uneven practice, with different populations and countries responsible for the majority of emissions. In 2019, flights departing from airports in the United States emitted 23 per cent of global airline passenger transport-related CO_2, two thirds of these emissions coming from domestic flights. The three largest aviation markets, the United States, the EU (19 per cent) and China (13 per cent), were responsible for over half of all airline passenger CO_2 emissions (ICCT, 2020: 10).

Secondly, within mature aviation markets such as the UK's, despite the increased popularisation of flying, it remains the case that a minority of highly mobile frequent flyers account for the majority of emissions from aviation. In England, an estimated 46 per cent of all households participated in flights in 2017–2018. But the top 20 per cent of flyers accounted for approximately three-quarters of all flights (Büchs and Mattioli, 2021: 95–100). Globally, 'super-emitters', the 10 per cent of the most frequent fliers, some of whom can undertake up to 300 trips per year, emit more than half of global CO_2 emissions from commercial air travel. When added to non-CO_2 radiative forcing impacts, this suggests that 'super-emitters' might contribute to global warming at a rate that is 225,000 times higher than the global poor (Gössling and Humpe, 2020: 9). And given that flying is a highly income-elastic activity, inequalities are likely to accentuate as the social and economic impacts of the COVID-19 pandemic unfold – low-income groups and other less privileged groups reduce air travel more than richer households when economies enter recession (Büchs and Mattioli, 2021: 99).

Such inequalities and environmental injustices are amplified when the impacts of flying on local communities living near airports and under flight paths are added to the disbenefits of aviation. Aircraft noise impacts on memory and learning in children, disturbs sleep, and has been linked to long-term health problems, including cardiovascular disease, as well as impacts on mental health through increases in stress and anxiety (Banatvala et al, 2019). People living under the flightpath at Heathrow Airport are 10–20 per cent more at risk of stroke and heart disease than those living outside the flight path (Hansell et al, 2013), while over 1 million people in the UK live in areas where aircraft noise over a 24-hour period is above recommended levels, with close to 600,000 people experiencing night-time aviation noise above 48 dBA Lnight, far higher than WHO recommended levels (AEF, 2016a: 5). At the same time, air pollution from aircraft exhaust fumes, road traffic at and around airports, and emissions from ground service equipment contributes to the risk of heart disease, stroke, lung diseases and lung cancer. Airport-related air pollution has been documented some 20 miles from runways.[5]

The social inequalities and environmental impacts generated in particular by commercial aviation problematise our motivations and justifications for flying. The expansion of flying has come on the back of rises in leisure and not business flights. It has been calculated that 57 per cent of international tourists, or 1.4 billion people per year, travel by plane (ICAO, 2019b: 19), while in the UK 'three times as many passengers take flights for leisure as fly on business' (Airports Commission, 2015a: 69). Yet, when asked in retrospect to rate the relative importance of the flights that they had undertaken, student frequent flyers deemed almost half of the leisure flights that they had undertaken to be of 'indifferent' importance, 'of limited importance' or 'not important at all' (Gössling et al, 2019: 8). The environmental impacts of such flights cannot so easily be dismissed.

Approaching the airports and aviation problem

There are multiple ways of describing and explaining the impacts and contradictions of airport expansion and the growth of aviation in the UK and beyond. Various studies have used different theoretical lenses to furnish competing ways of conceptualising the issue. One important strand of scholarship focuses on the political economy of the industry, and the planning and management of its expansion in the context of capitalism (Doganis, 2006; Bowen, 2010; Budd and Ison, 2020; Young, 2020). Other accounts emphasise the dominant logics of technocracy and scientific expertise at play in the planning and building of new airports, runways and terminals (Feldman and Milch, 1982, 1983), as well as patterns of local resident protest and campaigning (McKie, 1973; Perman, 1973), which for much of the 20th century were mostly focused on the problems of aviation noise, adequate compensation, fear of accidents and air pollution (Stevenson, 1972; Nelkin, 1974; Stratford, 1974; Bednarek, 2016), though this period also brought (in Japan notably) the emergence of radical social movements and wider ideological struggles, which formed alongside them (Apter and Sawa, 1984; Apter, 1987). At the same time, scholars emphasise the instrumental calculations by state institutions about the location of infrastructure, some focusing on the strategic interactions between the democratic state and the organisational structure and power of civil society (Aldrich, 2008), and others on the failures of planning processes and the governance of large infrastructure projects more generally (Hall, 1982; Feldman, 1985; Flyvbjerg et al, 2003).

More recently, a number of detailed accounts of the UK airport dilemma itself have appeared (Le Blond, 2019; Hicks, 2022). Le Blond's insider story of the plans to expand London's airport capacity underlines the discontinuities and pathologies of aviation policy and planning processes, which he characterises as the politics of 'muddling through', which is often applied to British policy-making more generally (Le Blond, 2019: 34; see also Feldman, 1985). According to Le Blond, the challenge for all stakeholders, both the aviation industry and local communities, is the absence of long-term policy stability, particularly the 'counter-decisions' that have reversed policies and commitments in recent years (Le Blond, 2019: 139). Drawing on his professional experience, he advocates an incremental approach that is predicated on providing for growth when it arises, coupled with a legal commitment to a defined level of development, the safeguarding of land and 'early, proactive and generous compensation' (Le Blond, 2019: 168).

8

An interesting facet of Le Blond's intervention is that he tends to downplay environmental issues and concerns. On the one hand, his analysis privileges concerns over noise and air pollution, while backgrounding climate change and rising emissions from aviation, even though he is confident that the 'noise impact' of an airport like Heathrow 'is probably not going to get any worse' (2019: 43). On the other hand, he accepts that climate change will have little impact on the growth of passenger demand, either through increasing awareness of individuals of the impact of flying on the environment or through proposed schemes of emissions trading, reproducing claims that carbon emissions is a national and international issue rather than one consigned to individual airports (2019: 45). So, although he recognises the significant environmental challenges posed by UK airport expansion, he nonetheless argues that they 'can be met with strict controls, such as a night-flight ban and adherence to legal limits on air quality', together with the development of 'innovative measures' to deal with the problems of surface access, which include 'the electrification of the hotel and car park bus networks and the creation of gateways at the airport perimeter for private car access, alongside the [funding of] new rail links' (Le Blond, 2018: 13). Hence, in many ways, as we demonstrate in Chapter 3, Le Blond's analyses and recommendations resonate with that of Howard Davies and the Airports Commission (AC), repeating the latter's assertions that Heathrow expansion is the best option to meet growing demand for air travel compatible with UK carbon commitments (2019: 161–66).

By contrast, Celeste Hicks's *Expansion Rebellion: Using the Law to Fight a Runway and Save the Planet*, puts the contradictions between airport expansion and climate change at the heart of her narrative. Navigating the complex steps of the judicial review against the proposed third runway at Heathrow Airport in 2019, she charts how environmental lawyers constructed their case against the Airports National Policy Statement (ANPS) in 2018, in which they argued that the plans for the third runway were incompatible with the UK's international climate change commitments under the Paris Agreement, and that the government had failed to meet its duties under the Planning Act (2008) in giving the go-ahead for expansion. Drawing on her skills as an investigative journalist, Hicks's careful analysis recognises the limits of such legal strategies, and describes how the judicial review ultimately failed in the Supreme Court in December 2020. However, her study also underlines the symbolic capacity of legal challenges to hold decision-makers to account, and to disclose 'loopholes' and contradictions in the rationales for airport expansion. She also argues that legal challenges serve to delay plans for expansion, while capturing public attention and heightening the awareness of the climate emergency. Overall, in light of the Paris Agreement and the Heathrow case, her research demonstrates the increasing use of the courts by campaigners, while suggesting that new avenues of legal challenge will be required by campaigners and protesters, as existing appeals on the grounds of the Paris commitment to keep the rise in global temperature to 1.5 °C are exhausted and sidelined by the policy agenda of net zero (Hicks, 2022: 198).

Often focused on different objects, and viewed from different theoretical vantage points, it is noticeable that most accounts draw attention, either implicitly or explicitly, to the *politics* of aviation and airport expansion. Indeed, one clear message of existing studies and interpretations is that politics matters. Nevertheless, in our view, they fail to shed adequate light on the deep and persistent value conflicts underpinning the politics of airport expansion, which have become increasingly salient with the rise of environmentalism, eco-politics and the challenges of climate change, and they do not explain how and why particular strategies and tactics have been pursued by differently positioned actors and groups (Griggs and Howarth, 2013; 2019a). Existing interpretations also neglect the complex interplays between the way governments and states have sought to ensure the delivery of airport expansion, and the struggles for hegemony within and across the aviation sector, as well as the ethical and normative implications of such struggles for disclosing new counter-logics and alternatives to expansion.

The UK airports and aviation dilemma

Extending and developing our earlier analyses of citizen protests against airport expansions (Griggs and Howarth, 2002), and the different logics of policymaking (Griggs and Howarth, 2013), our book draws upon, deconstructs and reworks the existing interpretations to provide a more comprehensive account of the exemplary case of UK aviation expansion. We begin by problematising the UK airports dilemma in more concrete terms. At least since the mid-1960s, and certainly since the mid-1990s, there have been considerable economic and political pressures to expand the UK's airport capacity, especially in South East England. Major debates and conflicts about airport capacity were evident in the proposals to develop London's Third Airport in the 1960s and 1970s, mostly focused on the Roskill Commission and its recommendations, and airport capacity has been a bone of contention for many other communities and places affected by airport expansions across the country since that time. More recent endeavours to develop a national policy of aviation and airport expansion at the turn of the new millennium by the Labour government, and subsequent drives to build a third runway at Heathrow, have only intensified the ongoing controversies and struggles.

Less than a year and a half after the Brown government gave the go-ahead for a proposed third runway at Heathrow in early 2009, the new Coalition government imposed a moratorium on any new runways in South East England, only then to overturn this commitment following the deliberations of the AC and its recommendation to support the building of a third runway at Heathrow in 2015. The May government subsequently endorsed this recommendation 3 years later when it published the ANPS in 2018, though the ANPS was successfully challenged in the courts in March 2020, just as the COVID-19 pandemic led to the collapse of global air traffic, alleviating the immediate pressures for airport expansion, at least in terms of passenger numbers. The vacillations and uncertainties of Brexit, and the reversal of the legal challenge to the ANPS by the Supreme Court in December 2020, only served to complicate the saga further.

For nigh on 60 years, then, it is striking that despite the state sponsorship of aviation expansion, plans for the construction or expansion of new runways in the UK have often been delayed, stalled or simply cancelled. Policy reversals and failures, implementation gaps and government hesitations, citizen opposition and legal disputes in various spaces all mark the uneven trajectories of airport and aviation policy. As various Transport Ministers have lamented, the UK has failed to build a new full-length runway in the south-east since the 1940s, leaving the construction of Manchester's second runway, which became operational in 2001, as the sole major runway project successfully completed in this period, though this project itself engendered the emergence of new forms of environmental protest, which linked local communities and direct action protesters, and was heavily contested (Griggs and Howarth, 2002).

In short, one core issue that immediately animates this book arises from the inability of successive UK governments to devise, execute and implement their desired plans to expand airport capacity in the South East of England and across the UK, especially their failure to win the consent of affected subjects and constituencies. Although this issue can be named and characterised in various ways using different theoretical idioms, we draw mainly on Poststructuralist Discourse Theory (PDT) (Glynos and Howarth, 2007; Howarth, 2013; Laclau and Mouffe, 2014) to construct the puzzle as a *deep and intractable policy controversy*, which foregrounds opposed values and ideals about the role of aviation and airports in society at large. Such issues generate antagonisms and persistent disagreements, which are fuelled not simply by rival claims to expertise, but also by incompatible values and rival representations of the very policy problem to be addressed (Schön and Rein, 1994). Rather than the search for a rational solution within the existing terms of the policy and political debate, the airports issue is thus best viewed as an ongoing hegemonic battle between rival forces with opposed values about the rules and policies that should govern aviation, the polity, the organisation of social relations and our relations with the natural world in general.

The argument

In addressing these issues, the central argument of *Contesting Aviation Expansion* focuses on the primary role of politics in shaping the complex problems and proposed solutions of UK airports policy. Since the rapid development of modern aviation in the 1950s and 1960s there has been an increasing *politicisation* of the UK airport's issue, evident in growing citizen contestation, legal challenges and policy failures, at least in the eyes of the governing elites. Beneath the myriad disputes about the necessity, location and character of particular airport expansions reside deeper clashes of value driven by alternative visions of travel, consumption, leisure, social organisation and the way we ought to live.

Our main claim in the book is that successive UK governments have failed in their efforts to *depoliticise* the issue through the development of various technologies and techniques, and have been unable to broker a workable policy solution to their dilemmas. Instead, they have run up against the fundamental challenge of the political in its various guises: the multiple contradictions, growing antagonisms and ideological struggles, which mark the ongoing battle for policy hegemony in this overdetermined field. Alongside the ongoing concerns about noise, compensation, air pollution and the disruption of everyday life, this hegemonic struggle has been complexified by the growing salience of carbon emissions, climate change and eco-politics – locally, nationally and globally – as well as the emergence of new strategies and tactics, which are conducted in novel spaces and at different levels of the political order.

The elaboration of our argument corroborates and strengthens the pioneering work of Feldman and Milch (1982) on the importance of forecasting and numbers in shaping airport politics, while our analysis of the campaigns against airport expansion, particularly against proposals for a third runway at Heathrow, chime with Apter and Sawa's (1984) study of the struggles against Narita Airport in Japan during the 1970s and 1980s, albeit without the accompanying political violence. We also build upon Hicks's focus on the growing importance of legal challenges and battles in airport politics, especially in the case of Heathrow, but elsewhere too. Unlike Le Blond (2019), however, we place greater emphasis on the growing significance of climate change and rising carbon emission for characterising and resolving the airport problem, and our book sets out a series of demands that in our view have to be satisfied to tackle the issue. Our detailed characterisations of UK cases over an extended time period, especially the peculiar path dependency of Heathrow Airport, also contributes contextual detail to Aldrich's (2008) path-breaking study of the site location of 'public bads' (such as dams, nuclear power stations and airports), which is focused mainly on Japan and France. Hence, we endorse the importance of the organisation and strength of civil society in explaining the politics of airport expansion, but also highlight the peculiar path dependency of Heathrow Airport, and the great planning disaster surrounding Roskill and the mythical third London airport, and the inconsistencies of forming and exercising political will right up to the present.

Table 0.1: Problematising the politics of 'predict and provide' in UK aviation policy

	Problems	Critical conjunctures
P1	Building an aviation industry in post-war Britain.	1946–1958
P2	Dealing with growing consumer demand in South East England.	1968–1973
P3	Enhancing competitiveness and meeting growing consumer demand in progressively deregulated skies.	1986–1992
P4	Balancing demands for expansion with environmental constraints.	2000–2003
P5	Making aviation and airports policy sustainable in a context of unprecedented climate change.	2010–2011
P6	Increasing airport capacity in South East England, protecting the position of London as a global city, and balancing demands for expansion with environmental constraints.	2012–2015
P7	Coping with legal challenges and COVID-19 in the face of dislocations and radical critique of the aviation industry.	2020–2021

Problematising the problematisations

Our analysis of the critical problematisations of airports policy in seven key historical conjunctures, corresponding to seven problematisations (see Table 0.1), and the genealogical narrative that we piece together on their basis, shows that the actual and perceived political costs of expansion at various moments has produced delay and policy reversal, epitomised by the current stalemate blocking the expansion of Heathrow. Such costs were allied to the inability of government or the industry to constitute an effective political will, as well as the changing dynamics and imperatives of electoral and party politics, all of which were played out in a context of unpredictable events and changing pressures. Indeed, over time, shifting institutional rules and configurations, fluctuating economic markets and changing demands came together to focus political attention on different policy problems and issues.

In analysing the way these questions were addressed by the main actors and institutions, the broad sweep of our genealogy concludes that the implementation of the logic of 'predict and provide' in different conjunctures has only served to politicise the expansions and infrastructure projects that were proposed or decided upon. Local communities, groups and politicians vigorously opposed proposals in their own backyards and constituencies, and often blocked or delayed expansion plans (see Table 0.2). Over time, particular demands about specific expansions in dispersed areas and regions were contingently connected together to forge more universal national coalitions (such as AirportWatch) against aviation policy, provoking in turn

Table 0.2: The anti-airport expansion campaigning community: local groups

No Third Runway Coalition (Heathrow)	Stop Luton Airport Expansion (SLAE)
HACAN (Heathrow Association for the Control of Aircraft Noise)	Aircraft Expansion Opposition Southampton (AXO)
Stop Heathrow Expansion (SHE)	Group for Action on Leeds Bradford Airport (GALBA)
Teddington Action Group (TAG)	
Richmond Heathrow Campaign	Stop Bristol Airport Expansion (SBAEx)
West Windsor Residents Association	Bristol Airport Action Network (BAAN)
Stansted Airport Watch (incorporating Stop Stansted Expansion)	Stop Airport Expansion and Noise (SAEN Southend)
Gatwick Area Conservation Campaign (GACC)	Edinburgh Airport Watch
Communities Against Gatwick Noise Emissions (CAGNE)	Stop Expansion of Manchester Airport (SEMA)
	Campaign Against the Re-Opening of Manston Airport (CARMA)
Luton And District Association for the Control of Aircraft Noise (LADACAN)	Aircraft Noise Action Group: Newcastle Airport

pro-expansion coalitions like Freedom to Fly and Back Heathrow. Moreover, this politicisation generated novel methods of campaigning and political struggle, including direct action and legal activism; the disclosure of new dimensions of politics, especially with respect to the environmental and ecological issues; and the construction of different political spaces, such as protest camps, corporate meetings and the courts, within which to conduct their campaigns.

In the face of political resistance, and as decisions and planning became more complex and controversial, governments have brought forth a panoply of supplementary political and ideologico-fantasmatic logics designed to secure the consent or compliance of affected parties, and to defuse the growing antagonisms constructed against governments and powerholders. One of the principal aims of government has thus been to try and depoliticise aviation policy. Such supplementary logics have taken the form of different technologies of government – public inquiries, expert commissions and national consultations – coupled with a battery of data-gathering and decision-making techniques, including cost-benefit analysis, forecasting, scenario planning and statistical probabilistic modelling. But they have also involved the invention and elaboration of new rhetoric, fantasmatic images and the use of various heresthetic operations, often operating alongside the more formal avenues of representation and interest mediation, in the repeated quest to engineer a policy settlement to facilitate aviation expansion and economic growth.

Finally, it has brought the development of new institutions and public bodies designed to engage and involve affected local residents, airport communities and everyday citizens in the management of issues like noise, air quality and compensation, as government and corporate interests, including airlines and airports, have sought to legitimise plans and operations. Such institutions include, for example, the Independent Commission on Civil Aviation Noise (ICCAN) and the Community Engagement Board for Heathrow Airport (HCEB). The ICCAN was established in 2019 with a 2-year mission to assess the management of aviation noise across the UK, and to generate alternative ways of working for the aviation industry, government and local communities, though it ceased to operate on 30 September 2021. The HCEB, whose strategic objectives were shaped around the two roles of an Airport Consultative Committee (ACC) and a Community Engagement Board (CEB), was set up in the wake of the recommendations of the Airport Commission to smooth over the construction of a third runway at Heathrow. Its function was to enable communities to scrutinise, challenge and effectively contribute to the decisions made by the Airport.[6]

But in many respects these endeavours to legitimise and win support have also failed. In fact, the plans and proposals for expansion or development have been immensely complicated by a growing awareness of deepening environmental problems, such as climate change, new concerns about air quality and the financing of large-scale projects in an era of neoliberal governance where governments are reluctant or seemingly unable to finance projects from the public purse. At the same time, campaigners have also skilfully exploited different technologies to re-politicise aviation, while contesting plans for expansion across alternative arenas and spaces, including parliament, select committees, universities and other scientific bodies, the different trenches of civil society, the media, the law courts and so on. Indeed, within and across these different arenas, protesters and campaigners have used multiple strategies, tactics and forms of agency, including lobbying, direct action and media campaigns, while building novel alliances and equivalences between heterogeneous demands. In other words, efforts to depoliticise aviation have exposed the complex dialectics of politicisation and depoliticisation, and their impact on the struggle for policy hegemony.

Over the years, as the regime of expansion, and its political rationality of 'predict and provide', has come under growing and sustained political pressure, so the problem of aviation has mutated into a deep policy controversy, which is proving increasingly difficult, if not impossible, to resolve politically. Counter-hegemonic demands and visions have begun to percolate in different spaces and sites, as the dominant logics of economic growth, leisure and mobility have been challenged in the name of alternatives modes of pleasurable living – conjuring up the possibility of a 'new' politics of aviation to which we endeavour to contribute through the articulation of a manifesto for aviation degrowth. Here the critico-normative aspect of our study advances a counter-hegemonic project that builds on Thomas

Princen's (2005) logic of sufficiency and Kate Soper's (2020) proposals for an alternative hedonism, which are set within the demands, ethos and institutions of radical democracy. Drawing on the work of Ernesto Laclau, Chantal Mouffe, William Connolly and others, our conception of radical democracy involves the democratisation and transformation of various social spaces, including aviation and transport, in the name of eco-egalitarian principles and ideals.

The method of genealogy

To explore our puzzles and test our initial orientating intuitions, we use the method of genealogy as developed by Friedrich Nietzsche and Michel Foucault (1977, 1984, 1988).[7] Most famously employed by Nietzsche in his critique of modern Western morality, genealogy is a methodological tool that focuses on the contingent emergence of values, practices, policies and ideas, which are seen to be the product of disparate events, reversals, inversions and occluded struggles with no necessary connection or essential evolution (Nietzsche, 1994). Such sequences have to be carefully pieced together into a counter-narrative by the researcher, who is not an objective or impartial observer, but inextricably enmeshed in the values and norms that are probed and evaluated. In certain respects, genealogy shares a family resemblance with the method of process tracing, which is a fundamental tool of qualitative analysis (Collier, 2011). However, unlike standard historical or social science approaches, it is explicitly concerned with problems and pathologies in the present, starting with practices, institutions, identities and political forms that engender critical attention, while seeking to unsettle and deconstruct our normal understandings and expectations.

But this focus on contemporary conditions does not mean that current impasses or dilemmas are explained by recourse to an origin whose *telos* accounts for present discontents, and neither does it seek to interpret the past simply via our own theoretical concerns and interests. Nor does it presume a series of disparate events that appear to have little or no connection between them. Both pure continuity and discontinuity are disturbed in this approach, as our empirical gaze is expanded to embrace a field of dispersed events and processes, and the focus is on the subtle interweaving of seemingly inconsequential and marginal ripples, which may (or may not) come together to create significant movements and effects. The present stimulates inquiry but does not pre-determine its outcome.

In short, genealogy is not just a more complicated manner of narrating events and processes, and nor is it a new historical method, which offers a more nuanced way of periodising things in terms of intersecting and overlapping series and emergences, though the latter are noticed and drawn upon. Instead, genealogies are designed to uncover exclusions, expose inversions and bring to light new possibilities that have been overlooked or forgotten by the sedimentations of existing trajectories, with their baked-in projections and determinations. Its method is thus critical and normative, indicating new possibilities and currents, while problematising seemingly fixed temporalities and teleological images of development and evolution.

Finally, in equal measure, power and exclusion are of capital significance, as the investigative gaze is directed at elements that are foreclosed (or marginalised) in the historical process, as well as the production of new hierarchies and dominations. Attention is thus focused on the strategies and rhetorical expressions that lead to the foregrounding and acceptance of some forms, and the marginalisation of others. Hence, the perspectivism associated with this approach enables the genealogist to shuttle between the conjunctural and structural elements of the examined phenomena, seeking to strike a balance between their competing demands. Indeed, the genealogical intervention may lead to a revision of the accepted interpretations of the very dimensions themselves, thereby leading to a reorientation of our perceptions and evaluations. What was taken to be fixed and taken-for-granted, and thus structural, may be shown to be mutable and contested.

The particular and the universal

Cast in more methodological terms, our focus on the logic of aviation expansion investigates and presents a case study of UK airports politics and policy since the 1940s. Or rather, more precisely, it represents a series of cases or problematisations, which have been constructed to work together in tandem. Nonetheless, this choice of method and its research strategies require some further elaboration. In general, as Moran puts it, case-studies 'throw light on old arguments and illuminate new ones'; but though 'the light of a single study shines brightly ... its beam is always narrow'. This means that for a case study to produce maximum enlightenment it should exemplify phenomena, while also providing a perspicuous representation of features that are 'common elsewhere' (Moran, 1986: 144). This chimes with Albert Hirschman's observation that meaningful social science is not necessarily best served by the search for lawlike causal explanations, which are based on universal and general models of social change – the cognitive style of paradigmatic thinking – and whose aim is to test and prove general theories. Instead, it should also seek to understand complex social realities – the 'unique constellation of highly disparate events' as he puts it – which, while introducing a healthy degree of contingency in the form of unique or overdetermined processes, still enable us to illuminate wider processes and social trajectories (Hirschman, 1970: 339). It is the latter style of cognitive reasoning, which permits and encourages us to move freely between singular cases and their more universal implications, which guides this study. More so, if the claim can be sustained that singular cases distil a whole domain of social and natural phenomena, then their role and function is enhanced further.

Our previous research has led us to the hypothesis that the UK airports policy and aviation politics does indeed display this *exemplary* quality. Indeed, even a cursory understanding of this issue demonstrates that the problems and controversies it discloses are not unique. On the contrary, the struggles to develop large scale infrastructure projects like airports (but also roads, railways, nuclear power stations, wind farms and so forth) bring into play issues about: the relationships and tensions between economic growth and environmental protection; the complex interplays and dependencies between the natural and the social world; the dialectics of politicisation and depoliticisation; the logics of neoliberal governmentality and the role of different technologies and techniques in the management of such projects; and the role of numbers in shaping, underpinning and questioning the dominant logics of accumulation, financialisation and consumption in late capitalist societies. The airports dilemma also provides a vantage point to criticise and evaluate our dominant institutions and ways of living, while constructing and projecting alternative interim visions. But *if* in fact it does so, and *how* exactly it does so, remain open questions until the empirical results have been analysed and presented; at this point our hypotheses remain undecided and unelaborated. A core task of this book is therefore to explore whether such intuitions do indeed hold, and then to set out their wider implications and ramifications.

Statements, signifiers and tropes

More concretely, in conducting our research on these themes since the mid-1990s, we have collected together an exhaustive archive of the primary empirical data on each of the problematisations that have been examined, including policy documents, public statements, speeches, manifestos, media representations, campaign posters, leaflets and so forth. Of particular importance was the array of policy documents surrounding public inquiries and expert Commissions, as well as the extensive media representations of such events. With respect to the latter, we canvassed a wide ensemble of materials in the national and local press in the UK and elsewhere. In particular, we focus much attention on the AC and its aftermath, describing and analysing the vast set of papers and reports produced and disseminated in its name, while critically evaluating their public discussion.

At each stage of our analysis, we undertook repeated readings of the texts, using 'manual processing' to isolate and describe the articulation of demands, the drawing of equivalences and differences, as well as the framing of problems and solutions and the employment of particular signifiers and rhetorical tropes. We paid particular attention to the identification of the core statements that emerged or disappeared across different problematisations (Keller, 2013: 97). Drawing on the work of Foucault, we define *statements* as 'serious speech acts' that are enunciated by actors when describing their practices and programmes in particular historical contexts (Foucault, 1972). Here the notion of a 'speech act' highlights the performative dimension of their utterances and written expressions – 'saying as doing' – while the idea of 'serious' captures the way these linguistic performances seek to accurately describe their beliefs, thoughts and practices (Dreyfus and Rabinow, 1982: 45–56). Our readings of texts thus explored how core statements were reiterated by specific actors in different policy spaces and arenas, assessing the resonance and take-up of statements by different actors and hegemonic projects, as well as the transformation of key statements over time (Griggs and Howarth, 2019b; Griggs et al, 2020).

In isolating and documenting specific statements and signifiers, as well as the overarching rhetoric of airport expansion, we engaged in a process of articulation, moving between our empirical data and our research puzzles. We assembled and described the logic and character of different discourses through our judgements and our background knowledge of the aviation policy sector, as we mediated between our theoretical assumptions and the discourses at play. In so doing, we were able to identify the seven problematisations of aviation policy that form the basis of our study. This means that we did not simply discover different problematisations and technologies of government residing in the text, but named and constituted them by using our situated ability and judgement; we then tested our characterisations and explanations against the developing evidence.

Outline and organisation of the book

Our genealogical narrative in this book pinpoints seven *problematisations* in the evolution of UK airports policy since 1945, each combining different strategies, technologies and techniques of government, as the government and state pursued its logic of 'predict and provide' in aviation. In problematising the various problematisations that emerged in these different conjunctures, we focus on the construction of the problems, the proposed solutions, the technologies and rationalities that were elaborated to tackle the problems, the outcomes, specific sites of the problems, discursive framings and the political struggles that ensued.

We present these genealogical interpretations in Chapters 2, 3, 4 and 5, in which we argue that 'predict and provide' yielded and required different types of technologies and policy instruments. Chapter 2 examines the state sponsorship of commercial aviation from the 1940s and 1950s until the early 2000s, and the aftermath of New Labour's 2003 Air Transport White Paper (ATWP). Chapter 3 investigates the work of the AC, focusing on its efforts to provide ideological cover for the Conservative government and generate a depoliticised evidence-based consensus for expansion at Heathrow Airport. Chapter 4 examines the repoliticisation of aviation policy in the aftermath of the AC, investigating how anti-expansion campaigners in February 2020 used the legal arenas of judicial review – what might be seen as a counter-technology of government – to mount an initially successful legal challenge to the third runway. Chapter 5 pulls together the contingent and sometimes overlapping strands of our genealogy by displaying the technologies, techniques and policy instruments that came into play, and their implications, thus providing the means to compare and contrast the seven problematisations of airports and aviation since the 1940s. It then plunges into the extreme turbulence experienced by the aviation industry and UK airports policy during the triple crises of Brexit, the COVID-19 pandemic and the impending climate catastrophe, showing how this new conjuncture has brought the aviation industry, airports and indeed many parts of social and economic life in the UK, and across the globe, to a decisive crossroads.

Against this background, Chapter 6 and the Conclusion shift our attention towards the normative and policy implications and lessons of our study. Chapter 6 reflects upon and explores the possibilities of a radically democratic settlement in aviation, and the policy recommendations, scenarios and proposals that can deliver an effective green transition. Our Conclusion foregrounds the primacy of political practices and decisions in shaping the character and trajectories of our genealogy. Here we analyse the linkages between political costs and the creation and exercise of political will, showing how this factor played a crucial part in explaining airports policy and the development of the regime of aviation expansion. Chapter 1 sets out our theoretical approach to the dialectical complexities of politicisation and depoliticisation, connecting such relationships to our concepts of discourse and politics, to which we now turn.

1

Depoliticisation, discourse and policy hegemony

> The Airports Commission has been described as a once in a
> lifetime opportunity to secure the UK's aviation capacity for
> the future, but delivery of the long term solution it ultimately
> recommends needs cross-party political agreement. Our panellists
> describe the process of 'depoliticising' the eventual scheme, so that
> it doesn't get derailed by short term political considerations, and
> how it can be delivered, effectively, in as short a time as possible,
> within the UK's democratic processes.
>
> (Runways UK, 2014a)

On 16 January 2014, as its founding event, Runways UK convened a major
conference on airport expansion in the UK. The event was entitled 'Airport
Infrastructure for a Future Britain', and it was hosted and moderated by the
broadcaster Kirsty Wark. Describing itself as a 'neutral platform for scheme
debate' (Runways UK, 2014b), the new network was one of a plethora of
groups and initiatives that has sought to influence the development of UK
aviation policy in recent times. One of its afternoon panels – 'Achieving
Cross-party Agreement and Delivery' – discussed the 'delivery of the long-
term solution' required to satisfy the UK's aviation capacity needs. The
panellists included Lord Adonis, the former Labour Government Secretary
of State for Transport, and Nelson Ogunshakin, the Co-Chair of National
Infrastructure Plan Strategic Engagement Forum, which was set up under the
Coalition Government. It was not insignificant that the event was chaired by
Baroness Valentine, who was then the chief executive of London First, the
pro-Heathrow expansion business group campaigning to get the proposed
third runway back on the political agenda. In order to frame the discussion,
the introductory preamble in the Conference programme explicitly asked
its panellists to describe the process of 'depoliticising' the 'eventual scheme'
that would be proposed by the AC. The latter was chaired by Sir Howard
Davies, and finally reported on 1 July 2015, following the May general
election (Runways UK, 2014a: 7). In her formal welcome to conference
delegates, Baroness Brenda Dean, chair of the Runways UK Advisory
Group, and former chair of the pro-expansion Freedom to Fly coalition,
noted with some frustration how 'the UK has never had a calm, detailed

and broad debate on what we best need as a nation from aviation', adding that the aim of Runways UK was to 'lift the debate to a level of informed knowledge and to create an unbiased forum to help in reaching the right long-term answer' to the UK's aviation needs (2014a: 3).

Such explicit calls to depoliticise the provision of aviation infrastructure resonate with one of the core puzzles animating this book: the inability of successive UK governments to devise, execute and implement their desired plans to expand airport capacity in South East England and across the UK, especially their failure to win the consent of affected subjects and constituencies. This chapter sets out our theoretical approach to address this anomaly by using the resources of PDT to clarify the dialectics of politicisation and depoliticisation, and their impact on the struggle for policy hegemony. We begin by intervening in contemporary debates about the concept of depoliticisation, which discloses a number of questions for further investigation and clarification, after which we develop our core assumptions, showing how the interacting logics of politicisation and depoliticisation are intimately intertwined, and how they can be further specified through the concept of hegemony and antagonism. In particular, we connect the dialectics of politicisation and depoliticisation to the logics of equivalence and difference, and the production and dissemination of fantasmatic images and narratives, before turning to the multiple rationalities, technologies and techniques through which government seeks to make controversial issues 'governable' or tractable. More concretely, what we term the *logic of depoliticisation* consists of a process, a state of affairs and an attendant set of practices, where all three elements are intimately connected to 'the primacy of politics'; these aspects will be unfolded as we proceed. Such concepts and logics provide us with the criteria to describe and evaluate the various practices of depoliticisation that have been employed by the pro-expansion project. We conclude by connecting these theoretical concepts and logics to the problems of policy analysis in the field of UK aviation and the struggle for policy hegemony.

Debates in contemporary political theory and science

Discussions of depoliticisation in contemporary political science and philosophy are heavily marked by the rise of neoliberal forms of capitalism and governance – sometimes labelled the 'anti-democratic offensive' – and a growing scepticism about the efficacy of liberal democracy in resolving the acute crises and mass disaffections that have emerged since the collapse of communism and the much-vaunted 'end of history' (Fukuyama, 1992; Laclau and Mouffe, 2014). Indeed, the neoliberal critique and radical rejection of the social democratic consensus and the post-war Keynesian welfare state in the UK, the US and elsewhere during the 1970s and 1980s, and then its spread to a number of other contexts, has led some theorists to highlight the eclipse of democratic politics and civic engagement in the name of free markets. The emergence of Third Way politics, which endeavoured to steer a course between traditional socialism and free-market capitalism, coupled with growing concerns about a perceived widespread apathy and disenchantment among citizens of liberal democracies, has also led some analysts to rethink the concept and role of depoliticisation as an organising motif of contemporary politics.

And despite the recent resurgence of populist politics of various types, as well as the rise of ethno-nationalism and political extremism across the world, the problematic of depoliticisation still resonates today in many quarters. Ongoing theoretical debates about politicisation, depoliticisation and repoliticisation have disclosed a helpful horizon of concepts and questions for further investigation. In *Why We Hate Politics*, Colin Hay seeks to account for the 'disenchantment' of politics in the age of neoliberalism by providing a new perspective on the concepts of politics, politicisation and depoliticisation (Hay, 2007: 153). Specified in terms of its 'content', and not as a 'domain' of action or practice, Hay defines politics as 'the capacity for agency and deliberation in situations of genuine collective or social choice', stressing that 'politics does not, and cannot, arise in situations in which human purpose can exert no influence', in part because politics 'is synonymous with contingency; its antonyms are fate and necessity' (Hay, 2007: 77).

Building on this conception, Hay's three types of depoliticisation invert his logic of politicisation, where the latter arises because an issue – or proto-issue – becomes the object of 'public deliberation, decision-making and contingency, where previously it was not' (Wood and Flinders, 2014: 154). Hay then offers his threefold typology, in which 'the most basic form of politicisation (Type 1) is associated with the extension of the capacity for human influence and deliberation which comes with disavowing the prior assignment of an issue – or issue domain – to the realm of fate or necessity' (Hay, 2007: 81), while 'issues may then become further politicised when they develop into the focus of a concerted pattern of public deliberation as if they have suddenly become identified as issues of collective, rather than individual or private, wellbeing' (Type 2) (Wood and Flinders, 2014: 154). Traditional beliefs, for example, or embedded cultural assumptions may be found wanting, or scientific discoveries and technological advances may disclose new opportunities to shape practices in the world, which were not previously thought possible, or which are regarded as questionable in existing horizons (Hay, 2007: 81).

The second type of politicisation also assumes multiple guises, ranging from organised petitions to influence MPs through to the generation of alternative evidence and direct action street-blockades, as campaigners seek to insert issues or proto-issues into the public arena by making them visible through ideological and political struggle. Such politicisations may then be projected into the governmental sphere (Type 3), which may become part of the parliamentary debate and agenda, leading to the production of new legislation and responsibilities for 'government departments and similarly "governmental" processes' (Wood and Flinders, 2014: 155). In short, Hay's logic of politicisation foregrounds the contingent and contested arrangement of socio-political spheres in modern democratic orders, whose boundaries are shaped by ongoing hegemonic practices, governmental reorganisations and developing institutional patterns across the world.

Yet, as many commentators have noted in the age of neoliberal governance, the main vector of change points to the *depoliticisation* of political decision-making through practices like delegation, privatisation and denial (Burnham, 2001, 2006; Pollitt and Talbot, 2004; Mair, 2013; Flinders and Wood, 2014; Wood and Flinders, 2014: 155). Developing this logic, the first type of depoliticisation (Type 1) in Hay's initial conceptualisation refers to the effective relegation of 'issues previously subject to formal political scrutiny, deliberation and accountability to the public yet non-governmental sphere', which for Hay can display 'two general forms': first, the transference of responsibility from 'governmental to public or quasi-public authorities' and, secondly, the displacement of areas of 'formal political responsibility to the market (through privatisation)' (Hay, 2007: 82). Hay's claim here is not that the issue has been effectively decontested or depoliticised, but that it has been moved to a domain that is less overtly politicised or vulnerable to politicisation. As Flinders and Buller (2006a; 2006b) put it, the issue has been subject to a process of 'arena-shifting', where Gordon Brown's decision to switch responsibility for setting interest rates to the Bank of England in 1997 is often cited as a paradigmatic case of this logic (Fawcett and Marsh, 2014).

A further step in the logic of depoliticisation (Type 2) consists in a process in which an issue (or responsibility) is displaced from the sphere of formal political deliberation to the private domain, thus rendering it a matter of 'domestic deliberation or consumer choice' (Hay, 2007: 85). For example, the individualisation of issues such as pollution, debt or crime, in which moral and political responsibility and culpability is placed on individual behaviour and choice, rather than the decisions of politicians, structural conditions or institutional actions/non-actions, if successful, represents this kind of depoliticisation. Hay also suggests that the development of societal values may result in the depoliticisation of various issues, including debates about gender, race, or sexuality, as public attitudes and moods wax and wane, carrying both positive and negative implications from a progressive point of view. Some previously relevant markers of difference, such as race, gender or sexuality, may become irrelevant with respect to equal employment opportunities, though, equally, other social identities (such as religious orientation) may continue to remain invisible and thus discriminatory, or at worst they may become the grounds for explicit targeting and othering in the media and other parts of civil society, and thereby re-politicised (Hay, 2007: 85–6).

Although often missed, yet for that and other reasons perhaps the most significant form, a third type of depoliticisation (Type 3) brings about 'the transfer of responsibility from the space of deliberation (the "political" realm) to that of necessity and fate (the "non-political" realm)' (Hay, 2007: 86). Processes of 'de-secularisation', for example, may reintroduce appeals to divine authority, leading potentially to an effective depoliticisation of issues pertaining to gender inequality, or indeed to a re-confirmation of excluded or marginalised sexual identities, which had been previously emancipated. Appeals to inexorable logics of globalisation may also serve to remove choice and political debate about alternative economic policies and strategies (Hay, 2007: 86–7). Hence, Type 3 depoliticisation returns previously contestable and contingent issues to the domain of necessity and fate, thereby occluding their ultimately political character. Neo-conservative and various theocentric perspectives, for example, might wish to exclude certain beliefs, orientations and social questions (such as gay marriage, the legalisation of drugs, abortion and so forth) from political debate and democratic negotiation, while neo-liberals might wish to naturalise the space of the free market, immunising it from democratic demands and state interference (Foucault, 2008).

Hay's intervention has spawned a rich literature on the dynamics of politicisation and depoliticisation, which has sought to refine his initial categories, while seeking to apply the approach to pressing policy issues and empirical cases (for example, Bates et al, 2014; Jessop, 2014). Endeavouring to develop a second generation of research on depoliticisation, Wood and Flinders (2014) have broadened the ideas put forward in the first wave of research on this topic by pushing beyond the limits of what they term 'governmental depoliticisation', which is understood as a 'mode of statecraft' instituted by politicians to deflect blame and accountability from governments as decision-making is placed at 'one remove' from the centre (Burnham, 2001, cited in Wood and Flinders, 2014: 157), and by questioning the way 'a continued focus on "arenas" may lead to a still narrow and relatively static conceptualisation of politicising', which they detect in the work of Hay and Blühdorn (Wood and Flinders, 2014: 161). More positively, endorsing the work of Greta Krippner (2011: 146), they call for more attention to be directed towards other aspects of depoliticisation, which are less focused on the 'social location of decisions' and more concerned with their 'content'. In other words, they argue for a 'more dynamic approach' that can shift 'the focus of analysis from arenas to discourse' (Wood and Flinders, 2014: 161).

Using Lukes's metaphor of the three 'faces' of power to 'impose a degree of analytical order' on a complicated series of theoretical interventions and empirical investigations, while drawing on Schmitt's concept of the political, Wood and Flinders distinguish three faces of depoliticisation (Wood and

Flinders, 2014: 156). In their revised typology, *governmental depoliticisation* captures the displacement of issues from 'the governmental sphere to the public sphere, as elected politicians endeavour to delegate to arm's-length bodies, judicial structures or technocratic rule-based systems that limit discretion'; *societal depoliticisation* highlights the transfer of 'issues from the public sphere to the private sphere by illuminating and privileging the role of choice and "capacity deliberation", as well as the shift towards individualised responses to collective social challenges'; *discursive depoliticisation* comprises the relegation of issues from the 'private realm' to the 'realm of necessity', where 'things just happen' and their contestability and 'contingency' is lacking (Flinders and Wood, 2014: 165). This third, and presumably most encompassing and radical face of depoliticisation, thus foregrounds 'the role of language and ideas to depoliticise certain issues and through this define them as little more than elements of fate' (Flinders and Wood, 2014: 165).

Hay is broadly supportive of these proposed revisions, as are we, but correctly questions Wood and Flinder's idea of a separate category for 'discursive depoliticisation', accurately noting that 'there is a discursive component to all depoliticisations (whatever their type)', so that 'it is unhelpful to think of discursive depoliticisation as being involved only in depoliticisation processes of type 3' (Hay, 2014: 299). Nonetheless, as we shall argue, the very concepts of discourse and the discursive are deeply contested notions, and they can be constructed and empirically used in different and even competing ways. Hay also queries their new typology because 'it associate[s] too closely the mode of depoliticisation with the arenas or sites from which/to which responsibility' is transferred, where such processes are not just restricted to delegation, privatisation and ideological concealment, and he strongly criticises their affirmation of Schmitt's (2007) stark concept of the political, predicated on a fundamental opposition between friend and enemy, whose overly normative connotations deny pluralism and nuance in the analysis of (neo-liberal) forms of governance and policy-making (Hay, 2014: 299; 296–98).

Building an agenda

In the main, we agree with many of Hay's correctives of Flinders and Wood's suggestive reflections and classifications. We can see the virtues of accepting that 'decision making, agenda setting and preference shaping can all ... be more or less politicised – and each might be seen to be associated with different types or modes of politicisation and depoliticisation' exhibiting different linkages and articulations, and using this as the basis of a new research agenda (Hay, 2014: 299). In fact, one of the main aims of this book is to develop this agenda, both theoretically and empirically. Moreover, we affirm the dynamism of depoliticisation processes, where there is often an overdetermination of types and elements, so that the processes are uneven and not linear. We also accept that 'there is a discursive component to all depoliticisations (whatever their type)' (Hay, 2014: 299). But, going further, we argue that the very notions of discourse and the discursive need to be clarified and articulated, and then linked theoretically to depoliticisation.

So, in elaborating our alternative approach, we need first to clarify our concepts of discourse and politics, and then connect these ideas to our understanding of the logics of politicisation and depoliticisation. We also need to problematise other issues that have remained implicit or unexamined in the current debates. For one thing, we must revisit the structure–agency debate, inquiring as to whether the logic of depoliticisation is a function of the intentional choices and strategies of politicians and administrators, or whether it is the effect of social or ideological logics that are embedded in social relations and structures. Or, indeed, as we shall argue, whether it is better to develop a more sophisticated theoretical framework that brings out the complex dialectic of structure and agency. We also need to clarify the idea of a distinctive *logic* – or *logics* – of politicisation and depoliticisation, where the idea of 'logic' straddles the divide between simple correlations and causal mechanisms, while elaborating our approach in relation to the different spaces in and through which norms and practices are politicised and depoliticised (Glynos and Howarth, 2007). Finally, we need to clarify the distinction and relationship between depoliticisation as an outcome or process, and we need to consider and tease out its normative implications. It is to these questions that we now turn as we set out our theoretical approach.

Logics of politicisation and depoliticisation: mechanisms, strategies and tactics

In our approach, discourses are partly constituted in relation to threatening objects – real or imaginary – where the latter's symbolic presence is deemed to block or impede the identities and interests of the discourse in question (Laclau, 1990: 17–18). Put more fully, discourses are articulated *against* other discourses through the construction of antagonistic relations, which divide friends from enemies, though at the same time they also align with other forces and discourses.[1] In so doing, following Laclau and Mouffe (2014), we affirm the primacy of politics, in which the political involves the contestation of established social hierarchies and exclusions, and thus the division of society into hostile camps, as well as practices that aim to institute new relations and social orders. The construction of social antagonisms between subjects involves an equivalential operation in which discursive resources external to a social arrangement or setting are used to negate an oppressive relation: for example, a hierarchical relation between management and workers may in certain circumstances be deemed unjust or exploitative by drawing on a discourse of rights to render the injustice visible. Moreover, the logics of equivalence and resonance also enable demands to be linked together by annulling the particular content of their identities in favour of their *common negation* of an oppressive force, thus making possible the creation of political frontiers that divide society. By contrast, logics of difference furnish the means to complexify systems of social relations by expanding the boundaries of inclusion/exclusion to incorporate previously antagonistic elements. In so doing, the logic of difference pluralises and multiplies social identities, pushing political frontiers to the margins of society (Laclau and Mouffe, 2014: 113–20).

The creation of a *hegemonic* discourse is the result of complex struggles in which opposed political forces – 'discourse coalitions' or 'hegemonic projects' – seek to 'universalise' their particular storylines and interests either by connecting together different demands and identities to establish a new order, or by integrating demands and identities into an increasingly capacious regime. An emergent hegemonic project accomplishes this by articulating a common discourse, which can win the support of a significant portion of affected parties, while securing the compliance of others. And, of course, the achievement of hegemonic dominance also involves the exercise of force and coercion against antagonistic elements that remain opposed to the new discourse. Finally, a key condition of this approach is that all such elements are contingent and unfixed, so that their meaning and identity is only partially fixed by articulatory practices. In short, then, all objects and social practices are discursive, as their meaning and position depends upon their articulation within socially constructed systems of rules and differences (Laclau and Mouffe, 2014: 91–101; 120–31).

In this perspective, it follows that all practices of depoliticisation are both articulatory and symbolic, involving the intertwining and overdetermination of contingent elements, where the identities of such components are modified by the practice in question. More concretely, the *logic of depoliticisation* consists of a process, a state of affairs, and an attendant set of practices; all three elements are intimately connected to what we shall call the primacy of politics. The primacy of politics captures the way in which a social relation or system is contested, instituted and transformed, where the moment of politics is the point at which a relation, policy or institution is made visible and challenged in the name of an alternative mode (Glynos and Howarth, 2007: 113–17). Conversely, the logic of depoliticisation involves the covering-over and thus the sedimentation of this originating moment (Laclau, 1990: 33–6).

Using these terms, it follows that politics reactivates the founding moments of relations and proposes new ways of doing things, though this does not imply that such reactivations always assume the same forms and terms that were evident in their original emergence and constitution. By contrast, depoliticisation as a *state of affairs* refers to a relatively sedimented and naturalised system of relations, while the *process of depoliticisation* comprises the bundle of practices that achieves the outcome of stabilising or decontesting a set of relations, policies or procedures that have been – or are being – contested. Finally, *practices of depoliticisation* include the array of actions, interventions, manoeuvres, strategies and tactics that bring about a state of affairs that might be characterised as depoliticised.

Deferring to expertise

The *practices of depoliticisation* suggested by our approach are complex and varied, so they are worth unpacking in more detail. Consider, first, the temporary displacement of issues through the establishment of independent public commissions or inquiries, which are authorised to propose acceptable resolutions of the problem. Such instruments are replete with their own dramaturgy of performances, scripts, settings and stages (Hajer, 2005). They often take the form of technocratic and elite modes of decision-making, and are thus rarely political and democratic in the sense that they involve affected groups and communities in the production of an acceptable agreement. In his discussion of the transition from non-wage to wage labour in capitalist societies, Offe (1984: 113) characterises such strategies as the scientisation of politics, which 'functions to unburden the system of political decision-making both socially ... and temporally'.

The recourse to experts sidelines the demands of stakeholders who cannot make claims to have the requisite scientific legitimacy and puts in place a 'temporary buffer zone' for politicians while the expert inquiry takes place (Offe, 1984: 113). In fact, this recourse to expertise is part of a wider shift towards discourses of policy-making, which question the effectiveness of representative democracy to resolve policy problems, and narrowly construct policy-making as the domain of 'ahistorical models, correlations, mechanisms or processes' (Bevir, 2010: 3). Indeed, in the field of airports policy, Feldman and Milch's (1982) classic comparative study of eight proposed airport developments in five capitalist democracies concludes that the scientific expertise, ideological prejudices and business *mentalité* of airport managers led them generally to conceptualise the development of airports along narrow and technical lines, often disregarding other policy options (such as managing demand), the social impacts of the proposed developments and the neglect of the political prerequisites for the successful implementation of such projects.

This said, competing social interests will mobilise alternative forms of expertise, while expert judgements will be open to competing interpretations, and the effectiveness of such interventions will 'emerge only in the course of conflict-ridden attempts to apply them' (Offe, 1984: 113). In these terms, then, appeals to expertise are part of a contingent discursive struggle, which produce politicising and depoliticising effects, as different actors seek to shift blame and credit for actions and/or legitimise alternative forms of expertise in an effort to pluralise access to the policy arena (Meriluoto, 2021; Kettell and Kerr, 2022).

Decontesting the terms of discourse: framing and rhetorical redescription

Against this background, the action of decontesting the *terms* of political discourse – pushing certain concepts and notions into the background with the aim of neutralising or naturalising their appeal – is an important dimension of depoliticisation (Freeden, 1996). Decontestation may often be achieved by the technique of rhetorical redescription, whereby rival and neighbouring terms are inverted and re-evaluated so as to rework their normative import. Otherwise designated as the trope of *paradiastole*, this rhetorical operation involves the substitution of one term for another, thus altering the moral character of an act or behaviour (Skinner, 2002: 183). For example, in his book *The Passions and the Interests*, Albert Hirschman (1977) seeks to explain the way in which individual self-interest and 'the pursuit of personal gain' became a core 'human virtue' in the early modern period in Western Europe, underpinning the discourse of modern social science, and providing important norms and values in liberal conceptions of society.[2] Hirschman's engagement with the issue focuses on the subtle interplay of vices and virtues in the collective social imaginaries of different forms of society. As Little suggests, using this device on a very general level, it can be argued that 'power' captures the underlying ethic of the ancient world, 'honour' underpins feudalism, and 'greed' and 'self-interest' represent and constitute the 'spirit of capitalism' to use Weber's expression (Little, 2013). Moreover, according to Hirschman, there was a vital evolution in our thinking about the passions and the interests in the early modern period, in which the previously hegemonic ideal of heroism and honour was inverted and replaced by the idea of avarice.

More pointedly, the vice of avarice became the virtue of pursuing one's own 'self-interest' (Hirschman, 1977: 42–8). In exploring this change, Hirschman focuses on the rhetorical mechanisms, operations and logics through which this complex inversion and transformation occurred and was embedded. Put simply, he argues that different ideals are connected to passions and affects, and that the role of clashing passions and affects are vital in changing ideals (Little, 2013). Moreover, he goes on to show that in the texts and discourses of key early liberal thinkers, such as David Hume and Adam Smith, interest is constructed as a passion, which can regulate and temper other more 'unruly passions' (Hirschman, 1977: 15), so that the passionate pursuit of interests or avarice can replace its prior association with vice and begin to function as a virtue (Hirschman, 1977: 65–6, 111–13).

In short, as Adelman puts it, early modern thinkers like Hume and Smith were able to transmute once antonymic terms like 'interests' and 'passions' into synonyms, so that overall social improvement is only progressed when each particular individual pursues their own private interests (Adelman, 2014: 517).

According to Skinner, and as it is illustrated in the work of Hirschman, *paradiastole* applies to the normative re-characterisation of certain actions. But for us it can also be applied to objects and projects, such as proposals to build new or extended airports. For example, in the critique of New Labour's proposals to expand airports after the ATWP (2003), much attention was focused on the allegedly unsustainable and politically unacceptable plans to build a third runway at Heathrow. Yet, the subsequent redescription of Heathrow as a singular and indispensable global hub, which is therefore vital to the UK economy and its needs of connectivity and access to competitive markets, provided pro-expansion groups with the rhetorical ammunition to get Heathrow extension back onto the political agenda during the Coalition government.

The production of empty signifiers

As we have noted, the practices of politicisation and depoliticisation are connected to the structuring of social relations, especially the division of society or particular spaces in society into antagonistic camps through the interacting logics of equivalence and difference. The logic of equivalence involves the linking together of a number of different and potentially competing demands and identities through their common opposition to a defined enemy. Here the production of an empty signifier not only represents the 'absent fullness' of the multiple demands that are woven together, but it also negates the various antagonistic others against which it has been constructed (Laclau, 1996). In this way, the production of empty signifiers constitutes a particular decontestatory mechanism, whose role is to mask any differences in a coalition or project, while stabilising a field of antagonistic relations, where signifiers can float freely and be articulated by rival coalitions and projects. But once this enemy has served its purpose in partly constituting a new overarching identity, the role of an empty signifier is to partially fix the meanings of a signifier by overcoming discursive instability and social antagonism. The attainment of hegemony in a field or society is thus connected to the construction of empty signifiers, whose function is to displace conflict and politicisation.

Such rhetorical operations often go hand-in-hand with the strategic aspect of the logic of depoliticisation. For example, William Riker has inventively supplemented formal rational choice theory by articulating the role of rhetoric in constructing and dismantling political coalitions (Riker,

1986, 1996). What Riker has named the role of heresthetics – the art of strategic manipulation – consists of a whole battery of operations, which are used by social actors to achieve certain goals. Such operations include decisions about which groups of agents are deemed to be significant in a particular situation; creating novel actions and political practices that subvert sedimented norms and routines; framing and reframing how opponents and rival actors evaluate outcomes so as to achieve specific goals; moving issues from a politicised to a non-politicised arena and vice versa; and changing the perceptions and import of individual preferences by multiple rhetorical interventions and processes (Riker, 1996; Shepsle, 2003: 309–10; see also Griggs and Howarth, 2013: 35–6). While such techniques and practices can be used generally to achieve a desired outcome, they are also vital in overcoming conflict and ending dispute, thus partaking of what we have termed the logic of depoliticisation. While each practice or intervention involves political actions, their outcome can be to sediment, pacify and depoliticise antagonistic relations and situations. For example, in the case of UK aviation, governments have endeavoured to shift policy decisions from one domain to another, trying even to remove the issue from the political fray altogether, while campaigners have sought to contest policies by moving the issue and its focus of attention to what they view as a more favourable site of struggle, such as law courts and the media.

The logic of difference

Another strategic mechanism, though arising from within PDT, is the logic of difference. As against the logic of equivalence, which supplies the means for campaigns and projects to connect different demands by stressing their opposition to something that negates them, the logic of difference enables actors to decouple linked and overdetermined demands, so that they might be marginalised, displaced or addressed in a punctual fashion. The logic of difference thus involves the disarticulation of equivalential chains of demands via various practices of challenge, institutionalisation, deflection or negation. Generally, then, this logic is marked either by the differential incorporation or even co-optation of claims and demands, where their cutting edge may be blunted, and/or it is accompanied by the pluralising of a regime or practice to new demands and claims, where those in a social field acknowledge and accommodate difference (Laclau, 2005: 129–30).

In many respects, therefore, the logic of difference speaks to the way in which claims and demands are managed by powerholders, so that a dominant practice or regime is not disturbed or modified in a fundamental way. What is more, in many modern societies, it is the government and the state, both as actors and in terms of their dominant institutional and organisational roles in society as a whole, which are vital elements in the development and execution of such strategies, and thus in the accomplishment of such goals. This is certainly the case if we return to the politics of sustainable aviation in the UK. Indeed, it is our contention in this book that during the last three or four decades at least, the British government and the UK state has actively sought to mediate between the contradictory pressures for more airport expansion, tighter environmental regulation and greater accountability to local communities, though it has remained committed to the overall expansion of UK aviation. More concretely, one of the ways that we shall explore these issues is by focusing on what Michel Foucault and more recent Foucauldian scholars have named the rationalities, technologies and techniques of government, and we shall say more about this later. But first we turn to the role of fantasmatic images and narratives in our account of the logic of depoliticisation.

Fantasmatic images and narratives

Rhetorical and heresthetical mechanisms like framing and the logic of difference can help us to account for the way in which various grievances and demands can be depoliticised and rendered manageable within a particular discursive practice. But in some cases, an even better means of depoliticising a politicised issue or social relation, and thus exercising power, is to prevent contestation from occurring in the first place. One way to address this issue would be to wheel in a theory of ideology that places much of its explanatory emphasis on the role of deception and various forms of fake consciousness that preclude subjects from seeing and comprehending their 'real interests' (Lukes, 2005). However, this epistemic focus has been rightly criticised in various quarters for presuming that such interests exist and can be detected, and that a researcher or analyst can completely bracket out their own values and ideals and reach objective judgements (for example, Foucault, 1980: 118; Žižek, 1994; Freeden, 1996; Laclau, 1996). So how is it possible to capture an exercise of power that works to prevent subjects from translating dislocatory experiences into demands, grievances and challenges without recourse to a notion of ideology as false consciousness?

Here we make use of Slavoj Žižek's endeavour to develop a Lacanian inspired theory of ideology through his concept of 'social-ideological fantasy' (Žižek, 1989: 28–33, 124–8). In *The Sublime Object of Ideology*, he reformulates Marx's conception of ideology, which he neatly summarises as: 'they do not know it, but they are doing it', as well as the cynical view of Peter Sloterdijk, which he formulates as: 'they know very well what they are doing, but still, they are doing it', substituting instead the idea that the subjects of ideology 'know that, in their activity, they are following an illusion, but still, they are doing it' (Žižek, 1989: 28, 29, 33). He begins this reworking by distinguishing between and relating the notions of symptom and social fantasy. Locating its origins in the work of Marx, he argues that Freud and Lacan's psychoanalytic concept of the symptom (which is manifest, for example, in various compulsions, lapses and obsessions) represents a 'certain "pathological" imbalance' in a structure or belief system, whose negative effects also 'function' to constitute and form the structure in question (Žižek, 1989: 21).

Put differently, symptoms refer to those seemingly heterogeneous and 'impossible' elements in a social formation, which are essential and necessary for its functioning and reproduction – both subverting *and* sustaining the logics and principles of their 'own universal foundation' (1989: 21). And in order to illustrate this paradoxical phenomenon, Žižek focusses on the ideal of freedom in bourgeois society. Freedom in liberal capitalism assumes different forms – 'freedom of speech and press, freedom of consciousness, freedom of commerce, political freedom and so on' – but also includes the freedom of the worker to sell their labour power as a commodity, where this last instance of 'choice' actually undermines the universal ideal of freedom itself by ensnaring the worker in relations of exploitation, subjected to the extraction of surplus value via the logic of capitalist production (Žižek, 1989: 21–2). Here, and elsewhere in his reflections on populism, Žižek makes the related point that the proleteriat in the capitalist mode of production occupies an equally contradictory position, in which it is both required for the generation of profit and the system's reproduction, yet systematically excluded and foreclosed by its logic, functioning as that point at which the 'existing social order encounters its own unreason' (1989: 23; see also Žižek, 2006: 565–6).

After introducing the idea of the symptom, he goes on to affirm that ideology operates at the level of *doing* and *acting*, rather than *knowing* or *thinking*. Highlighting the role of money in capitalist societies, and developing what is often an overly simplistic reading of Marx's theory of commodity fetishism – his critique of the 'fantastic' inversion of the relationship between things and social relations in the buying and selling of commodities (Marx, 1976: 165) – he claims that individuals are generally aware that money is simply a token for economic exchange, and that its possession gives them a right to a portion of the social product. In this respect, the subjects of capitalism know that there is 'nothing magical' (Žižek, 1989: 31) about money, and that it is simply a token for economic exchange, whose possession gives them a right to a portion of the social product. But though subjects appear to be conscious of their fetishisation of money in practice, using it to buy and sell things, as if it possessed an agency of its own, or remain cynically and knowingly detached from its operation, when they are 'interpellated' as subjects of capitalism they remain ignorant of the full force of bourgeois ideology, which leads them to act 'as if money, in its material reality, is the immediate embodiment of wealth as such' (Žižek, 1989: 31). Indeed, what their actions occlude, according to Žižek, are the distortions and mystifications embedded in the very structures and relations of capitalist society, thus giving rise to the fetishistic illusions or 'ideological fantasies' that guide and enmesh social behaviour – the exploitative and concealed 'act of commodity exchange' itself (1989: 31):

> What they do not know is that their social reality itself, their activity, is guided by an illusion, by a fetishistic inversion. What they overlook, what they misrecognize, is not the reality but the illusion which is structuring their reality, their real social activity. They know very well how things really are, but still they are doing it as if they did not know. The illusion is therefore double: it consists in overlooking the illusion which is structuring our real, effective relationship to reality. And this overlooked, unconscious illusion is what may be called the *ideological fantasy* ... The fundamental level of ideology ... is not that of an illusion masking the real state of things but that of an (unconscious) fantasy structuring our social reality itself. (Žižek, 1989: 32–3)

In this model, then, 'the subject can "enjoy his symptom" only in so far as its logic escapes him' (Žižek, 1989: 21). Moreover, an individual's belief in a fantasy is not an internal component of their cognitive or mental apparatus, but is embodied and reiterated in their social activities, so that fantasies are not secret or 'hidden in any unfathomable depths', but crystallised in buildings, texts, films, jokes and public actions, albeit in a distorted fashion (Žižek, 1997: 3–7).

One upshot of the installation and acceptance of ideology is the effective depoliticisation and objectification of social processes in capitalist societies, such as commodification, accumulation and exchange, which are actually political through and through. At the same time, it is to endorse Marx's critique of the eternalisation of the laws of political economy in the discourse of classical political economy, and the inscription of class struggle and politics in the theoretical categories and real abstractions (like money and the commodity), which are produced and reproduced in capitalist societies. What is clear is that Marx performs the task of *politicising* the endeavour by the dominant intellectual and cultural voices to *depoliticise* the contingent and contested laws and abstractions of capitalist societies. More specifically, with respect to our empirical analyses, we shall draw attention to the way in which numbers, quantification and the logic of forecasting have also come to function as fetishised, 'real abstractions' in the ongoing debates about UK airport expansion, shaping policymaking, negating opposition and structuring the terrains of argumentation.

In this perspective, then, fantasies are materialised in particular narratives, objects and images, with which subjects can identity, and they procure an enjoyment for those caught in its thrall (Žižek, 1990). Fantasies thus structure a subject's 'lived reality' by concealing the ultimate contingency of things and social relations, and by naturalising the various relations of domination within which a subject is enmeshed (Glynos and Howarth, 2007: 147;

see also Glynos, 2021). More precisely, fantasmatic storylines promise completion if they are realised, or implosion or disintegration if they are not (Stavrakakis, 1999: 108–9, 2007: 189–210). In the case of UK aviation, for example, such fantasmatic narratives are evident in those discourses in which aviation is connected to promises of unbridled economic growth and global connectivity, when properly supported and encouraged, while obstacles to its expansion are presented as bringing about catastrophic consequences for the British economy and populace.

Seen in these terms the role of fantasies is to manage or keep at bay the inevitable contingencies and uncertainties that interrupt the social orders we are compelled to inhabit, ensuring their smooth reproduction and facilitating their depoliticisation. Indeed, the 'success' of a fantasy is sometimes 'evident' in its invisibility: the fact that it supports social reality without our being conscious of it. By contrast, the visibility of fantasmatic figures and devices – their appearance *as* fantasies – means that they cease to function properly in this regard. The underlying frame that structures enjoyment and identity thus becomes manifest and open to challenge, opening up the potential for the re-politicisation of existing 'taken-for-granted' arrangements.

Rationalities, technologies and techniques of government

The role of rhetoric, images and fantasies – the whole panoply of *mentalités*, ideological and intellectual predispositions, linguistic representations and so forth – provide useful tools to analyse the processes of politicisation and depoliticisation associated with the emergence and negotiation of policy dilemmas. But, as Peter Triantafillou and others have correctly suggested, if we want to critically explain the ways in which new problematisations are constructed and navigated, we must also focus on the 'physical, material and technical dimensions of these processes', including 'concrete techniques of data production, forms of decision-making, methods of comparative analyses, schemes for the dissemination and exchange of knowledge and policy-making procedures', as well as the objects of such interventions and their particular properties and resistances (Triantafillou, 2012: 22). Needless to say, this broadening of our theoretical horizon is perfectly compatible with our conception of discourse, which stresses the role of articulatory practices in constructing the meaning of objects and processes in certain ways, though it discloses such relations in more explicit ways.

In exploring this dimension, we focus on the specific rationalities, technologies and techniques of government, which Foucault gathered together under the name 'governmentality'. In a series of lectures at the *Collège de France* more than 40 years ago, Foucault coined this word to capture the art of governing in terms of 'conduct' – the 'conduct of conduct' – reactivating earlier meanings of the signifier, as he sketched a genealogy of such practices and carefully tracked their different forms and modalities (see, for example, Foucault, 1982: 220–1, 1991, 2008). Mining these lectures, Miller and Rose elaborated the idea of *technologies of government* to address processes of problematisation in the political domain (Miller and Rose, 1990; Rose and Miller, 1992), where *rationalities of government* refer to the types of knowledge, forms of reasoning and modes of calculation, which inhere in the art of governing, while *technologies of government* capture the multiple 'devices, mechanisms and procedures', which are used 'to render a problem governable' (Triantafillou, 2012: 23). As Triantafillou puts it, Miller and Rose build on Foucault's concept of power-knowledge to argue that technologies of government are not just the instrumental means to reach a set of assumed political objectives, because the rationalities and technologies of government are bound together and 'co-constitute' one another. That is to say, while governmental technologies form the means to mould and guide the *problems* of government, as well as the different modes through which to reflect upon them, governmental rationalities privilege certain technologies and ways of governing over others (Triantafillou, 2012: 22–3).

Such analytical distinctions and relations can be further complexified. Mitchell Dean helpfully distinguishes between *technologies* and *techniques* of government, where technologies comprise 'types of schooling and medical practice, systems of income support, forms of administration and "corporate management", systems of intervention into various organisations, and bodies of expertise that are assembled through particular governmental programmes', while techniques consist of 'systems of accounting, methods of the organisation of work, forms of surveillance, methods of timing and spacing of activities in particular locales'. At the same time, technologies of government can be further split into *intellectual* technologies, which include 'the use of statistical tables, graphs, reports and forms, and all other means of the eliciting, recording, memorising and transporting of information', though this is not an ontological separation dividing the ideational and material dimensions, but a convenient analytical device (Dean, 1994: 187–8).

We draw on these elements to develop our approach, though tailoring the resources to our puzzles and locating them within our overall framework. First, following the later Heidegger reflections, technologies of government are not just reducible to the particular forms of equipment, tools and instruments that are used by governments to achieve an end or purpose. Attention should also focus on the particular ethos – the *way* of approaching and '(en-)framing' an issue or problem under discussion – where modern technology is governed by a logic of mastery, in which a knowing and expert subject seeks complete control over an object it wishes to dominate (Heidegger, 1962, 1977). Seen in these terms, the question of technology forms part of what Timothy Mitchell has called the emergence of 'techno-politics' and 'techno-power', which he introduces in *Rule of*

Experts (Mitchell, 2002) as a critical tool to explain large-scale infrastructural projects such as the building of the Aswan Dam and the reorganisation of economic practices and relations in the period of neo-liberal globalisation. Supplementing his earlier concerns with the role of disciplinary power and bio-power in making possible the 'power to colonise' Egypt in the 19th century (1991), Mitchell argues that the emergence and hegemony of 'techno-power' is the central organising logic of 20th-century Egypt. In his view, various forms of expertise, like engineering or economics, have no autonomous scientific status, as it is the practices associated with 'the projects themselves' that 'formed the science', and the human agency associated with engineering only 'seems to come first' (Mitchell, 2002: 37). In fact, it was through the 'necessary misapprehension' and concealment of these practices, and their underlying assumptions, that techno-power was produced and operated: 'Overlooking the mixed ways things happen, indeed producing the effect of neatly separated realms of reason and the real world, ideas and their objects, the human and nonhuman, was how power was coming to work in Egypt, and in the twentieth century in general' (Mitchell, 2002: 52).

More specifically, in terms of our puzzle and research questions, the important aspect of making the policy controversy governable involves engaging the public and affected parties in the construction and resolution of the issue. For us, then, technologies of government can be defined as *those particular bundles of concrete techniques or policy instruments, which are deployed by governments to engineer policy agreements among affected parties and communities, in their desire to secure consensus and tackle potential opposition to decisions, thereby making a controversial issue 'governable' or tractable.* This working definition can be augmented by also stressing the techniques that experts and decision-makers use in addressing policy problems. In general, for analysing our puzzle, and its particular field of practices, we concentrate our attention on the techniques of government related to the selection and analysis of data, the empirical methods, diagrams and ratios, and so forth, which are used by experts to problematise and frame the decisions to be taken. Techniques are thus integrally bound up with the power of numbers and quantification.

Taken as a whole, then, our approach focuses on the different ensembles of rationalities, technologies and techniques that come into play in the problematisations of UK airport expansions since the 1950s. But it should also be stressed that the linkages between elements are contingent and not necessary. For example, as we shall see in the case of UK aviation, while a certain rationality or strategy – for example, the logic of 'predict and provide' – can remain more or less consistent over time, it may be connected with different technologies. Equally, we should stress that our conception of rationality is not understood as an unchanging essence, but will always be modified in different ways in each articulation (see Table 1.1).

Table 1.1: Rationalities, technologies and techniques of government

Concept	Paradigm cases	Examples
Rationality or Social Logic of Government	'Predict and provide'	London's Third Airport (1968–1973)
Technology of Government	Public inquiry	Heathrow Terminal 5 (1995–1999)
	Expert commission	Airports Commission (2012–2015)
	National public consultation	Air Transport White Paper (2003)
Technique of Government	Cost-benefit analysis	Roskill Commission (1968–1971)

Struggles for policy hegemony

In operationalising our theoretical approach, we shall avoid precise and exhaustive definitions of policy, governance and policy analysis, agreeing with Colebatch that such terms are used differently across multiple spaces in relation to and as part of the practices and processes of governance (Colebatch, 2002a, 2002b). As Hogwood and Gunn (1984) argue, the notion of policy is best seen as a heuristic device, which captures various phenomena and practices, including a field of activity, expressions of intent, specific proposals, decisions of government, a process and series of decisions. Nonetheless, our working definition of policy can be further extended by focusing on the complex struggles for *policy hegemony*, that is to say, by describing the conditions that are required for a policy to be constructed, accepted and implemented by a relevant set of social actors and institutions in particular contexts. This gaze directs our attention to the different spaces where struggles occur and decisions must be taken, including the particular sub-systems of a specific policy domain, where policy programmes are formulated and proposed, and then finally accepted. But it also includes the state and administrative institutions where policies are implemented and sedimented, such as the Department for Transport (DfT), as well as the wider societal levels (local, national and international) where policy decisions are made and within which institutions are embedded.

In general, our concept of hegemony builds upon the work of Antonio Gramsci and post-Marxists, such as Stuart Hall, Ernesto Laclau and Chantal Mouffe. As Perry Anderson notes, 'Gramsci extended the notion of hegemony from its original application to the perspectives of the working class in a bourgeois revolution against a feudal order, to the mechanisms of bourgeois rule over the working class in a stabilized capitalist society', and he used the concept to undertake '*a differential analysis of the structures of bourgeois power in the West*' in a highly original fashion (Anderson, 1976: 20). But, whereas the emergence of hegemony in the Marxist tradition is mainly designed to focus on the overall dynamics and structures of national social formations – or 'historical blocs' as Gramsci puts it – it must be elaborated in a much more fine-grained fashion when doing policy analysis in specific sectors.

More fully, the achievement of policy hegemony – or policy and societal 'closure' to use Hajer's (1995) terms – for a particular policy or programme, and thus the partial and temporary resolution of a societal problem, can be arranged on a spectrum that runs from the winning of the active consent of a large majority of relevant subjects, on the one hand, to its coercive imposition on a reluctant and sceptical public on the other. Degrees of support and compliance for proposed projects can then be plotted along this axis, where different positions can be measured in terms of the level of consent or acceptance that is constructed and manifested. In fact, it is possible to delineate three levels of hegemony: policy hegemony, institutional hegemony and societal or cultural hegemony (Griggs and Howarth, 2013: 31). In brief, and building on our previous research, *policy* hegemony refers to the making and implementation of law, legislation and administrative guidance about a particular issue; *institutional* hegemony captures the organisational spaces and branches of public authority involved in the development and implementation of public policies, which may or may not be connected to groups and associations in civil society through various formal and informal networks; and *societal* or *cultural* hegemony focuses on the wider norms and values that constitute and underwrite the different forms of 'common sense' in society as a whole.

Such levels and spaces form a loosely interconnected system of processes and practices, though it is also important to stress that they do not necessarily coincide in a strict and watertight way. For one thing, policy hegemony may be realised in one subsystem, without the accomplishment of institutional or societal hegemony. At a basic level, for example, policy may not be carried out in expected ways as street level bureaucrats modify plans and policies in their implementation. More acutely, fundamental policies or programmes may be adopted but not sedimented in the dominant rules that govern particular departments of state, or policies may be reversed as old or former interests and imperatives embedded in an institution or organisation are reasserted and new governments are formed. Equally, policy change does not translate automatically into a shift in the organisation of a state apparatus, or in the underlying beliefs, norms and values of the wider public. In this sense, the conditions for hegemonic success in the policy realm are a change in legislation or laws; the transformation of those institutions that are charged with implementing new rules and regulations, or at least the winning of sufficient compliance among powerful actors within an institution (which usually involves some form of organisational transfiguration); and the winning of consent and compliance among wider sectors of society. Hence, the creation of policy hegemony is a complicated practice, requiring political successes, broader institutional innovation and wider socio-cultural changes. Indeed, we can analyse and assess hegemonic successes in the policy domain via these parameters. However, it is noteworthy that the attainment of hegemony does not need the *total* consent of subjects, whether active or passive, and does not entail their complete compliance. Instead, it only implies the securing of significant support or acquiescence – 'the taking of the "leading position"' – in core sites and institutions of society, and remains 'always contested' (Hall, 1988: 7).

Of course, the question of hegemony would not arise if a policy proposal or programme was readily endorsed by subjects without contestation – the unlikely situation that a controversial policy or programme is accepted without antagonism or disagreement. In most circumstances, as with UK aviation, this is most certainly not the case. Indeed, as we have noted, various policy proposals have been intensely politicised and met with considerable debate and dispute. In such circumstances, if policies are not simply to be imposed upon reluctant and resisting subjects and communities, then either the opponents have to be persuaded of their virtues and benefits, or efforts have to be made to disguise or even mislead affected parties into accepting proposals, which go against their expressed preferences and 'real interests' via the construction and dissemination of ideologies and rhetorical devices, though we have already raised serious objections about the coherence and efficacy of the latter. Overall, in dealing with overt and intense politicisation, where no consensus or legitimate compromise can be constructed, governments and elites often endeavour to *depoliticise* their proposals through various strategies and tactics, in order to secure their enactment and implementation.

Conclusion

Paradoxically, there is a significant tendency in political theory and science to either disavow antagonism and contestation in the name of expertise, moral principles and legal procedure, or to insulate the concerns, demands and interests that arise from such practices from government or the official public sphere, or to transfer them to more manageable domains and sites. By contrast, our conception of politics and the political highlights the role of conflict and antagonism, allocating a primacy to their construction, management and effects in different social and political spaces. Indeed, by using the resources of PDT, we have interrogated the evolving field of depoliticisation studies in political science and theory, while developing the concepts and logics that can illuminate specific instances of such processes. Conceding what we have termed the logics of politicisation and depoliticisation an ontological priority in our approach, we have thus elaborated the various general mechanisms and strategies at work in their operation.

But though such mechanisms and practices are accorded an *ontological* status in our theoretical approach, it is important that they are articulated and fleshed out in relation to specific domains of empirical phenomena. At this *ontical* level, two particular sets of processes come into view: the dynamics of the neoliberal conjuncture that accelerated in the 1970s and 1980s, marking governance and policy-making practices in this period, and then the specificities of our concrete case study – the politics of UK airport expansion – which illuminates and exemplifies the abstract logics and processes that are in play.

In short, our conceptual scheme enables us to cast light on the objects, processes, rationales, effects, strategies and counter-strategies, technologies, techniques and counter-technologies and overall structuring of the dialectics of politicisation and depoliticisation, generally and in our problematised case study. It thus precipitates questions about:

1. The specific targets of depoliticisation: what are the particular objects of depoliticisation – the issues, decisions, demands, policies, practices and so forth?
2. The practices and processes of depoliticisation: how is depoliticisation carried out?
3. The specific reasons for depoliticisation: why and how is it embarked upon as a strategy and practice of government?
4. The outcomes of (attempted) depoliticisations: do they work, and if so, to what degree (which raises normative, critical and functional issues)?
5. The strategies and counter-strategies of depoliticisation: what are the politics of politicisation, depoliticisation and repoliticisation, bringing into play the processes of dislocation, reactivation, the production of new demands and so forth?
6. The links between depoliticisation and technologies of government: how are the logics and processes of depoliticisation related to the technologies and techniques of government?
7. The relationships between depoliticisation and the dimensions of space and time: how does it shape the different spaces and temporalities of law, civil society, the political system, the logics of planning, EU, international organisations and treaties, and so forth, and what in turn are their different impacts and effects on practices of depoliticisation?
8. The connections between depoliticisation, discourse and hegemony: what are the precise mechanisms, strategies and tactics of depoliticisation, and how are they discursively mediated and articulated?

We shall now turn to our genealogical investigation of the emergence and contestation of UK aviation policy.

2

Governing by numbers: fantasies of forecasting, 'predict and provide' and the technologies of government

In the final years of the Second World War, the UK aviation industry was singled out in the corridors of power as a strategic driver of post-war recovery (Barnett, 1995; Engel, 2007; Edgerton, 2018: 189–90). This state sponsorship rapidly coalesced around a regime of aviation expansion which was predicated on a predominant social logic of 'predict and provide' (Adams, 1981; Dudley and Richardson, 1998). 'Predict and provide' was inscribed in the apparatus of the state and government, spelling out an administrative rationality that informed the energies of ministerial staff in planning and delivering additional airport capacity, where the latter was deemed necessary to meet the predicted exponential growth of passenger numbers. Hence, aviation policy was strategically pared down to the interdependent and 'troublesome' tasks of determining the timing of new airport infrastructure, deciding on or making a case for particular sites or locations and ushering proposed developments through planning processes and any local opposition. In other words, decisions over the need for, and the siting of, additional runways and terminals, came to rest on the predictive capabilities of the practices of forecasting and quantification of future passenger demand.

This chapter explores how the knowledge and expertise of forecasting brought into play complex political processes of data accumulation, calculation and modelling in the realm of aviation and airport expansion. We show how the DfT, in its various guises, constituted a wealth of categories, assumptions, economic models and statistical techniques, which sought to normalise expectations of expansion, putting in place complex assemblages of alternative projections of air travel across the UK and individual airports. Paradoxically, practices of forecasting provided a framework and a stage for core decision-making in the present, while effectively projecting the making and implementation of concrete decisions into a depoliticised space of the future. Along this pathway, the magical currency of numbers and the logics of quantification enabled the DfT to position itself as a 'centre of power', which could marginalise all but the most expert and powerful of citizens and groups.

However, despite assembling these statistical and modelling tools, we argue that in the field of airport and aviation expansion provision did not always follow prediction. As passenger numbers continued to expand, the persistent political controversies about the location and timing of new airport capacity dislocated the logic of 'predict and provide', exposing increasing tensions and contradictions. From the early 1960s onwards, governments of all political persuasions engaged in long drawn-out and heavily politicised struggles over the site of the third London Airport and airport expansion in South East England (Le Blond, 2019). By the end of the 1990s, such protest and organised resistance to airport expansion, which had its origins in rising noise pollution and widespread concerns about the local quality of life, had become emblematic of the struggle against climate change and the wider movement for environmental sustainability and justice.

Against this background, the second half of the chapter characterises and evaluates the different technologies that governments used in their endeavours to manage the dislocations and oppositions to expansion. Here we draw attention to three principal technologies: public inquiries, expert Commissions and national public consultations. Our claim here is that such technologies of government were designed to take aviation policy out of the political domain, or at least to dilute their political toxicity. In so doing, they included a strong investment in the personal reputation of appointed chairs and inspectors; the framing and staging of policy debates and the narrow specification of terms of reference; the privileging of appeals to scientific data and calculative reasoning; and the reiteration and reinforcing of the state's monopoly of the public interest. However, despite the efforts to constrain and negate opposition to expansion, these technologies were rapidly politicised by local residents and campaigners, who engaged in strategies of arena-switching and audience expansion. In short, we conclude that the post-war regime of aviation expansion was marked by complex and contingent logics of politicisation, depoliticisation and repoliticisation as governments, campaigners, airports and airlines strived to bring aviation in and out of the political domain, while the technologies of government that were used were either exhausted or bypassed.

The social logic of 'predict and provide'

In principle, the logic of 'predict and provide' simply assumed that there was rising demand for aviation in the UK that had to be met. Rising passenger numbers were mobilised to legitimise the building of new terminals, while future scenarios of aircraft operations combined with passenger numbers established the need for new runway capacity (Milch, 1976: 9). Hence, 'predict and provide' foreshadowed an almost 'bottomless' market for aviation (Milch, 1976: 16), while taking the promise of its economic and social benefits more or less for granted. It defined and extolled aviation and airport expansions as public goods, though they may just as easily be regarded as 'public bads', which impose net costs on affected individuals and communities, not to mention the environment (Aldrich, 2008: 3–4).[1] Whatever the case, practices of 'predict and provide' modelling were deployed to put the operational requirements of airports and carriers before any attempts to mitigate their impacts on local communities and the environment (Upham, 2003).

The art of forecasting

Among these practices, the science – or more accurately the art – of forecasting predominated. Wrapped in an ideology of 'high modernism' and the prospect of a fully quantifiable future, forecasting epitomised a particular form of speculative reasoning (Scott, 1998; Espeland and Stevens, 2008; Andersson, 2018). It interrogated the past to make calculated wagers on the future. Statistical methods of time-series regressions modelled the historical drivers of aviation markets and the relationships between them. Such historical drivers were then deployed to project future demand for air travel and patterns of consumption across different aviation markets (DETR, 2000a; AC, 2013c). The effect of such calculations was to compress time and space, as the future of aviation was constructed by extrapolating from the laws of the past, while gambling on their desired continuation in the future. Projected rises in Gross Domestic Product (GDP) and trade stepped in as primary determinants of passenger demand for business flights. Fluctuations in air fares and consumer spending were similarly designated as the drivers of rising demand for leisure flights.

But such causal assumptions and projections rested on contestable judgements, simplifications and categorisations (AEF, 2007). Take, for example, the 2000 forecasts that informed the preparation of the ATWP (2003) (DETR, 2000a). First, anticipated growth in GDP took centre-stage as an indicator of growing passenger numbers. Yet, in so doing, it overrode other considerations, such as the derived demand for flights, which rises and falls for example with changes in the opportunities for individuals to take holidays (Riddington, 2006: 311). Riddington (2006: 300) thus dismissed the statistical projections as little more than a 'trend forecast', which 'define, rather than find, a linear relationship between passenger numbers and GDP'. Secondly, the forecasts assumed that domestic GDP would grow by 2.25 per cent per annum over the 20 years from 2000 to 2020, even though this was a rate which the British economy only came close to achieving in 3 years from the 2008 global economic crisis through to 2019.[2] Thirdly, other variables such as travel by rail or the actions of government in managing demand were simply bracketed out of calculations (Riddington, 2006). Finally, many of the assumptions of the forecasters, including the belief that air fares would decline by 1 per cent per annum, were themselves based upon a series of contestable interpretations about the stabilisation and potential decline of oil prices, the absence of 'step changes' in aircraft technology and increased competition and deregulation within aviation markets (DETR, 2000a: 27). As Milch (1976: 15) points out, forecasts came to resemble 'inverted pyramids', whereby the implications of judgements and simplifications made at one stage of the process risked being amplified at another, so that forecasting was made 'increasingly unstable as it becomes [ever] more complex' (see Table 2.1). In fact, as late as the end of the 1970s, planners assumed that load factors, or the proportion of seats sold on an aircraft, were as low as 60 per cent for short-haul flights and 54 per cent for long-haul operations, building in to forecasts an 'immutable fact of life' that served to over-estimate the demands on capacity (Graham, 2018).

In the politics of aviation expansion, therefore, the 'accuracy' of forecasts was ultimately immaterial. For example, the case for the third London airport made by the 1963 Interdepartmental Review predicted that Gatwick and

Table 2.1: The Department for Transport forecasting model

National Air Passenger Demand Model (NAPDM)	• Generates forecasts of unconstrained demand. • Forecasts numbers of terminal passengers from, to or through UK nationally. • Splits demand into 19 different market segments. • Based on analysis of historical patterns of drivers of demand across market segments and how these might change in the future.
NAPDM feeds into	
National Air Passenger Allocation Model (NAPAM)	• Allocates national demand across 31 airports across UK. • Based on geographic origins of passengers, surface access transport costs and service frequency modelling. • Incorporates options of taking direct flights or travelling via hub in UK or abroad. • Incorporates a constrained forecast that provides a 'do minimum' baseline scenario.
Projections of passenger numbers and air traffic movements feed into	
Sub-models	• Modelling of UK future fleet deployed to estimate carbon emissions route-by-route from flights leaving UK. • Transport User Benefits Model assesses benefits to passenger of alternative policy options.
Examples of associated forecasts	• Forecasts of the UK Consumer Expenditure and UK GDP provided by the Office of Budget Responsibility. • Forecasts of oil and carbon prices established by the Department of Energy and Climate Change. • Forecasts of passenger data from the Civil Aviation Authority.

Source: Based on AC (2013c: 13–16).

Heathrow airports would be unable to accommodate all London air traffic by 1973, with an 'overspill' predicted at less than 20 million passengers. Yet by 1976 Gatwick and Heathrow actually received 28.9 million passengers. More generally, the capacity of existing airport infrastructure to accommodate further passengers was often and consistently underestimated, as were the technological developments that enabled larger planes to carry more passengers, a development which helped to shift attention from runway to terminal capacity (Hall, 1982: 21–4). Typically, forecasts of rising passenger numbers and air transport movements varied considerably over the 20 years of the controversy surrounding the third London airport. In 1971, the Roskill Commission predicted 82.7 million passengers going through London airports in 1985, compared to between 75.7 and 100.6 million estimated by the British Airports Authority (BAA) in its evidence to the Commission. Yet in 1972 BAA was to revise its prediction to 87 million, only to be followed in 1974 by the Maplin Review, which in the aftermath of the 1973 oil crisis reduced predicted passenger numbers to be between 58 and 76 million in 1985 (Hall, 1982: 40).

Importantly, forecasting brought into being a series of new *categories* which shaped the terrain of argumentation in aviation policy. The category of 'unconstrained' passenger demand, upon which forecasts for the 2003 White Paper were predicated, incorporated the need for additional capacity into the forecasts of the DfT (Upham, 2003). More broadly, the repeated juxtaposition of the categories of 'constrained' and 'unconstrained' demand in the discourse of forecasting served to focus debate on the opportunity costs of failing to deliver additional runways and terminals. Such juxtaposed categories highlighted the threat of foregone benefits or sacrificed enjoyment if additional capacity was not provided (Griggs and Howarth, 2013: 172–5). Concerns about passengers allegedly 'lost to the UK system' (those who would no longer travel by plane if additional capacity was not provided), threats of the potential migration of passengers to international competitors, worsening delays and increasing air fares and the horrific fantasy of 'capacity overloads' thus emerged as forecasts were often weaponised to offset opposition to expansion (Cairns et al, 2006: 34; Griggs and Howarth, 2013: 112–21). But in articulating the categories of passenger demand in this way the juxtaposition of constrained and unconstrained demand constructed a false dichotomy: in practice, of course, all policy frameworks imposed constraints on passenger demand, so the principal question was *how* 'constraining that framework should be' (FoE, 2013: 1).

Equally, the currency of forecasting functioned as the entry fee into debates over airport expansion. Technocratic arguments about statistical projections framed policy deliberations. Indeed, the task of contesting projections of rising demands on airports in the next 10 or 20 years, or the 'need' for expansion became the necessary, though often insufficient, means of opposition for external stakeholders and local resident groups (Milch, 1976; Hall, 1982). At the same time, the practices of data accumulation and calculation established new 'conduits of power', positioning the DfT as a nodal actor in the information flows that constructed the 'reality' of aviation policy (Rose, 1991: 676; see also Hacking, 1981). Forecasting thus pushed to the margins of policy debate all but the most 'expert' of 'expert citizens' (Bang, 2005). For example, in its 2013 submission to the AC's call for evidence on the DfT's models of forecasting, Friends of the Earth (FoE) highlighted such exclusionary dynamics, arguing that 'we do not have the technical expertise to present a detailed critique of the DfT forecasting approach' (FoE, 2013: 1).

Against this background, the politics of aviation policy was played out in the realm of the 'long-term': a spatio-temporality of speculated alternatives where troubling opposition could be displaced. In these projected imaginary futures, demands to regulate noise pollution or coordinate under-used capacity in the present could be summarily negated by mobilising predictions of technological change, inculcating effective regulatory mechanisms, or summoning up the immovability of consumer preferences. In a nutshell, forecasting was ultimately concerned with the political management of communication in the present. It was an investment in the 'manageable future', as well as a means of coordinating action in the present and depoliticising contentious issues of expansion in order to deliver an over-determined 'coming physical reality' (Andersson, 2018: 2). In other words, forecasting was less about envisioning a different future than stabilising support for the continual reproduction of the past. 'Long-term' forecasts in aviation ultimately boiled down to more of the same.

Overall, therefore, forecasting is best understood as the use of 'calculated power' (Rose, 1991: 673) to justify and legitimise sedimented policy discourses and goals. Writing in the 1970s, Jerome Milch (1976: 16) argued that policymakers were 'led to believe that forecasting [could] measure the shape of the future', and this 'overselling' of predictions owed much to the ideological 'grip' of numbers and quantification, offering what Peter Self (1975: 92) in his critique of numerology describes as the 'beguiling appearance (and nothing more) of scientific rationality'. Indeed, even though largely speculative, such forecasts were regularly 'accepted', and used in opposition to the more difficult logic of quantifying environmental impacts and considerations (Self, 1975: 166). Forecasts were thus in part a self-fulfilling prophecy, garnering support in the present for expansion in the future. The need or desire for additional infrastructure in the long-term created its 'own' demand or even accelerated demand above what was expected (Cairns et al, 2006: 36; Transport for London, 2013: 5). In practice, then, statistical projections did not 'merely inscribe a pre-existing reality', but 'constituted it' (Rose, 1991: 676).

Flaws and mounting opposition

Over time, despite the shifting role and character of the British state, the practical and ideological investment in the art of forecasting remained more or less continuous, though its precise forms were at times rejigged (DfT, 2002a: 35; AC, 2013c: 12; Le Blond, 2019: 88). Hence, the logic of prediction and quantification spread its tentacles into new issues, stretching into forecasts of carbon emissions in the 2000s, as well as the critical issue of noise pollution following the establishment of noise contours in the early 1960s. The Wilson Committee drew up Noise and Number Index (NNI) contours in 1963, as it sought to map and quantify the mean noise annoyances experienced by local residents around airports, developing the category of 'noise exposure' (Paul, 1971: 297). Taking the 35 NNI contour as the indicative boundary of where the average person was aggravated by aircraft noise disturbance, although the Wilson Committee recognised that people were a 'little annoyed' at 31 NNI, decision-making over noise in planning inquiries and departmental guidance was reduced to calculating the number of people living under flight paths within or above the 35 NNI contour, where 55 NNI signalled 'high annoyance' (Paul, 1971: 298; Brooker, 2008: 21). However, the measurement of NNI contours was inherently flawed (McKennell, 1969), and the 1961 survey around Heathrow upon which the NNI was based had generated insufficient data of the impacts on residents of repeated instances of moderate loudness from planes or intermittent instances of loud noise from flights. It also equated the impacts of noise during the day with the impacts of noise at night, calculating noise contours according to the average exposure to aircraft noise on a summer's day from 7am to 7pm.

But, most importantly, the NNI could not account for the subjective impacts of noise, in which individuals living under a flight path experienced noise differently. Writing at the turn of the 1970s, Paul (1971: 300) stated that 'in the present state of knowledge we cannot count the numbers who will be annoyed by aircraft noise', concluding that 'NNI contours are used because they are thought to be better than anything else'. Such metrics were to remain in place until the findings of the 1985 Aircraft Noise Index Study ushered in the use of the alternative measure – 57 dB LAeq – which calculated the noise levels of aircraft in decibels (57 decibels was estimated to be the level that triggered significant annonyance in communities), and the average of sound energy from all aircraft in an area throughout the 16 hours from 7am to 11pm (Brooker et al, 1985). Even so, this transition to Leq measures did little to tackle the subjective nature of responses to aircraft noise and community annoyance (Brooker, 2008).

What is more, as aviation expanded, the political rationale of 'predict and provide' was to generate increasing opposition and protests from communities, especially from the 1960s onwards with the rapid growth of noise from jet engines. Such sustained opposition decoupled the twin elements of 'predict' *and* 'provide': for while forecasting advanced demands for increased airport capacity within political circles, persistent policy controversies emerged around the siting and timing of additional infrastructure to meet this projected demand. The location of the third London airport thus came to dominate the policy agenda in the 1960s (McKie, 1973; Roffrey, 2012; Le Blond, 2019). Struggles over its location and expansion in South East England were to continue throughout the 1980s and 1990s, bringing sustained opposition from local residents at Stansted, Gatwick and Heathrow. Such campaigns were to expand beyond the particular demands of conservation and community well-being to embrace universal demands for environmental justice as awareness of the impacts of flying on climate change increased. In the late 1990s, local residents joined forces for the first time with direct action environmentalists to contest the building of a second runway at Manchester (Griggs et al, 1998; Griggs and Howarth, 2002). This struggle began to imitate the strategies and tactics of the anti-roads movement, echoing the arguments that had discredited the logic of 'predict and provide' in road building. And the growing political pressures had their effects: by the ATWP (2003), the New Labour government was at pains to point out that its aviation policy and predictions for expansion were not another case of 'predict and provide'.

We shall now turn our attention to how different technologies of government were deployed to offset the political opposition to airport expansion. Endeavouring to manage the timing and site location of new airports, runways or terminals – the predominant problems that arose from the logics of 'predict and provide' – politicians and officials drew upon and transformed an ensemble of technologies, coupled with their attendant techniques of analysis and policymaking, which were designed and arranged to exclude opposition and depoliticise aviation expansion. We begin by examining their use of the quasi-judicial forums of public inquiries, before turning to the creation of the Roskill Commission on the Third London Airport in the late 1960s, and the therapeutic technologies of community engagement advanced by the New Labour government in the run-up to the ATWP (2003).

Public inquiries

Planning inquiries are heavily structured and formal examinations of proposed developments where appointed inspectors assess arguments for and against planning applications, gathering evidence from witnesses before taking a decision to grant or refuse development. Such inquiries are established when developers appeal against the refusal of local planning authorities to grant their planning applications, as in the case of the Stansted

Airport Public Inquiry in 2021, where Manchester Airports Group appealed the decision of Uttlesford District Council to refuse planning permission to increase the capacity of the airport. Similarly, Bristol Airport appealed the February 2020 decision of North Somerset Council to reject its plans for expansion, with the ensuing public inquiry opening in July 2021. But, more importantly for our analysis, public inquiries can also be the result of the Secretary of State deciding to 'call in' a planning decision and take it out of the hands of local planning authorities. In a similar way, appeals can also be 'recovered', as they fall under the jurisdiction of the Secretary of State. In such circumstances, the Secretary of State can deem the development to be of national importance or highly disputed, as in the case of Terminal 5 at Heathrow. The final decision on proposed developments thus reverts to the Secretary of State following a public inquiry and recommendations by planning inspectors (Butcher, 2018: 7–8).

Against this background, and understood as a technology of government, public inquiries have been constructed and used as independent forums to deliver a rational and impartial assessment of the plans for additional airport capacity, be it a new terminal, runway or a relaxation of the caps on passenger numbers (Kemp, 1985: 177). In the UK context, public inquiries were held for the proposed expansion of Stansted in the middle of the 1960s; the Fourth Terminal at Heathrow at the end of the 1970s; the North Terminal at Gatwick, a new terminal and safeguarding of land for a second runway at Stansted, as well as the prospects for a Fifth Terminal at Heathrow in the 1980s; the Second Runway at Manchester and the Fifth Terminal at Heathrow in the 1990s; and the expansion of the passenger planning cap at Stansted in the 2000s. Most recently, in 2021, public inquiries have considered expansion plans at Bristol and Stansted airports, while the Secretary of State in 2022 'called in' plans for expansion at Leeds Bradford and Luton airports (although Leeds Bradford subsequently withdrew its planning application in March 2022).

Formally, inquiries operate as temporary arenas of institutional scrutiny or advice, where local stakeholders and interested parties present evidence and contest arguments for and against infrastructural development. In practice, they effectively form a quasi-judicial, adversarial arena in which the right to be heard and listened to is exchanged for the duty to abide by the decisions of an allegedly neutral and independent Inspector who presides over proceedings, although the final approval for development can rest with the Secretary of State (Griggs and Howarth, 2013: 119; see also Kemp, 1985; Owens, 2002).

The adversarial space of public inquiries privileges the logics of legal argumentation, which are performed through 'proofs of evidence', rebuttals and written statements of the case for or against expansion. Pre-inquiry meetings with interested parties determine the timetable of the inquiry, while also reaching agreements about the proof of evidence formats, procedures and sitting hours, and the presentation of outline statements of the case. In the specific inquiries that are relevant for our problematisations, local campaigners and developers were represented in such proceedings by solicitors and barristers, often at significant cost. Experts were also called by opposing sides to support their case and challenge that of their opponents (Rough, 2011).

Typically, rival arguments contested the justifications for increased capacity and the veracity of passenger forecasts, while disputing claims over jobs and economic benefits, as well as the cost and funding of projects and the required levels of compensation and mitigation. Much argument was focused on estimates of the impacts of expansion on the environment and the quality of life of local residents, especially with respect to aircraft noise and air quality, surface transport and road access, wildlife habitats, listed buildings and sites of special scientific interest (see, for example, the Manchester airport second runway public inquiry (Butcher, 2010)). The breadth of information and documentation presented at such inquiries is also worth noting. For example, the inquiry for the Fifth Terminal at Heathrow airport opened in May 1995 and by April 1998 had received over 600 proofs of evidence and some 20,000 written statements from the public (Williams and McKenna, 1998).

It was imperative that the performances and interventions enacted in these 'staged events' should adhere strictly to the 'rules' of legal argumentation. Campaigners and activists were thus advised, if not obliged, to present evidence that avoided emotive statements and which could be defended under cross-examination. They were urged by experienced organisers and lobbyists to dress conservatively, to 'act like the other parties at the inquiry ... and argue in ways that are similar to theirs [the developers]' (AEF, undated: 6). In its guidance to local campaigners, for example, the Aviation Environment Federation (AEF) (undated: 6) showcased the work of Brian Ross and his colleague, Mike Young, from Stop Stansted Expansion (SSE) at the 2007 Stansted 'Generation 1' Public Inquiry. Ross and Young, who had careers in corporate finance and accountancy, challenged the economic benefits of expansion at Stansted, legitimising their calculations by using the Treasury's own methodology – the *HM Treasury Green Book* – as well as the discount rate assumptions used by the DfT, and the findings of the Stern Review on the economics of climate change (which was published in 2006) to conclude that 'the economic impacts [of expansion] are substantially and demonstratively negative' (Ross and Young, 2007: 12). Public inquiries were, therefore, an arena for expert citizens to act politically in a highly regulated space of engagement, where the logics of quantification could often prevail.

In these quasi-legal spaces, the critical target audience for local campaigners was the Inspector, who at the end of the inquiry was to make recommendations to Ministers, as was the case in airport developments where the planning application had been 'called in'. FoE (2020: 9) went as far as to advise campaigners to 'remember' that 'the Inspector is your friend, is impartial and does not work for the developer'. Hence, the strategic aim in presenting the case against expansion was to 'help [the Inspector] make a decision, by teasing out arguments that [they] will ultimately use to help support [their] decision' (AEF, undated: 5). In such efforts to shape the decision of the Inspector, the singular advantage of campaigners was usually perceived to be the mobilisation of local knowledge, leading local campaigners to invest in the power of rational dialogue and reasoning. Indeed, within some opposition ranks, the public inquiry was perceived to be a 'level playing field' in which 'Davids with good arguments have won over seeming Goliaths' (AEF, undated: 1).

However, the function of the Inspector was not to question the direction or validity of government policy, but to assess plans for development against the application of land-use planning regulations, development rules and the objectives of government policy. In other words, Inspectors were mainly influenced by arguments that challenged the 'material considerations' or 'soundness' of planning proposals, not the strength of local opposition. The terms of reference of the inquiry were set by government, often resulting in a narrow framing of the decision-making process, as in the Gatwick inquiry of the 1950s, where they constrained any questioning of the need for a third London airport and alternatives to expansion at Gatwick (McKie, 1973: 45, cited in Griggs and Howarth, 2013: 119).

Equally, it was alleged by many campaigners and affected parties that the design of public inquiries distorted communication processes, defining and legitimising what constituted 'relevant' arguments and evidence (Kemp, 1985; Blackman, 1991). For one thing, the foregrounding of planning issues biased opposition towards technical rather than social value considerations (Blackman, 1991: 312). Wider questions of the public interest were effectively monopolised by government and pushed to the margins of public inquiries, because it was assumed that national issues could not be decided locally. Moreover, this logic was amplified by the construction of public inquiries on a site-by-site or case-by-case basis, which not only removed the definition of the public interest from the realm of debate, but often pitted the expansion of one airport against expansion at another, thereby fragmenting or hindering the emergence of national opposition to aviation policy. It is indeed striking that this ideology of the public interest enabled the discursive construction of local residents as NIMBYs (Owens, 2002), while drawing equivalences between aviation expansion and the national interest.

Overall, public inquiries played the strategic political function of a 'safety valve', allowing the public to 'blow off steam' via heavily constrained channels of opposition (Drapkin, 1974: 243, cited in Rough, 2011: 24). Embodying state power, they acted as legitimising arenas whereby already identified sites for expansion 'gain[ed] justificatory force through association with the supposedly open, democratic characteristics of the public inquiry process' (Kemp, 1985: 178). Yet local residents, campaigners and communities often demurred. For example, at the public inquiry into the second runway at Manchester airport in the mid-1990s, participants cast doubt on the process of the inquiry, concluding that they 'won' the argument but lost the 'decision' (Griggs and Howarth, 2002). Importantly, even if the Inspector was able to make recommendations to government, the final decision to approve plans for development rested with ministers. In practice, therefore, in the words of Widdicombe (1978: vii), government 'combine[d] the roles of advocate for the scheme and judge of the objections to it' (see also Appleyard, 1983: 113–14).

By the late 1990s, then, traditional strategies of fighting public inquiries were increasingly discredited. For many local campaigners who experienced the personal dislocations of 'lost campaigns', recommendations made by Inspectors were too easily overturned or ignored by government. In his evidence to the House of Commons Procedure Committee in 2002, Roy Vandermeer QC, the Inspector at the Heathrow Terminal 5 Inquiry, claimed that 'many members of the public took the view that [the inquiry] was all really rigged' and questioned ' "Why are we wasting this time?" '[3] The Inspector at the inquiry into the fourth terminal at Heathrow had recommended a cap on flights at the airport and that there be no fifth terminal. In fact, previous constraints imposed on expansion by Inspectors were repeatedly reactivated by local residents who were able to assemble narratives of 'broken promises' and government failures (Stewart, 2008). Stop Stansted Expansion thus opened its submissions at the public inquiries into capacity at Stansted airport in 2007 and 2021 with the conclusions of Graham Eyre QC, the Inspector at the 1983 inquiry into Stansted expansion, who argued that the expansion of Stansted to accommodate 25 million passengers per annum would be 'nothing less than a catastrophe in environmental terms (SSE, 2007: 2, 2021: 2). Significantly, Alan Boyland, the Inspector of the 2007 inquiry, argued in his final report that he did 'not regard Eyre's conclusions as constraining, still less prejudging, mine on the current proposals, and respectfully suggest that the Secretaries of State should not regard them so either' (Boyland, 2008: 578).

In fact, as Sharman concluded, as early as the beginning of the 1970s, the 'British practice of seeking to expose and justify an airport proposal at a local public inquiry, though it has had some good results in some cases has become increasingly inadequate to prevent a polarisation of forces for and against each proposal' (Sharman, 1975: 50). Public inquiries were quickly politicised, highlighting contestable views of the public good (Owens, 2002: 952) and open to strategies of disruption that transformed them into 'arenas without rules' (Dudley and Richardson, 1998). They were the primary institutional site where the public could question the location of airports (Rough, 2011: 25), and they enabled interests outside government to bring new forms of expertise and knowledge into the decision-making process (Dudley and Richardson, 1998). Indeed, despite the quasi-judicial character of the inquiry, and the government's monopolisation of the public interest, Inspectors had some discretion to interpret 'the brief liberally to permit debate on the wider public interest' (Levin, 1979: 21; Blackman, 1991: 314; Rough, 2011).

Such discretion was the necessary condition of the role of the Inspector, forming an integral part of the depoliticising narrative of public inquiries. But this discretion opened up potential for further politicisation. For example, Roy Vandermeer QC, the Inspector at the Heathrow Terminal 5 Inquiry, underlined how at the start of the inquiry in 1997, the most recent incarnation of government policy was the Airports White Paper (1985), which was described by a Junior Minister as 'yellow around the edges'. Vandermeer himself also found the Inquiry's terms of reference to be 'vague', concluding that in such conditions 'it was very difficult after that to stop people considering aspects of policy when you have an out-of-date document or an old document and some doubt cast upon it by a member of the then Government'.[4]

Public inquiries were also part of a chain of settings and venues engaged in decision-making over airport expansion. Arguments presented at inquiries can be picked up by the media, 'dropped' into Parliament, and tied to other demands and campaigns. Campaigners were increasingly quick to grasp such opportunities to challenge the perceived democratic legitimacy and underhand incrementalism of government decision-making. At the 2007 inquiry into the expansion of Stansted, SSE called as a witness, Aqqaluk Lynge, a member of the Inuit Circumpolar Council and the United Nations Permanent Forum on Indigenous Issues, to give evidence on the impact of climate change on the ecosystem of Inuit communities. Making the link in his evidence between flying and rising carbon emissions, the Inuit leader implored airlines not to 'melt away our future' (Lynge, 2007). His appearance was seized upon by the SSE Campaign director, Carole Barbone, to open up new political frontiers and expose the inconsistencies of government policy, arguing that 'if Gordon Brown [then Prime Minister] doesn't grasp that nettle [stopping expansion at Stansted] then his claims about acting to address global warming will be exposed as mere platitudes'.[5]

Such strategies were part and parcel of attempts by campaigners to shift the venue of decision-making beyond the confines of public inquiries, while constructing broader political coalitions against expansion. Undoubtedly, such politicising practices triggered the 'many years of partial and almost secret decision-making by Government' regarding the site of the third London airport, particularly following local and parliamentary campaigns to enforce the decisions of the Inspector at the Public Inquiry (1965–1966) into the development of Stansted airport (Lichfield, 1971: 157). The Inspector at the inquiry concluded that the case for the development of Stansted as a 'national necessity' was not proven (Wraith, 1966; Roffrey, 2012: 97).

But the government subsequently internalised the policymaking process within the corridors of Whitehall, delaying the publication of the Inspector's report, while putting in place an Inter-Departmental Committee to review the case for expansion at Stansted. It ultimately reiterated its support for a third London airport in May 1967 in a White Paper, before announcing in November 1967 that the development of Stansted airport would go ahead under a Special Development Order, which granted approval for the project through a parliamentary vote without the need for a further public inquiry (McKie, 1973; Roffrey, 2012). However, the government soon backtracked as opposition in and outside Parliament continued and grew in strength with the formation of the Stansted Working Group and the intervention in July 1967 of J.W. Brancker, who was the technical advisor at the public inquiry. Writing in the *Times* newspaper he disclosed that the Stansted inquiry had had assurances that government would not over-rule its recommendations (Roffrey, 2012: 97–104). Amidst such political uncertainty, Anthony Crosland, President of the Board of Trade, announced the launch of a new inquiry into the third London airport in the middle of February 1968. It was to be chaired by the High Court Judge, Eustace Roskill.

Bring on the experts: the Roskill Commission

After concerted political opposition to the development of Stansted, the Roskill Commission was an attempt by government to deliver a 'fair and impartial' decision by taking the issue of the third London airport out of the political domain. The appointment of Roskill, as Peter Hall suggested at the time, brought into being the 'coolness of a judge-conducted inquiry' (1968: 939), and Roskill was instructed to 'ensure fair play for objectors [while] six other expert Commissioners (one an economist) would cover the various technical aspects of the decision' (Self, 1970: 8). Roskill himself was conscious of the need for the Commission to 'establish public confidence' in its decision-making, noting at the outset that he and his fellow Commissioners had to convince the public that 'its work would be impartial, unbiased and entirely uninfluenced by what had gone before' (cited in Waters, 1971: 203–4; Commission on the Third London Airport, 1971: 10).

The workings of the Commission were 'judicial in form' (Self, 1975: 155). Its public hearings followed the practices and performances of the law courts and public inquiries. The 74 days of its stage five hearings took place at the Piccadilly Hotel, inviting a rollcall of witnesses to state their cases and be cross-examined by senior counsel. The seven Commissioners sat 'mainly silent upon a dais ... while the flower of the planning bar argued [in front of them]' (Self, 1970: 8). Politics was frequently associated with 'subjective judgements' and 'deep emotions', as Roskill and his team followed a 'quasi-judicial' logic of assessment, which sought to 'identify accurately each component part of the problem', then 'ascertain which component part interacts and possibly conflicts with others', before correlating any potential interactions. Such an approach maximised the 'rational and coherent' treatment of elements, while minimising 'subjective or intuitive judgements' (Waters, 1971: 204).

Cost-benefit analysis ...

Cost-benefit analysis (CBA) was chosen as the appropriate technique to implement this approach. It was advocated by the then President of the Board of Trade, Tony Crosland, who was an economist with a growing interest in environmental policy, though 'he quickly saw that there was a serious problem in identifying all the factors concerned with the location of airports' (Graham, 2018). CBA has its origins in the application of welfare economics to public policy issues (Pierce, 1971), itself a further product of the post-war rise of quantification (Rose, 1991; Porter, 1995; Espeland and Stevens, 2008), or what Self calls the 'econocracy', that is, the 'belief that there exist fundamental economic tests or yardsticks according to which policy decisions can and should be made' (Self, 1975: 5). In the political context of the late 1960s, epitomised by the Wilson government's investment in economic planning and science – the 'white heat' of the scientific and technological revolution – these underlying assumptions, and their adoption by Roskill and his colleagues, established the Commission as the 'very epitome of rational decision-making' (Self, 1970: 8).[6] Such framings went some way in legitimising this new technology of government, laying down the conditions to ensure public confidence in the decisions that Roskill was designed to produce.

Lending itself to the quasi-judicial logic of the Commission, CBA rests on the assumption that the multiple factors informing a decision can each be translated into a common language, often money, and quantified in relation to one another. The process of quantification and equivalence thereby allows decision-making to weigh up the costs and benefits of undertaking a particular course of action. Within this model of decision-making, the optimal course of action emerges from this act of translating factors into a common criterion and then weighing up the costs and benefits, such that in an 'ideal cost-benefit analysis ... the best decision would end as a simple exercise of addition and subtraction' (Self, 1975: 8). Peter Hall went so far as to characterise the work of the Roskill Commission as 'based on the most rational, dispassionate procedure of analysis that good minds could devise', although this did not stop him opposing its final recommendations

(Hall, 1971: 145). At the beginning of the public hearings in the Piccadilly Hotel, the counsel for the government devoted a whole day to explaining the methodology underpinning its analysis (Self, 1975: 155), though even a leading planner, Colin Buchanan, who was a member of the Commission, and who was ultimately to publicly dissent from its collective conclusions, admitted his difficulties in understanding the method of CBA.

The Commission, supported by a 23-strong research team, initially considered a long list of 78 sites over 20 counties, which was whittled down to 20 and finally to four sites some 40 miles from London: Cublington, Foulness (later Maplin), Nuthampstead and Thurleigh. Foulness came thirteenth out of the 20 sites on the longlist, owing in part to its expense and surface access costs, but it was shortlisted for its novelty (Hall, 1982: 29–38). For each site, the Commission calculated the costs of an extensive list of factors from airport, road and rail construction through to passenger and freight user costs, interference with military flights, losses to agriculture, falls in the quality of life and so on. The exercise was designed to identify the 'least-cost site', where differential costs, rather than total costs, were used to readily permit a comparison across the sites. As such, the best site for each factor was awarded a '0', while other sites were then weighted accordingly. Significantly, total costs were initially communicated by the Commission but were subsequently withdrawn as 'misleading' (Self, 1975: 158–9). The costs of each factor were then aggregated together to generate the overall 'costs' for each site. Cublington, located in between Birmingham and London, came out on top in the rankings using this calculus, generating the lowest costs of all the sites (see Table 2.2).

... and its discontents

Understandably, despite widespread recognition of the efforts of the Commission, and 'the methodical and majestic way in which [it] sailed from its uncertain beginnings to its very firm end' in a context of intense publicity and scrutiny (Lichfield, 1971: 157), much of the criticism at the time came to rest on the Commission's use of CBA. On the one hand, its work was derided not as a form of CBA, but as a simple relative evaluation of the costs of the four sites, which did little to assuage the presumption that 'a third airport at any one of the four alternative sites can be justified on economic grounds' (Mishan, 1970: 223). On the other hand, it was seen to undervalue the costs of the greatest concern to local communities by attributing too much weight to airspace movement costs and passenger user costs, and by providing insufficient explanation of how these costs were calculated (see Adams, 1970: 3; Self, 1975: 157).

Notably, the Commission faced accusations that it had undervalued: the non-material benefits of the countryside and a noise-free environment,

Table 2.2: Roskill Commission and cost-benefit analysis: differences from lowest-cost site (£ million discounted to 1982)

		Cublington		Foulness		Nuthampstead		Thurleigh	
		High time values	Low time values	High time values	Low time values	High time values	Low time values	High time values	Low time values
1	Airport construction		18		32		14		0
2	Extension of Luton		0		18		0		0
3	Airport services	23	22	0	0	17	17	7	7
4	Meteorology		5		0		2		1
5	Airspace movements	0	0	7	5	35	31	30	26
6	Passenger user costs	0	0	207	167	41	35	39	22
7	Freight user costs		0		14		5		1
8	Road capital		0		4		4		5
9	Rail capital		3		26		12		0
10	Air safety		0		2		0		0
11	Defence		29		0		5		61
12	Public scientific establishments		1		0		21		27
13	Private airfields		7		0		13		15
14	Residential conditions (noise, off-site)		13		0		62		5
15	Residential conditions (on-site)		11		0		8		6
16	Luton noise costs		0		11		0		0
17	Schools, hospitals and public authority buildings (including noise)		7		0		11		9
18	Agriculture		0		4		9		3
19	Commerce and industry (including noise)		0		2		1		2
20	Recreation (including noise)		13		0		7		7
	Aggregate of inter-site differences (costed items only) high and low time values	0	0	197	156	137	128	88	68

Source: Table 16. *London Third Airport sites: summary cost/benefit analysis*, Commission on the Third London Airport (1971) Report, London: HMSO, p 119.

failing to account for the costs of disruption to the quality of life of those living next to the airport; the disruption caused by residential displacement and aircraft noise; and the impacts on environmental intangibles such as wildlife and landscape depreciation or loss. The difficulties in quantifying the costs and benefits of such factors led to allegations of bias in the calculations underlying the results of the work of the Commission, which were seen 'not only [as being] materialistic and philistine but also discriminatory against low-income groups'. In fact, the Commission had failed to recognise that those who might benefit most would be those living and working in London, and not those living next to the planned airport (Adams, 1970: 5, 9; see also Mishan, 1970; Self, 1975).

Issues such as aircraft noise were indeed pushed to the margins of its calculations by the design and use of the method of CBA, or at least how it was implemented by the Commission. Alan Walters, an economist on the Commission, disclosed the methodological difficulties at the opening hearings of the Commission when he announced that 'we can read evidence which takes the form of a large number of complaints [about noise], but it is very difficult to put numbers on it and to put it into a consistent system of valuation' (Hall, 1968: 942). The Commission first drew upon the work of the Wilson Committee, accepting the noise contour of 35 NNI as the boundary of the 'acceptable' range of aircraft noise disturbance experienced by those living under flight paths, even though the limits of these metrics were widely acknowledged, particularly the equating of noise experienced during the day and night, as well as evidence to suggest that some individuals experienced significant noise disturbance even within lower NNI contours (Paul, 1971).

Faced with the individual and subjective nature of noise, as well as the differential capacities of some individuals to 'exit' and move out of the area, the Commission subsequently resorted to calculating predicted movement in property values as a surrogate indicator of the costs and benefits of expansion and aircraft noise on local communities, while accounting for the costs of the insulation and moving of public buildings, as well as falls in efficiency for industry and losses in enjoyment for outside leisure activities (Flowerdew, 1972: 36). Yet the depreciation in housing values indicated at best 'what someone will pay to escape noise rather than what [the individual] needs to be compensated for enduring it' (Paul, 1971: 319). Indeed, although it had the advantage of being a factor that could actually be measured, Self (1970: 9) underlined how any estimate of the costs of noise nuisance and opportunities of airport expansion, which was tied to the movement of house prices, was 'bound to be a lemon'. Such estimates, according to Self, invariably masked the individual subjective valuations of such issues, disregarded the fact that most people do not even calculate the specific price of such issues, and relied upon the assessment and use of 'imputed prices' on an 'imputed market which shifts with circumstances', not least housing supply.

Nonetheless, in extolling the virtues of the method of CBA, the Commission was able to deflect opposition to its decisions onto its methods and techniques of analysis, and thus away from the need for aviation expansion per se (Self, 1970: 9; Lichfield, 1971: 157). In fact, it was the ranking of different sites and the final calculation of costs that caught the attention of local campaigners, for as Self (1975: 93) argues the 'fixing of eyes upon the techniques of final evaluation shifts attention from the intervening process and the reasoning behind them'. The dominant assumption of the need for a third London airport and the continual rise of passenger numbers to reach 200 million in 2000 was not challenged by the Commission. More importantly, the rise in air traffic was straightforwardly assumed to be a benefit, such that the ' "base load" of benefits [was] not measured for each site' (Adams, 1970: 6). Increases in volumes of traffic were again assumed to be 'some natural and inevitable phenomenon', which failed to capture how supply leads demand in aviation, such that new infrastructure and the charge made for them sets the limits of expansion (Adams, 1970: 6–7). To ram home this failing in the work of the Roskill Commission, Adams (1970) re-ran its calculations and accounting assumptions to demonstrate how they enabled a case to be made for Westminster in central London to be the site of the next London airport.

Discursive framing

More pertinently, the work of the Commission was structured by its terms of reference, in which it was asked to 'inquire into the timing of the need for a four runway airport to cater for the growth of traffic at existing airports serving the London area' (Fordham, 1970: 308; Hall, 1982: 30). This framing accepted the need for a third airport for London and prepared the ground for a four-runway airport to cater for presumed growth. On the one hand, such assumptions structured the way that the Commission deployed CBA, shaping for example its understanding of the land required for development, the size of workforce to be employed at the airport, and the extent of population growth as a consequence of its construction, as well as biasing the exercise towards the interests of transport users. On the other hand, the whole CBA exercise was carried out without any questioning of the benefits of a new airport, which were taken for granted (Self, 1975: 157), and the economic case for expansion was not part of the terms of reference (Mishan, 1970: 226).

Seen in this way, the work of the Commission became yet another exercise in 'predict and provide', boiling down to the timing and location of new infrastructure. In fact, in line with the logic of forecasting, the Commission rested its analysis on past patterns of behaviour and development, viewing the new airport as 'a marginal addition to the established airports of the country' (Lichfield, 1971: 170). It assumed, for example, that passengers in the Midlands would continue to travel to London airports for flights, which privileged an inland airport, and it was obliged by the terms of reference to reject expansion at existing airports such as Heathrow. In the absence of a national plan or airport strategy, the Commission had little choice but to invest its faith in the analytical power of CBA (Self, 1975: 164). In short, in exuding a style of policy reasoning that privileged utilitarian calculation, the Commission endeavoured to depoliticise its decision-making processes, while concealing and rationalising the logic of airport expansion (Stone, 2012: 380). It did so by foregrounding CBA as a form of modern scientific and economic rationality, while politically its quest for objective quantification based on a rhetoric of numerology was dressed up in terms of 'protecting society from the subjective preferences of the official or politician' (Self, 1975: 92).

But, in making such claims and operating in this way, the Roskill Commission downplayed the role of political judgement, as well as the definition of the categories that informed its analyses or calculations (Foster, 2001: 17; Graham, 2018). It thus removed the 'corrective check' of politics, yielding instead a 'spurious and slipshod way of dodging the issues' (Self, 1975: 92). The effect was to divert attention away from the value judgements and conflicts that underpinned the categories and calculations made for the assigning of numbers and weightings to different factors (Self, 1975: 93). Calculative reasoning requires in the first instance the production of categories and value judgements about how we give meaning to the world around us, and this practice entails political reasoning or 'the reasoning of sameness and difference, of good and bad or right and wrong' (Stone, 2012: 382; see also Stone, 2021). It leads Self to conclude that CBA is 'more dependent on value judgements incorporated in the analysis than is true of most types of expert information' (1975: 11), with which our analyses and judgements concur.

In pushing to the background the criteria and values informing its judgements, coupled with its efforts to remove political reasoning from the domain of aviation policy altogether, the Commission's reliance on the techniques of CBA brought it into conflict with the traditional logic of planning (Foster, 2001: 16). The technique of CBA led to a focus on interests, the disaggregation of problems, as well as a logic of economic quantification and measurement, which stands in marked contrast to a logic of planning that privileged (and still to some degree privileges) legal discussions about the merits of developments, empirical studies and imaginative synthesis (Self, 1975: 168). Tellingly, Lichfield, one of the consultants appointed to advise the Joint Counties submission to Roskill, commented that the Commission was undecided as to whether it was a transport investment or a land-use planning inquiry. He concluded that the Commission imported into its decision-making an economistic interpretation of CBA, which was designed to deliver the efficient use of scare resources. In so doing, it did not adapt its method of working to the demands of regional planning, and thus failed to calculate the direct and indirect impacts of an airport on urban and regional development, and most notably the equity and distributional effects of such decisions, which were foregrounded in the logic of planning (Lichfield, 1971: 173–5; Self, 1975: 161–2).

Such tensions were amplified by the judicial logic of Roskill, which relied on precedents and the assembling of facts; although this form of reasoning is not obviously at odds with CBA in terms of its techniques, it did jar with the logic of planning. Ultimately, it was the conflict between these different logics that the Commission was unable to avoid (Waters, 1971: 204). Colin Buchanan, the key planner on the Commission, eventually broke ranks with other members of the Commission by publishing a letter of discontent that argued for Foulness over Cublington (Commision on the Third London Airport, 1971: 149–60; see also Buchanan, 1981: 46–8). In this intervention, he stressed the environmental impacts of an inland airport and the benefits of Foulness as a means of promoting growth to the east of London, while questioning if CBA was being used mainly to argue against Foulness, thereby paving the way for the destruction of rural space between London and Birmingham (Commission on the Third London Airport, 1971: 154–60) Importantly, Buchanan argued that the logic of planning did not just require a comparison of costs, but a coordinated and broad policy framework against which to appraise alternatives, as well as a political dialogue about public values and the potential contradictions between economic development and environmental protection, both of which were absent in the work of Roskill (Self, 1970).

The Roskill Commission promised to be the gateway to a brave new world of rational and efficient decision-making and infrastructure planning. Drawing on the most advanced techniques of economic analysis, and established to provide an independent, impartial and objective solution by experts and technocrats to a practical problem, its practices chimed with the new atomic age when the white heat of the technological revolution would lead to a greater control and predictability of the social and natural world. The age of experts and rational calculation based on the infallible evidence of numbers seemed to have dawned. Yet it ended up delivering a solution that even one of its own expert Commissioners disowned, and was never implemented, while it seemed to work in a depoliticised bubble that popped when politics erupted all around – and even within – its paper-thin membrane. In short, therefore, the Commission is best viewed as a utopian 'showpiece' exercise in rational and modernist policy-making, which ended in 'defeat' and 'comeuppance', as the 'minority report' of Buchanan 'which had passages of purple prose but no quantification, triumphed' (Foster, 2001: 16).

Of course, proponents of CBA in and around the Transport Ministry mounted a rear-guard action, attacking the calculations and assumptions of Roskill, its over-estimation of passenger numbers and its failure to grasp the extent of opposition to Cublington. But blame was placed squarely on ministers and officials for their failure to establish in advance the criteria that should have guided the final recommendations of the Commission – a failure which made 'rational project selection logically impossible' (Foster, 2001: 17) and exposed the limits of CBA in determining choices between alternatives (Graham, 2018). In the light of the political indecision that followed, and the absence of any government explanation for rejecting its recommendations in terms of CBA, the Roskill Commission came to represent the 'high' and 'low' points of CBA, the 'debacle' of its inquiry into the third London airport leading to falling support and 'credibility' for this technique among politicians, administrators and the public (Foster, 2001: 16–17). The 'triumph' of the planner Buchanan owed much to the fact that he better captured the 'national mood than his contemporaries' (Graham, 2018). Confronted by staunch political opposition and growing environmental demands, when it finally reported in January 1971, the Commission's recommendation for a new airport at Cublington in rural Buckinghamshire was 'already stone dead' (McKie, 1973, cited in Needham, 2014).

In April 1971, amidst the growing fallout, the Heath government rejected Cublington, plumping for Maplin or Foulness on the east coast. But this was not the end of the story. The Treasury, which supported the arguments of Roskill in favour of Cublington, feared that Maplin, if built, would only be able to operate with a state subsidy. It began to obstruct progress on plans for the construction of the east coast airport, and its delaying tactics provided time for opposition to the proposed airport to come together. Airlines, in particular, argued against Maplin, having little interest in moving their operations away from Heathrow (Needham, 2014). Three years later, in the midst of the oil crisis of the 1970s, it came as little surprise that the whole project was abandoned by the Wilson Labour government. The 'great planning disaster' – the 'policy fiasco' – which the entire episode of the quest for London's mythical third airport was retrospectively and aptly named, ended not with a bang, but a whimper (Needham, 2014).

A national public consultation

After some 20 years of discussion surrounding the third London airport, and 3 years of the Roskill Commission, the government reverted to the tried and trusted technology of public inquiries to push through new terminals at Gatwick, Heathrow and Stansted and a new runway at Manchester. However, as a technology of government, the public inquiry was also coming under growing pressure. By May 1997, the incoming Labour government faced a build-up of demands from both proponents and opponents of airport expansion. The Manchester Inquiry and the approval of the second runway had given the go-ahead for the first new runway since the Second World War. The Terminal Five public inquiry had taken over 3 years, and although Labour was to approve the building of the new terminal at Heathrow, growing pressures had built up across the industry.

In short, the technology of the public inquiry was increasingly discredited. For proponents of expansion, it was an overly long drawn-out exercise, which created uncertainty for investors and increased the costs of expansion in an increasingly competitive and deregulated aviation industry. For opponents, it was an exercise of top-down hierarchical governance, which formed part of the democratic deficit in aviation decision-making and planning. At the same time, the campaign against the second runway at Manchester airport had brought the direct action politics of the anti-roads movement into the arena of aviation. The campaign led to the forging of new coalitions between local residents and direct action campaigners, the so-called 'Vegans and Volvos' alliance, thus establishing the potential for new alliances, which linked struggles against particular airport expansions to a wider anti-aviation politics, as well as the universal issue of climate change (Griggs and Howarth, 2002, 2013: 126–64).

In response to such mounting pressures, the New Labour government announced its intention to deliver a new White Paper that would establish a plan for airport infrastructure for the next 30 years. It thus proposed to move away from the dominant rationalities of public inquiries, internal reviews, the commissioning of studies by specially chosen 'taskforces', and indeed the Roskill Commission, which favoured particularistic arguments and decisions about the development needs of individual airports and the merits of one site location over another, while potentially fragmenting any particular opposition to expansion. Writing in the early 1970s, David Perman had expressed dismay about the absence of a national plan for aviation, noting that 'airlines, local authorities, airport users, business, travel agents, workers and environmentalists [are] in the position of having to fight each battle as it arises without relevance to the battle being fought in the neighbouring airport area' (1973: 32). Against this background, Labour thus prepared to launch a national public consultation, which was to institute the space both for an overall long-term strategy for the country as a whole, and the emergence of a universal challenge against various particular airport expansions and, indeed, in some quarters the aviation industry itself. It is to this technology of a national public consultation that we now turn.

The purpose of the New Labour government's national consultation was to prepare the ground for a strategic plan for aviation for the next 30 years. Hence, the 1998 transport white paper, *A New Deal for Transport*, sub-titled *Better for Everyone*, called for a national, long-term, integrated and sustainable approach to aviation, which would coordinate development between regional and national airports, while delivering improved access to public transport networks and ensuring that aviation met the external costs of its impacts on the environment (DETR, 1998; Le Blond, 2019: 88). In 2000, the government published a consultation paper, *The Future of Aviation*, which was accompanied in the summer of 2002 by a series of seven regional air services studies. In practical terms, the consultation process involved 28 options for airport expansion at 14 different locations, and a swathe of technical reports and studies (Upham, 2003). *The Future of Aviation* consultation collected some 550 responses, while the regional studies, notably the South-East and East of England Regional Air Services Study (SERAS), received some 500,000 representations, including opinion poll responses, as well as organisational and individual submissions (DfT, 2003: 18). Almost half of the responses came from members of the Royal Society for the Protection of Birds objecting to the inclusion of a proposal for a new airport at Cliffe, an area of significant importance for wildlife, particularly birds. Options for expansion at airports gathered different levels of objections: around 5,000 for Gatwick, 8,000 for Heathrow and 24,000 for Stansted (Le Blond, 2019: 89).

The publication of *The Future of Aviation* effectively reannounced New Labour's intention to 'consult widely', reiterating the importance of 'taking into account the views of all interested parties' (DETR, 2000b: 6). It presented its engagement with stakeholders as an 'open consultation', which meant that it invited comments on any 'aspect of aviation' considered important by respondents, and it declared that responses to the consultation would be 'a significant input to the white paper' (DETR, 2000b: 6). In general, the aim of the Labour government was to generate a 'framework that integrate[d] economic, social and environmental objectives' (DETR, 2000b: 18). Cognisant of growing ideological and political concerns about the growth of aviation and the prospects of airport expansions, the consultation advanced a position of 'sustainable aviation', which would strive to 'balance' the economic benefits of air travel against its environmental impacts (Griggs and Howarth, 2013: 165–91). The consultation documents were thus the first significant government publications to underline aviation's impact on climate change (Le Blond, 2019: 88).

The rhetoric of the new government was at pains to distance itself from the social logic of 'predict and provide', which had been discredited by the anti-roads movement, and by local protests against airport development that had challenged the addiction of government to aviation expansion. In typical fashion, the publication of the *Future Development of Air Transport in the UK* consultation document for South East England (DfT, 2002a: 33) expressed its opposition to 'predict and provide', declaring that the use of forecasting did not signal a 'commitment to the politics of "predict and provide"', which 'would only be the case if Ministers were to decide to provide airport capacity to meet unconstrained demand without regard to the consequences'. The logic of forecasting was thus reduced to a 'starting point for assessment', and its objective was merely to identify 'what additional airport capacity would be needed if demand were to be met, either fully or partially, so that we can then appraise the positive and negative impacts of that additional capacity, and only then come to a view on what, if any, degree of expansion is appropriate' (DfT, 2002a: 33).

Such rhetorical appeals about 'balancing' demands presented the role of government as an arbitrator or regulator of the public interest, positioned as the sole body able to forge agreement across the interested parties in the field of aviation. In its consideration of the submissions received to the *Future of Aviation* consultation document, the DfT declared that the response to different demands was 'not simply a question of counting votes, Ministers will have regard to all relevant matters in taking decisions in the national interest' (DfT, 2002b: 2). Much like the political logic of public inquiries, the construction of the national interest was employed to negate local opposition to expansion, for it was stressed that the definition of the national interest could not be decided at the local level. But, at the same time, any definition of the national interest privileged the economic benefits of aviation, foregrounding its contribution to 'inward tourism' and the export of services, which it quantified at some £7.4 billion in 2000 (DfT, 2002c: 6).

In this way, aviation was enveloped in a fantasmatic narrative, which reinforced the belief that it was a 'great British success story and one of the major strengths of the UK economy, both now and for the future' (DfT, 2002c: 5). The rhetorical appeal of this fantasy was consistently conveyed through numerical assessments, which purported to quantify its economic contribution. Key policy texts and reports contained multiple references to the Oxford Economic Forecasting report, which estimated that the aviation industry contributed some £10.2 billion to the British economy or 1.4 per cent of GDP in 1998, while employing over 180,000 people (DETR, 2000b: 26). The consultation document for South East England duly promised that additional airport capacity would generate 80,000 new jobs directly or indirectly in the region, as well as £18 billion or more in 'direct quantifiable benefits' (DfT, 2002c: 8). Yet, simultaneously, the beatific dimensions of this 'great British success story' and 'our' dependency on it, were equally portrayed as being at risk from the horrific dimensions of 'capacity overload' at UK airports and competition from rival airports, notably Amsterdam and Frankfurt, which were challenging Heathrow's market superiority as a global hub (Griggs and Howarth, 2013: 172–3).

Despite the caveats of fully or partially meeting rising passenger demand by balancing the social, economic and environmental impacts of aviation, in practice the foundations of its predictions of rising passenger numbers retained the troublesome category of 'unconstrained demand' (Upham, 2003; Le Blond, 2019). When published in December 2003, the ATWP thus forecast a growth in demand from 200 million in 2003 to between 400 and 600 million in 2030, while underlining that 'previous forecasts have proved conservative' (DfT, 2003: 23–4). It cunningly equated the rise in passenger demand to merely two return trips on average per year for each UK resident in 2030, pointing out the then current average of one return trip per year, while ignoring the social inequalities associated with 'frequent flyers'. At the same time, rising climate change emissions from aviation were displaced to the international arena and the market, where they were quantified as 'costs' to be 'taken into account', and addressed through global collaboration, economic incentives and emissions trading schemes (ETSs), as well as technological fixes through which it was estimated the aviation industry could achieve a '50 per cent reduction in CO_2 production by 2020' (DfT, 2003: 31, 39–41; HMT and DfT, 2003).

Noise pollution was ultimately subjected to a three-pronged strategy: noise impacts were to be controlled, mitigated by insulation, or compensated through support for the costs of relocation (DfT, 2003: 35–6). As the arbiter of the national interest, the government's efforts to 'balance' competing demands thus came down firmly on the side of expansion, endorsing a forecasted doubling of passenger numbers, calls for global emissions trading and investment in technological fixes. Taken together, these policy commitments would effectively relieve individual airlines and national airports of their emissions responsibilities, perpetuating a fantasmatic discourse of sustainable aviation, where airport expansion was made compatible with environmental protection and the fight against climate change (Griggs and Howarth, 2013: 185–6). Indeed, the White Paper backed the construction of two new runways in South East England by 2030, first at Stansted by 2012, and then at Heathrow between 2015 and 2020, as well as new runways at Edinburgh and Birmingham airports, and runway extensions, new terminals and other facilities at airports across the country (DfT, 2003: 11–14).

Overall, the technologies and techniques of consultation that were put in place were highly limited. The NOP questionnaire in the south-east consisted of 20 primary questions, eight of which were focused on personal details around airport use, modes of travel to airports, age and professional background. Other questions revolved around the endorsement of government policy, the importance attributed to environmental mitigation and economic demands, support for hub airports, noise mitigation and preferences of site location (NOP, 2002). It is striking that no opportunity was offered in the questionnaire for individual comment. As with public inquiries, it was a 'have your say' form of consultation, which mainly allowed communities to let off steam. Information giving and the placation of contestation and difference predominated, all designed to deliver a process of therapeutic consultation. Moreover, in keeping with the positioning of the government as the guardian of the national interest, the whole consultation exercise did not seek to transform existing preferences or create the conditions for a reasoned dialogue over the future of aviation. Rather, it simply harvested the preferences of individuals and organisations, leaving government to attempt to accommodate such preferences in a so-called 'balanced' deal. In other words, it consisted of a process of accommodation that was then internalised and incorporated within the corridors of government (Griggs and Howarth, 2013: 130–4).

However, as a technology of government, the idea of a national consultation, and the positioning of the state as an arbiter of the national interest, exposed the government directly to the antagonistic demands of various forces and groups operating in the field of aviation. When asked whether or not government should expand aviation to meet the demands of consumers, or limit the negative effects of expansion, some 35 per cent of responses, identified primarily as environmental organisations, individuals, residents' groups and local authorities, argued that 'current growth patterns should not be allowed to continue because the costs were too high'. Yet 30 per cent of respondents, who were identified as members of airports, airlines and other aviation-related organisations, advocated policies that would 'respond to the demands of consumers and allow current growth patterns to continue' and mitigate negative impacts (DfT, 2002b: 3). In other words, the consultation exercise left the government vulnerable to the underlying politicisation of airport expansion, while not providing it with the tools or processes to build any policy settlement in the field.

In fact, in an effort to further politicise the process of consultation, the SSE campaign accused the government of failing to comply with its own code of consultation. It argued that the 4 months deadline to reply to the consultation did not meet the government's own demand to give interested parties 'adequate time' to engage with government, 'lend[ing] support to the view that the Government has already made up its mind and is merely going through the motions'. SSE also contended that the consultation document did not give sufficient weight to the case against expansion, and it also challenged the NOP questionnaire, which it argued did not give an opportunity to state grounds against expansion. Indeed, the leadership of SSE called for its membership to boycott the questionnaire and write directly to MPs (SSE, 2002a). In short, the consultation did little to address the absence of trust towards government, which earlier policies and commitments to expansion had engendered across communities.

The SSE also brought a judicial review against the consultation process because it excluded Gatwick from consideration for expansion, disclosing tensions within the anti-expansion groups. The government had excluded Gatwick on the grounds that a 1979 agreement between BAA and West Sussex County Council meant that there was no possibility of a new runway at the airport before 2019 and that any airport would be operational only by

2024. However, the consultation document pointed out that a new runway would be needed in the south-east by 2024, leading the SSE leadership to argue that Gatwick should be included in the consultation and that the exclusion of Gatwick was a breach of the positive duty under the Human Rights Act 1998 and the European Convention on Human Rights to protect the rights of people at Stansted regarding their homes, private lives and peaceful enjoyment (SSE, 2002b). At the same time as the consultation unfolded, the SSE leadership accused the government of withholding documents and closing down debate, making the consultation 'look more and more like a sham' (SSE, 2002c).

One important upshot of these responses was that the consultation exercise was quickly politicised by local campaigners and opponents to expansion. Indeed, as the formulation of the white paper progressed over the next 3 years, the exercise ultimately provided the space for the emergence of two rival hegemonic projects, hardening the political frontiers that were emerging about airport expansion and other environmental issues too. On the one hand, it brought together the formation of AirportWatch – an anti-expansion coalition that united individual campaigns against particular airport expansions – while drawing equivalences between anti-expansion struggles and the fight against climate change, multinational companies, global inequalities and democratic failings. On the other hand, the formation of Freedom to Fly provided a space and organisation to defend the need for additional airport capacity, as it sought to provide ideological cover for the Labour government to launch a programme of expansion.

So the publication of the ATWP (2003) brought even starker lines of difference and antagonism, which continued to divide the field of aviation policy. In opening its consultation, New Labour strived to outline a 'balanced' approach to airport expansion, thus foreshadowing and mediating a new settlement in aviation. But, if anything, it had achieved the opposite, providing the space for rival coalitions to emerge. Indeed, its White Paper (2003) had only added fuel to the flames, coming out in favour of the largest programme of airport expansion since the end of the Second World War.

Conclusion

The social logic of 'predict and provide' served as an administrative-political rationality that crystallised the UK state's sponsorship of commercial aviation, which resides at the heart of its policy-making and governance of airports. Aviation policy was predicated on the projection of future demand and the construction of additional airport infrastructure that could accommodate the expectations of additional passengers. Such imperatives and strategic tasks privileged the knowledge and expertise of forecasting, bringing into play complex processes of data accumulation and calculations. The DfT and its agents assembled a wealth of categories, assumptions, economic models and statistical techniques, which sought to normalise expectations of expansion. Predictions of rising passenger numbers and threats of 'capacity overload' were frequently weaponised in efforts to reignite and solidify the ideological grip of aviation among the ruling political class. The logic and rhetoric of forecasting thus functioned to ground processes of decision-making over airport capacity in a future, depoliticised space, where all modes of behaviour and technological changes, including shifting consumer preferences or the introduction of wider, quieter and fuel-efficient planes, could be schematised and articulated through different statistical techniques and models to support economic growth and defuse political opposition.

However, the installation and maintenance of this regime of aviation expansion was strongly contested. The failure of the planning of the third London airport dominated policy in the 1960s and 1970s, while by the end of the 1990s representatives of the aviation industry were exasperated by the fact that that the second runway at Manchester was the only new runway constructed in the UK since the end of the Second World War. Yet proposals and plans for expansion had only served to mobilise growing opposition from communities and environmentalists, who articulated demands for the protection of local landscapes, the regulation and mitigation of noise and other impacts on airport communities, and growing concerns about the impact of aviation emissions on climate change. Indeed, the contradictions and dislocations of the social logic of 'predict and provide' were progressively exposed: prediction was not always followed by provision. And, if the complex calculations of forecasting endeavoured to depoliticise aviation policy, the location of future infrastructure provision was rapidly politicised.

In response to the contradictions and politicisation of aviation policy, governments rolled out multiple technologies of government in an effort to negate, deflect and manage challenges to expansion. In this chapter, we have examined three different types of government technology: public inquiries, expert Commissions and the practices of therapeutic consultation. Such technologies all attempted to take the making and implementation of aviation policy out of the political realm by transferring it into quasi-judicial or deliberative spaces, where local residents and campaigners were conceded a highly constrained right to 'have their say'.

Using such technologies, the government pursued various strategies and tactics of depoliticisation. First, successive governments invested in the personal reputational power of the chair of the Commission or the inspector of the inquiry. Secondly, they framed the staging of debates and public engagement through the definition of terms of reference of any inquiry, commission, or consultation. Thirdly, they privileged rational methods of investigation and evaluation, confining the contestation of policy to the domain of calculative reasoning and quantification, which reached its height with Roskill's endorsement of CBA. Finally, government monopolised the definition of the public interest, locating its definition firmly in the realm of the national state and its particular imperatives.

Yet such technologies of government and their attendant techniques and rationalities were vulnerable to practices of politicisation by local residents and campaigners. Persistent protesters and local residents developed innovative strategies and tactics in their campaigns and representations, switching arenas and widening their audiences. Tightly scripted public inquiries slipped into 'arenas without rules', in part paradoxically because inspectors, in their efforts to demonstrate 'impartiality', could not prevent their use as public spaces in which citizens contested local and national policy. But even such technologies of government did not exhaust the space of politics, as campaigners were able to move their opposition in and out of different domains, especially the media, parliament and political parties, seeking to broaden their audiences. For example, while Roskill operated within the confines of the analytical parameters of CBA, local campaigners mobilised within the realm of party politics to undercut the findings of the Commission. Similarly, the national consultation established by New Labour created the space for the forging of equivalences between different local campaigns, brokering a more universal opposition to expansion, which was then linked to campaigns against climate change. In short, the regime of expansion was a constant 'dance' of politicisation, depoliticisation and repoliticisation, in which government, campaigners, airports and airlines competed to bring aviation in and out of the political domain, while technologies of governance were exhausted or bypassed. Such was the messy politics of policy hegemony in the field of aviation and airports policy, as new decisions and strategies were to develop in the wake of the Coalition government that took power in May 2010.

3

The anatomy of an expert Commission: Howard Davies, rhetorical reframing and the performance of leadership

The New Labour government's ATWP (2003) confidently set out its ambitious plans for airport expansion for the next 30 years. But its delivery was dogged by major setbacks and reversals. For one thing, its vision of the policies and practices of sustainable aviation were discredited by an anti-expansion campaign of local resident groups, scientific and environmental lobbies and direct action environmentalists, as well as institutions internal to the British state, not least the House of Commons Environmental Audit Committee (EAC). The anti-expansion campaign also voiced its concerns and demands in various arenas, exposing the intensifying contradictions between proposed airport expansions, aviation's rising carbon emissions, and the challenge of climate change. Indeed, by the end of the 2000s, as public awareness of climate change grew stronger, environmental protesters and activists had successfully turned the practice of flying into an emblematic issue in the struggle to tackle climate change. Although the Brown government had given the go-ahead for the building of a third runway at Heathrow in 2009, it was to be the last throw of the dice for a government that had in many ways already lost the argument in favour of expansion. It was no great surprise when the courts blocked proposals for the third runway in 2010, only weeks before the general election (Bowcott et al, 2010).

The arrival in office of a Conservative-Liberal Democrat coalition after the closely fought 2010 general election made possible a challenge to the embedded expansionist 'predict and provide' policies. In opposition, David Cameron, the then leader of the Conservative Party, had grabbed hold of the issue of climate change as part of his efforts to detoxify the party, announcing his 'no ifs, no buts, no third runway' slogan to opponents of expansion at Heathrow in 2009 – a pledge that was to haunt his and future governments in the next decade and beyond (Jenkins, 2016). The Coalition's 2010 Programme for Government duly promised to stop the expansion of airports in South East England, and the subsequent appointment of Justine Greening as Secretary of State for Transport in October 2011 – a vocal opponent of expansion at Heathrow – seemed to confirm the Coalition's commitment to move away from 'predict and provide' policies. In the Foreword to the July 2012 Draft Aviation Framework Policy, Greening dismissed traditional debates over airport capacity by arguing that any 'solution [to airport expansion] will have to be genuinely sustainable' and that 'a better balance than in the past needs to be struck between the benefits aviation undoubtedly brings and its impacts, both at a global and a local level' (DfT, 2012a: 5). Such sentiments resonated with her immediate predecessor, Philip Hammond, who had argued that Labour's 2003 White Paper was 'fundamentally out of date, because it fails to give sufficient weight to the challenge of climate change' and that 'the previous government got the balance wrong' (DfT, 2011: 4).

However, the Conservative Party came under increasing pressure from a highly resourced public campaign from the aviation industry, which exposed splits and rifts over airport expansion in the Cabinet and in the party, particularly in the shifting economic context of austerity and the fallout of the 2008 GFC. By January 2012, rumours were circulating that the Cameron government was to offer its support to a new London airport in the Thames Estuary, but retreated from doing so because of opposition from Deputy Prime Minister, Nick Clegg, and tensions in the Coalition (Orr, 2012; Winnett, 2012). Instead, in an effort to kick the issue of airport expansion into the political long grass, the Cameron government established the Airports Commission (AC) in September 2012, which was chaired by Sir Howard Davies. The government's return to an expert Commission indicated its desire to try once again to depoliticise the issue of airport expansion. And not only did the Cameron government push back the publication of the Final Report of the Commission until after the UK general election of 2015, but the fate of the much contested issue of airport expansion was to be decided by expert commissioners in much the same way as the infamous plans for a third London airport in the 1960s and 1970s. Importantly, the efforts to depoliticise airport expansion resided in the ability of the Commission to provide ideological cover for the Cameron government to perform a policy reversal. And this was confirmed when Justine Greening, a staunch opponent of a third runway at Heathrow, was moved from the DfT to the Department for International Development the day before the announcement of the Commission. Formally, the Commission was invited to deliver for government an 'evidence-based consensus'[1] on *where* and *when*, rather than *whether* there should be expansion (DfT, 2012b). It duly took up this invitation, ultimately coming out in favour of a new third runway at Heathrow Airport in July 2015.

This chapter investigates the work of the AC from its initial deliberations in 2012 to the delivery of its Final Report in July 2015, as we assess to what degree the Commission was able to deliver an 'evidence-based' policy settlement. We first discern and characterise the bundle of mechanisms, strategies, arguments and rhetorical claims at play in its discourse. Here we explore how the Commission deployed legitimising appeals to independent expertise; transformed the economic boosterism of aviation into the strategic advantages of connectivity; marshalled the techniques of forecasting and prediction; and redefined information-giving and transparency as forms of engagement. In particular, we demonstrate how the Commission strategically framed aviation emissions and aircraft noise to negate opposition to expansion and how its 'performance of authority' was embodied in the 'reasonable' and 'neutral' position of the chair of the Commission, Sir Howard Davies.

Against this background, we conclude by evaluating the political work of the Commission, namely its efforts to depoliticise aviation, and the dilemmas it posed for campaigners over fears of incorporation, as well as the divisions it opened up among airports and airlines over fears of market competition. Politically, the AC successfully kept the aviation issue off the national political agenda in the run-up to the 2015 general election, during which a cross-party consensus on airport expansion appeared to be forming. It also satisfied the demands of the pro-expansion Heathrow lobby, which in itself was a programme success for the Cameron government. However, in disclosing the complex dynamics of politicisation and re-politicisation at work during the Commission's lifespan, we argue that it did little more than instil a temporary 'phoney war' in aviation policy. More fully, the Commission repeated the logic of 'predict and provide', and legitimised the embedded narratives of the economic benefits of aviation growth over its environmental costs, thus falling short of furnishing the 'evidence-based' settlement in aviation it desired. In fact, the publication of its Final Report in 2015 triggered another round of 'trench warfare' over plans to construct a third runway at Heathrow, and thus re-politicised aviation policy, much like the discrediting of the ATWP after its publication in 2003.

The work of the Airports Commission

The AC officially launched its inquiries and deliberations at the beginning of November 2012. Howard Davies, the chair of the Commission, was joined by five fellow Commissioners (see Table 3.1) with experience in aviation and aerospace, transport, infrastructure, energy and climate change (DfT, 2012c). The work of the Commissioners was supported by a Secretariat headed by the senior civil servant, Philip Graham, who had led the government high-speed rail strategy and worked on the Eddington Study into transport and economic growth. This administrative infrastructure was completed by two advisory groups: the Expert Advisory Panel, which was launched in May 2013, comprising 21 academic and policy consultants in environmental, transport and engineering issues, and the Sustainability Reference Group,

Table 3.1: The Commissioners

Sir Howard Davies (chair)	Former Director General of the Confederation of British Industry; ex-Chair of the Financial Services Authority; ex-Director of the London School of Economics (LSE).
Sir John Armitt CBE	Former Chair of the Olympic Delivery Authority; ex-Chief Executive of Network Rail.
Professor Ricky Burdett	Professor of Urban Studies, London School of Economics and Director of LSE Cities research centre.
Vivienne Cox	Former Chief Executive and Executive Vice-President of British Petroleum (BP) Alternative Energy; former member of the BP Executive Management Team.
Professor Dame Julia King	Vice Chancellor of Aston University; member of the Climate Change Committee (CCC).
Geoff Muirhead CBE	Former Chief Executive of Manchester Airports Group (MAG).

which brought together government departments, the Environment Agency, Natural England and English Heritage.

In an inauspicious start, one of the six Commissioners, Geoff Muirhead, the former chief executive of Manchester Airports Group (MAG) resigned from the Commission in September 2013. Muirhead had stepped down as chief executive of MAG in 2010, but he continued to carry out an 'ambassadorial role' for the airport group until January 2013. Once MAG purchased Stansted Airport in February 2013, SSE stepped up its accusations that Muirhead's presence on the Commission was evidence of a conflict of interest and an 'apparent bias' in the decision-making of the Commission (Thomas, 2013). Facing the heat, Muirhead resigned before the publication of the Commission's Interim Report in December 2013 (Parker, 2013).

Once underway, the rhythm and work streams of the Commission were structured by the requirement to deliver two reports to government. First, it had to produce interim conclusions on the need for additional airport capacity, making recommendations to improve the use of existing runways, which had to be delivered by the end of 2013. Secondly, it was instructed to appraise the potential schemes and sites for additional capacity, while its final recommendations for any additional capacity and its delivery were to be published by the summer of 2015. The Commission thus spent much of the first 12 months bringing together its assessment of long-term demand forecasts and capacity needs. Following the publication of the Interim Report in December 2013, its focus then switched to the establishment of the 'sift criteria', which were to guide site location assessments, the evaluation of different schemes and the determination of measures to mitigate – and compensate for – the impact of airport expansion on local communities.

Table 3.2: The Airports Commission: a brief chronology

September 2012	Sir Howard Davies to chair Airports Commission
November 2012	Membership and terms of reference announced
February 2013	Discussion Paper 01: Aviation demand forecasting
March 2013	Discussion Paper 02: Aviation connectivity and the economy
April 2013	Discussion Paper 03: Aviation and climate change
May 2013	Discussion Paper 04: Airport operational models
July 2013	Discussion Paper 05: Aviation noise
July 2013	Public evidence meetings in Manchester and London
August 2013	Long term options: proposals received by the Airports Commission
September 2013	Geoff Muirhead resigns from the Commission
October 2013	Speech by Howard Davies, Aviation Capacity in the UK: Emerging Thinking
December 2013	Airports Commission: Interim report
January 2014	Opening of public consultation: Appraisal framework; call for evidence on Inner Thames Estuary Airport
May 2014	Submission of three revised schemes for short-listed proposals
June 2014	Discussion Paper 06: The utilisation of the UK's existing airport capacity
July 2014	Discussion Paper 07: The delivery of new runway capacity
July 2014	Opening of public consultation: Inner Thames Estuary Airport studies
November 2014	Public consultation: assessment of short-listed proposals
December 2014	Heathrow and Gatwick public discussion sessions
May 2015	Opening of public consultation: Air quality
July 2015	Airports Commission: Final report; concurrent with publication of ten technical reports and two reports detailing analysis and responses to consultation on three schemes and air quality

Over the next two and a half years leading to its Final Report, the Commission released seven discussion documents, with calls for responses; held four public evidence and consultation days; and its Chair and Commissioners delivered many public speeches, as well as undertaking a series of over 150 meetings and site visits (see Table 3.2). It also invited submissions on how to make better use of existing airports and runways (receiving 75 submissions), as well as outline schemes for expansion (52 submissions). Upon publication, these outline schemes were open to 2 months of comment and the Commission received some 300 responses, while its campaigns to gather views on the proposed London Estuary airport generated some 3,000 representations (AC, 2013a: 20–1). Importantly, after the publication of its Interim Report, its stakeholder engagement included three periods of national consultation on its appraisal framework; its assessment of selected schemes for expansion; and a consideration of air quality. Proponents of short-listed schemes also submitted revised designs for expansion, which were made publicly available. The consultation on the detailed appraisal of these shortlisted schemes attracted over 70,000 responses (AC, 2015a: 94).

The Interim Report, which was published in December 2013, concluded that allowing for its forecasts of rising passenger numbers and existing capacity constraints, there was 'a clear case for one net additional runway' in the South East of England by 2030 and a potential case for a second runway by 2050 (AC, 2013a: 11–12). As it was unable to spread these growing passenger numbers to airports outside London and South East England, the Commission shortlisted three potential schemes to meet the expected demand: a new South Runway at Gatwick airport; a new Northwest Runway at Heathrow; and the lengthening of the existing Northern Runway at Heathrow. In the meantime, the Commission announced a series of measures to improve the use of existing infrastructure, including operational efficiencies in airspace use, performance-based navigation and time-based separation, as well as the proposed creation of an Independent Aviation Noise Authority (AC, 2013a: 12–13).

Notably, it provisionally rejected the construction of a new airport in the Thames Estuary because of its higher costs (five times those of the shortlisted options), environmental impacts and extensive surface access demands (AC, 2013a: 14). However, the Commission stated that it would undertake further work on the Thames Estuary airport and report in early 2014 – the Thames Estuary scheme had been resurrected and promoted by Boris Johnson, then Mayor of London, and was to become widely known as 'Boris Island' (Mulholland, 2009). And, in contrast to the decisions of the Labour government, options to expand Stansted Airport were also sidelined. The Commission argued that the volume of traffic through Stansted had fallen, estimating that there was 'considerable spare capacity' at the Essex airport. However, it suggested that transforming Stansted into an international hub airport would also be 'close to the cost of the Estuary airport option, highly disruptive to airspace and would not present the same regeneration opportunities', although it was retained as a 'plausible option for any second additional runway in the 2040s' (AC, 2013a: 15).

The Final Report was delivered to government in July 2015, some 7 weeks after the election of a Conservative government under the leadership of David Cameron. The Commission recommended the construction of a third Northwest Runway at Heathrow, while not entirely ruling out a second runway at Gatwick. The option of a new airport in the Thames Estuary had finally been abandoned once and for all in September 2014. The third Northwest Runway, the Commission argued, offered 'more

Figure 3.1: Proposed third runway at Heathrow

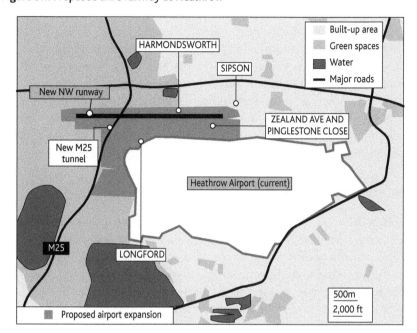

substantial economic and strategic benefits' than either expansion at Gatwick or the extension of the existing Northern Runway at Heathrow, while also 'strengthening connectivity for passengers and freight users and boosting the productivity of the UK economy' (AC, 2015a: 12). In comparison to Gatwick, with its short-haul market position, the Commission concluded that expansion at Heathrow would generate more long-haul destinations to emerging markets; offer more benefit to network carriers such as British Airways (BA); and cater for rising passenger numbers more quickly, while competing more effectively for transfer passengers (AC, 2015a: 19–22). The Commission's favoured scheme (see Figure 3.1) would nonetheless require the demolition of approximately 783 residential properties (compared to 167 for the second runway at Gatwick), as well as the construction of a tunnel to accommodate the M25 motorway on the boundaries of the airport (AC, 2015a: 232), while affecting up to 25 times more people with noise pollution than a second runway at Gatwick (AC, 2015a: 27).

However, a third runway at Heathrow was to be accompanied by a package of measures, which were designed to put in place a 'balanced approach' that mitigated the impacts on local communities (AC, 2015a: 10). In his Foreword to the Commission's Final Report, Howard Davies made it explicit that the function of such measures was to 'make expansion possible' after earlier plans for a third runway were 'set aside in the face of local opposition' (AC, 2015a: 5). The package of measures included: a ban on scheduled night flights between 11.30 at night and 6 o'clock in the morning; a legally-binding noise envelope; more predictable periods of respite; above market value compensation packages for those losing their homes; training and apprenticeship schemes for local people; more than a £1 billion community compensation scheme; an aviation noise levy; and the creation of an independent aviation noise authority and a community engagement board. Importantly, expansion at Heathrow was made dependent on further development being able to meet EU air quality limits, while a fourth runway at the airport was ruled out once and for all (AC, 2015a: 10–11).

First acts of power: framing the terms of reference

In this return to the technology of an expert Commission, it is imperative to stress that the efforts of government to frame political debates began well before the official work of the Commission even started, especially with the selection of the chair of the Commission and the definition of its terms of reference. Like other institutions and interventions of this sort, Chairs exercise a form of political agency, using their judgement to determine how a Commission is to be run, framing its investigation and shaping its recommendations (Wallis and Brodtkorb, 2020). The nomination of any Commission chair is indeed a significant moment of political communication – a symbol of political intent that is mulled over and second-guessed by those outside the corridors of ministries and parliamentary networks. Howard Davies, as he pointed out on more than one occasion, had no career experience in the aviation industry. He was an economist who had been Deputy Governor of the Bank of England (1995–1997), the first Chair of the Financial Services Authority (1997–2003) and Director of the London School of Economics (2003–2011).[2]

But even such established and recognised chairs are constrained by terms of reference, which guide the investigations and dialogue of Commissioners. Hence, terms of reference already represent an exercise in agenda-setting, as they structure the scope and methods of the operations of a commisison, strongly influencing its findings and recommendations. In this case, the terms of reference for the AC, if appearing less directive than those of the Roskill Commission, firmly shifted the framing of public debate back again onto the *where* and *when* – rather than the *whether* – of airport expansion. Howard Davies and his fellow Commissioners were thus charged with examining the 'scale and timing of any requirement for additional capacity' in the UK's airport infrastructure and were asked to deliver 'credible options' as to 'how any need for additional capacity should be met in the short, medium and long term' (DfT, 2012b).

More pointedly, the need for additional capacity was purposely tied to the task of determining the 'steps needed to maintain the UK's global hub status' (2012b; see also McLoughlin, 2012). On one level, this allusion to the importance of the UK's 'hub status' in the Commission's terms of reference merely repeated long-standing anxieties about the negative economic and social impacts of the failure to expand airport capacity, worries that arose from the dominant fantasmatic narratives that structured the perceptions about aviation and airports in the UK state. Yet they also went some way to acknowledging the demands of the intense campaign for further hub capacity in South East England, which had emerged after the 2010 moratorium. Indeed, framed in this way, the terms of reference gave prior weighting, if any were needed, to the strategic needs and advantages of Heathrow Airport, for Heathrow was widely recognised as the UK's only international hub airport.

Against this background, while the rhetoric of the Commission continued to stress its role as an 'independent review' of aviation capacity needs, its inward-facing work of assessing the options for expansion was increasingly shifted by its very terms of reference to the more political, outward-facing task of generating ideological cover for a policy reversal by the Coalition government. Hence, its discursive framing called upon the Commission to develop an evidence-based policy settlement in aviation, which would 'engage openly with interested parties', while offering government a 'detailed review' and 'high level assessment of credible long-term options'. The Commission was directed to 'build consensus [among local and devolved government and opposition parties] in support of its approach and recommendations'. In other words, the Coalition government demanded from the Commission a ready-made policy that could side-step or resolve political conflicts and provide the groundwork and analysis to 'accelerate the resolution of any future planning applications' (DfT, 2012b). Interestingly, for what followed, the design of the revamped technology of an expert Commission masked an already overdetermined outcome: Davies was expected to do the work of government, making the case for Cameron and the Conservative Party to support the third runway at Heathrow. It is to how Davies and his fellow Commissioners sought to deliver on this task that we now turn.

Performing authority: between quantification and judgement

From its launch, Howard Davies and his fellow Commissioners made concerted efforts to construct the AC as a purportedly neutral arena, which was governed by the rules of impartial professional expertise, effectively outside the day-to-day demands of politics. In the first instance, the Commission was at pains to draw boundaries between its way of working and that of previous attempts to broker a policy settlement in aviation. In their public utterances, Commissioners eagerly communicated that they had undertaken a 'fresh' assessment of the evidence (AC, 2013a: 20), claiming that the 'broad approach' of the Commission 'distinguish[ed] this exercise from others which have preceded it' (Davies, 2013). At the same time, they repeatedly positioned themselves as adopting an 'independent view, at arm's length from politics', insisting that the Commission had reviewed 'the evidence afresh without preconceptions' (AC, 2015a). In his speech on the emerging thinking of the Commission in October 2013, Davies (2013) thus distanced the Commission from the politicised legacies of past failures, repeating how 'the Commission began its work in a state of agnosticism' and insisting that 'none of us had taken a firm public view on the subject [of airport expansion]'.

Occupying a 'state of agnosticism', the Commission thus committed itself to 'follow a process which [was] comprehensive, rigorous, open and inclusive' (AC, 2013b: 5–7) with the aim of delivering a 'broad consensus of opinion' (DfT, 2012c; see also AC, 2013a: 21). At the presentation of the membership of the Commission, Davies himself declared that its future recommendations were to be grounded in the generation of a 'robust evidence base' (DfT, 2012c), while commission reports and documents, transcripts of public meetings, details of responses to consultations and scientific analyses and forecasts were all to be made available for consultation by interested parties. Claims to procedural and methodological vigour peppered the Final Report, showcasing the use of innovative methods such as Monte Carlo simulations to address uncertainty, Spatial Computable General Equilibrium (S-CGE) models, or multiple metrics noise cards. The 264-page Strategic Fit: Forecasts report, which was released as part of the documentation accompanying the Final Report of the Commission in July 2015, 'educated' the reader on the existing literature on aviation demand elasticities, with references to time-series econometrics models, multinominal logit models and probabilistic forecasting, as well as probability assessments, confidence ranges and load factors (see AC, 2015b: 19). Indeed, as part of the AC's commitment to transparency, campaigners on both sides of the aviation divide were bombarded with information and data. For example, the Consultation on Shortlisted Options for a New Runway in November 2014 (AC, 2014a) released a main consultation document, three business cases and a sustainability assessment for the shortlisted options, as well as a 20-page glossary, which amounted to some 530 pages of documentation. It was supported by over 60 technical reports and spreadsheets, which amounted to over 4,000 pages of analysis, including 889 pages on its appraisal of noise.

However, at the same time, the AC carefully reserved for itself a capacity and space for agency, appealing also to the role of judgement and reason, so as to distance itself from a purely instrumental logic of calculation and quantification. Hence, the Commission explicitly announced its intention not to allow the data to speak for itself. Methodologies of quantification only provided the means to explore and map the potential demands for additional capacity. And while the empirical data generated by the Commission was to be exposed to objective processes of validation and contestation, it recognised that there were multiple ways of 'reading' the data, offsetting opposition to its analysis by putting its final decision down to the judgement of individual Commissioners. In the November 2014 consultation document over the three short-listed schemes at Gatwick and Heathrow, Commissioners thereby noted how they were 'acutely aware' that 'the numbers of the report are not an end in themselves, but a representation of how each scheme may affect people', relegating the quantification of data to a tool to 'share ... information clearly and to facilitate comparisons between schemes' (AC, 2014a: 32). They thus retreated from 'attempting to set out in these [consultation] documents which of these impacts is the most important or matters most to people's lives', and acknowledged that 'people reading these documents can make their own judgments', as could the Commissioners themselves (AC, 2014a: 33).

Of course, in defining itself in this way, the Commission, like Roskill some 40 years before, masked the fact that the decisions over what data to generate or what categories to count *are* intrinsically political. In other words, interpretation does not just begin with the reading of the data, but with the very decision to generate it, and decisions about what categories to develop and use and which forms of data to gather. Yet, by bringing judgement back into its workings, the Commissioners gave themselves a little room for manoeuvre, so elevating reasonableness as the defining criteria of the success of its recommendations. As such, the work of the Commission came to rest on whether it was judged to have made a reasonable case for its conclusions, rather than on its capacity to engineer a consensus. The Commission thus asked stakeholders to assess whether they could 'accept that we [the Commission] have made an effort to grapple with the conflicting points of view and to produce reasonable responses to their points' (AC, 2013a: 4). Ultimately, it did not seek to manufacture a consensus, but sought the recognition or at least an acceptance that it had delivered 'well considered' outcomes. Indeed, this role for reason and judgement was installed in the first Guidance Document of the Commission, where Davies presented the Commission as a 'body without any vested interests or preconceived views, which is able to review the evidence dispassionately, to engage widely, to exercise its judgement and make well-considered and integrated recommendations' (AC, 2013b: 5).

Against this background, the Commission, and particularly its Chair, came to 'perform authority' in a distinctive way. Commissions often become known by the name of their chairs, and following this convention, the AC was soon renamed the Davies Commission in much public discourse. Moreover, amidst the sound and fury of competing projects and proposals, policy reversals and government vacillation, Davies exemplified the genre of science and scientific expertise embodying a dispassionate and reasoned engagement with the issues under consideration. Figures, tables, graphs, sophisticated methods of statistical analysis, presentations of different scenarios – the full panoply of verbal and visual rhetoric – were vital parts of the arguments and proposals made by the Chair, as he skilfully used the media and his various public interventions to present a 'reasoned elaboration' of policy (Friedrich, 1958: 29 in Hajer, 2009: 20).

In fact, his style contrasted with the other forces, individuals and agencies involved in the debate. It differed acutely, for example, from the passionate and visionary quality of Boris Johnson's performances, who sought to galvanise the public and key decision-makers around his idea of a new international airport in the Thames estuary. Whereas Johnson projected energy, enthusiasm and overriding ambition, Davies presented an image of balance, reasonableness, sobriety and calm. His style was indeed commended by politicians like David Cameron, who consistently emphasised his good standing and judgement. Perhaps more surprisingly, even some leading opponents of airport expansion were impressed with the manner and knowledge of the Commission's chair (personal communication with leading campaigner, 2014).

The logic of 'predict and provide' and the technique of forecasting

Even though Davies and his team of Commissioners declared that they would work differently from previous inquiries and commissions, the practice of forecasting – the staple rationality and technique of government in aviation policy – remained at the heart of their efforts to build an evidence-based consensus. Nevertheless, like the previous Labour government in its formulation of the ATWP (2003), the Commissioners devoted their energies to dissociating their analysis of future passenger numbers from the logic of 'predict and provide', which they derided as 'a simplistic process of projecting future demand, and then providing the infrastructure to meet that demand no matter the cost'. The Commission even went so far as to hold earlier techniques of 'straightforward prediction' responsible for past failures to reach any political consensus over the future of aviation (AC, 2013a: 18). Thus, although it declared the forecasting methodology of the DfT to be 'the most robust, peer-reviewed, tool available' (AC, 2014a: 21), it did not shy away from acknowledging the expressed criticisms and limitations of the work of the transport ministry, seeking to revise and update its forecasts (AC, 2013a: 103–4). As such, the Commission committed itself to processes of 'credible forecasting' and the pursuit of an 'inclusive and integrated approach' to how it calcuated its numbers (AC, 2013a: 19–20; AC, 2013c: 4; AC, 2015a: 39).

Unlike past inquiries, this 'integrated' methodology was designed 'not [to] look at airport expansion in isolation', but to 'consider how it interacts with the wider transport network, with broader policies in respect of economic growth, environmental protection, and quality of life, [as well as] how it affects different communities, businesses and localities' (AC, 2014a: 19). Typically, the Commission prided itself on how the proposed comparative assessment of shortlisted proposals took into account for the 'first time' the 'quality of life impacts' of 'a major infrastructure project' (2014a: 31). At the same time, it explicitly and frequently recognised the technical challenges and limitations to forecasting raised in responses to its February 2013 Discussion Paper (AC, 2013c), including the inability of existing models to account for uncertainty, inadequate classifications of emerging markets and groupings, the poor modelling of international transfer passengers and loose representations of airline and airport competition, each of which had been recognised in previous rounds of forecasting (AC, 2013a: 104). In an effort to counter such weaknesses, the Commission set out an array of methods and statistical models in the public domain, disclosing how it revised established definitions of emerging economies; decreased projections of the overspill from south-east airports into regional airports; undertook probabilistic forecasts to counter high and low forecasting; and remodelled overseas hubs and redefined input models, including updating oil prices (AC, 2013a: 105–6).

The incorporation of technical challenges to existing models of forecasting sat alongside sustained efforts by the Commission to recognise its reliance on plural modes of data, triangulation and peer review, while accepting the limitations of available evidence in certain areas (AC, 2014a: 21–2). First, it published four different forecasts, depending on whether capacity was constrained, and whether aviation emissions were subjected to carbon-trading or carbon-capped regimes (see Table 3.3). Secondly, it subjected these forecasts to sensitivity testing through the initial development of four different scenarios or 'potential futures': 'global growth'; 'relative decline of Europe'; 'low-cost is King'; and 'global fragmentation'. Such scenarios 'tested' passenger forecasts against alternative patterns of aviation market liberalisation, different market configurations of low-cost carriers and alliances between carriers, multiple patterns of long-term economic growth, and global or domestic climate change measures. Importantly, the Commission claimed that their scenario planning and multiple forecasting was deployed to address the uncertainties of prediction, while mitigating the risk of 'basing its analysis on any single likely pattern of future demand' (AC, 2014a: 21). Finally, as the work of the Commission continued, its three shortlisted options were tested against a fifth scenario, namely an 'assessment of need', which calculated future demand on the grounds of 'central projections for economic growth and other macro-economic factors' (AC, 2015a: 18).

Even so, the AC could not escape the 'ghost' of 'predict and provide'. It did not reject that logic, but rather argued for a more sophisticated methodology to deliver its forecasts. Despite its initial criticisms of the DfT forecasts, the Commission took as its 'starting point' those same aviation demand models (AC, 2013a: 104). Its modifications of such models did not undermine established patterns of rising demand for air travel. For example, the use

Table 3.3: Airports Commission: UK passenger forecasts

Airports Commission passenger forecasts (January 2014)			
UK: million passengers per annum (MPPA)	2020	2030	2050
Carbon traded; capacity constrained	248	299	400
Carbon traded; capacity unconstrained	261	323	448
Carbon capped; capacity constrained	247	295	389
Carbon capped; capacity unconstrained	259	297	377
Department for Transport passenger forecasts (2013)			
UK: million passengers per annum (MPPA)	2020	2030	2050
Constrained; central prediction	255.2	312.6	447.5
Unconstrained; central prediction	258.7	319.6	482.2

Note: Forecasts for Table 3.3 and Table 3.4 are available from Airports Commission, *Airport level passenger forecasts 2011 to 2050*, Available from: https://www.gov.uk/government/publications/airports-commission-airport-level-passenger-forecasts-2011-to-2050 [Accessed 27 February, 2023]; and Department for Transport, *UK aviation forecasts, January 2013*, Available from: https://www.nwleics.gov.uk/files/documents/df_t_aviation_forecasts_january_2013/DfT%20Aviation%20Forecasts%20-%20January%202013.pdf [Accessed 27 February, 2023].

of Monte Carlo simulations was more concerned with refining predictions by offering a 'better approach' to map uncertainty than 'tradition high/low scenarios' (AC, 2013a: 106). In addition, its underlying assumptions replicated the underlying beliefs and narratives of aviation growth in the UK state and industry, and presumed a continual rising demand for passenger flights. Thus, of the four scenarios generated by the Commission to test the need for additional capacity, only one scenario projected a decline in the growth of the aviation sector. And, more importantly, the Commission used one scenario – 'the assessment of need' – as its starting point for the assessment of the different shortlisted options. It is significant that the privileging of the assessment of need scenario was undertaken on the advice of the International Transport Forum of the Organisation for Economic Co-operation and Development (OECD), which argued that this consideration was appropriate given 'its incorporation of verifiable historic relationships in the growth and allocation of demand and, in particular, its use of central projections of economic and population growth, oil prices and other drivers' (AC, 2015a: 108). In short, it still privileged the narrow factors of previous 'predict and provide' exercises.

Taken together, the Commission's intricate patterns of rhetoric, methodological justification and argument rehearsed the fantasmatic threat of 'capacity overload' – tropes that had populated all post-war exercises in airport planning. In other words, its rationale followed well-choreographed steps. It first asserted the threat of capacity overload, underlining how Heathrow had been 'effectively full for many years', while Gatwick was 'completely full at peak times' (AC, 2015a: 75). It then listed a series of negative consequences of capacity overload, highlighting, for example, the threats to cheap travel, increased delay, poor connectivity to emerging markets, heightened environmental damage due to planes circling while waiting to land and in the absence of expansion the loss of '£21–23 billion to users and providers of airport infrastructure and £30–45 billion to the wider economy' albeit over a 60 year time period (AC, 2015a: 81). Finally, the Commission bolstered existing assumptions that there was little possibility of substituting capacity in London by the use of regional airports, because its modelling demonstrated that there were no effective regulatory measures to redistribute passenger demands away from London airports (AC, 2013a: 127). In any case, the privileging of international hub capacity had strategically excluded any sustained consideration of the 'spare' capacity of Stansted Airport in the deliberations of the Commission.

In making its claims, the Commission also decided to showcase the upper end of its predictions, emphasising that its carbon-traded forecasts predicted a doubling of passenger numbers by 2050 to approximately 470 billion passengers per year (AC, 2015a: 83). Like the assessment of passenger numbers at Heathrow and Gatwick, this prediction was not that much lower than that of the DfT (see Table 3.3 and Table 3.4), although

Table 3.4: Airports Commission: passenger forecasts for Heathrow and Gatwick

Airports Commission passenger forecasts (January 2014)				
Heathrow (HRW) and Gatwick (GTW): million passengers per annum (MPPA)		2020	2030	2050
Carbon traded; capacity constrained	HRW	75	81	90
	GTW	39	41	46
Carbon traded; capacity unconstrained	HRW	99	119	158
	GTW	34	37	49
Carbon capped; capacity constrained	HRW	75	82	91
	GTW	39	41	45
Carbon capped; capacity unconstrained	HTW	99	114	146
	GTW	33	32	36
Department for Transport passenger forecasts (2013)				
Heathrow (HRW) and Gatwick (GTW): million passengers per annum (MPPA)		2020	2030	2050
Constrained; central prediction	HRW	75.5	81.8	92.9
	GTW	37.3	40.6	44.2
Unconstrained; central prediction	HRW	86.6	109.4	170.1
	GTW	38.3	39.8	51.9

the Commission's carbon-capped scenario fell to 377 million passengers per annum in 2050 (2015a: 83). Yet, the Commission warned of capacity overload in the London airport system by 2030, at which date it predicted passenger demand would be 'choked off by constraints on capacity', even when the impacts on passenger numbers of a carbon cap and larger aircraft and increased passenger loadings were taken into account. More so, it showed how the 'threat' of capacity overload would only intensify over time, suggesting that without new runway capacity, unconstrained demand – even with carbon emissions capped – could not be accommodated across London airports in 2050 (2015a: 84). In short, the Commission left little doubt that the maintenance of the UK's competitive status as a global hub for aviation 'could not be achieved without new infrastructure being provided' (AC, 2015a: 85).

Supporting 'a thriving aviation sector': the rhetoric of economic boosterism

The Commission developed its case for increased capacity by drawing upon the dominant fantasmatic narratives of economic boosterism and spillovers, tapping into the accepted 'common sense' that 'a thriving aviation sector' was central to the economic success of the UK (AC, 2015a: 15, 69). Typically, as if such surmises were even needed, it drew attention to how air travel 'facilitates the movement of services and goods, workers and tourists, and drives business innovation and investment' AC, 2015a: 71). Such messages were rammed home by frequently mentioning the fact that 'the UK's strong services sector' relied on aviation, as well as 'British trade and manufacturing, particularly in highly technical industries such as pharmaceuticals' (AC, 2015a: 16; see also AC, 2013d: 12). Here the Commission tied the expansion of the export markets of these industries, particularly in emerging economies, to the availability and growth of air freight, notably at Heathrow, 'by far the largest and most important airport for freight' (AC 2015a: 73). At the same time, it feted the direct employment and economic value of the aviation sector itself, which was calculated to have a 'turnover of around £32 billion' and to have generated '£12 billion of economic output' in 2013, while 'employ[ing] 116,000 workers' and providing 'a valuable source of Government revenue through the collection of Air Passenger Duty (APD), which raised over £3 billion in 2013–14' (2015a: 74). Recycling the rhetoric of the ATWP (2003), it also aligned the economic and social contributions of aviation by noting how 'about half' of the British population had flown in the last year, often to 'visit friends and family abroad or to reach a holiday destination'. Alongside such claims, it underlined how aviation permitted businesses to 'recruit from a global talent pool for whom the ability to return home to visit parents and children is important' (2015a: 15), thus 'making a material contribution to the competitiveness of the UK' and contributing to 'higher levels of life satisfaction, general and mental health and happiness' (2015a: 70)

Besides these established narratives of the economic benefits of aviation expansion, the Commission made two rhetorical shifts which served to further negate opposition to expansion. First, it challenged the distinction between the categories of leisure and business flights, arguing that all flights are composed of a combination of business and leisure travellers. The Commission's assault on these established categories in aviation discourse attempted to disarm opponents of airport expansion who, in the context of aviation's growing carbon emissions, ultimately questioned the reliance of business on aviation and the legitimacy of expanding airports to cater in practice for increased leisure flights. Instead, the Commission explicitly acknowledged that leisure travellers ensure the 'density' of the UK route network, maintaining the 'connectivity that [UK] businesses require to compete globally' (AC, 2015a: 71).

Secondly, the Commission transferred its economic justifications for expansion onto the argumentative terrain of connectivity and global competitiveness, thus supplementing its appeals to the direct economic benefits of airport expansion. On the one hand, the hard-to-oppose discourse of connectivity drew equivalences between 'air connections' and the maintenance of exports markets, in a global economy whose 'centre of gravity' was 'moving eastward and global supply chains becoming more complex' (AC, 2015a: 16). On the other hand, the demand for connectivity accentuated the need for a global hub airport to maintain competitiveness, justifying further the recommendation of a third runway at Heathrow. Here the Commission rearticulated the fantasmatic narrative of aviation expansion by suggesting that the failure to expand capacity would lead to the UK losing out to its rivals in emerging markets, which would be exacerbated in the political context of austerity and the aftermath of the 2008 GFC. In the words of the Commission, 'in a complex and competitive global environment, it would be short-sighted and perilous to place the UK's world-leading connectivity at risk by failing to address these constraints [of airport capacity]' (AC, 2015a: 17).

The total economic benefit of its preferred Heathrow scheme – a new Northwest Runway – was calculated by the Commission to be £69.1 billion – a headline figure which made no references to the costs of expansion or the differences across carbon traded and carbon capped scenarios. The total benefits of £69.1 billion for a carbon traded Northwest Runway fell to £46.2 billion in a carbon capped scenario. But after taking into account the calculations of net present value, including disbenefits and scheme and surface costs, the projected value of the Northwest Runway at Heathrow fell to £1.4 billion under carbon capped conditions. In such scenarios, the construction of a second runway at Gatwick outperformed the Northwest

Runway, generating £5.5 billion over the projected period (AC, 2015a: 147). However, the Commission argued that this performance advantage of Gatwick was 'outweighed by the stronger overall benefits delivered by the Heathrow scheme, particularly if it is privately financed' (AC, 2015a: 150), with repeated references to the freight and business passenger market advantages of Heathrow and its 'stronger performance' in local economic impacts (AC, 2015a: 149).

But this conclusion is hard to swallow because, when compared to Gatwick, any advantage of Heathrow was ultimately rendered immaterial by the significant larger costs of its expansion. In this vital element of its deliberations, it was very much a case of the Commission using its agency and independent judgement to sideline the stronger performance of the case of Gatwick under carbon capped scenarios, privileging instead the 'value' of the alleged broader benefits of job creation at Heathrow over other categories of evidence and outcomes in its own data. Ultimately, in any case, the Commission effectively bracketed out from consideration its own data by concluding that all schemes, which were to be delivered by private finance, 'make efficient use of public funds' and by asserting that 'the benefits clearly outweigh the costs', with the Northwest Runway offering the 'greatest net benefits' (AC, 2015a: 150).

At the same time, the mapping of aviation's 'economic spillovers' in terms of trade, business growth and job creation, particularly the use of an S-CGE model – one of the innovations in forecasting advanced by the Commission – were challenged by the Commission's own economic experts, who argued that the calculations of the wider impacts of expansion by Price Waterhouse Cooper should be treated with 'caution'. In May 2015, Professor Peter Mackie and Brian Pearce, who were advisors to the Commission on the economic case for expansion, outlined concerns about the over-weighting of the impacts of increasing seat capacity on productivity, unclear causal assumptions, 'hard to explain' results and the promotion, particularly within the media, of optimistic 'up to' results (AEF, 2015a; Mackie and Pearce, 2015). In their report, they cast doubt on the overall projections of the Commission: wary of 'double counting' and 'media exaggeration', they argued that the calculations of wider economic impacts should not be seen as 'additive', but as complementary calculations, which could not figure in the CBA of the Commission (Mackie and Pearce, 2015: 5). They also raised questions about how the Commission had modelled and accounted for carbon emission constraints in their calculations, dismissing the treatment of the Climate Change Committee's (CCC's) planning assumptions as 'inherently problematic' (Mackie and Pearce, 2015: 1). Counselling 'caution', they concluded that 'care is required in assessing its [that is, the economic case's] robustness and reliability' (Mackie and Pearce, 2015: 5). Indeed, it is worth noting that, if the wider economic benefits associated with the Northwest

Runway were removed from the CBA undertaken by the Commission, the benefits of the proposed runway in a carbon-capped scenario would fall to a net social benefit of £9.7 billion, or a cost of £6.3 billion once the scheme and surface access costs were considered (AC, 2015a: 147). In its Final Report, the Commission persisted with its headline-grabbing prediction of benefits of £147 billion to GDP over 60 years (AC, 2015a: 129).

The public face of the Commission: engaging stakeholders in an 'open and inclusive' process

Throughout its deliberations, the Commission published a series of consultative discussion papers, undertook a programme of meetings and site visits, held public evidence and consultation sessions and carried out three consultation exercises (see Table 3.2). At the same time, the Commission trumpeted its openness and transparency, publishing on the web all of its documents, responses and even the minutes of its meetings. Transcripts of public meetings, details of responses to consultations and the analysis of the Commission were all made available for consultation by interested parties. By releasing this information into the public domain, the Commission was determined to render its decisions and reasoning available for public validation and contestation. After all, its terms of reference called for the Commission to do little more than provide 'opportunities to submit evidence and proposals to the Commission and to set out views relevant to its work' (DfT, 2012b).

In extolling the virtues of these high expectations, and then striving to meet them, transparency came to stand in for practices of consultation, so that in reality, actual engagement was often limited to the provision of written responses to released documents and staged public meetings. Indeed, in the guise of transparency, community groups were bombarded with technical information and data, which placed increasing demands on their capacity to engage with the work of the Commission. At the same time, the Commission's programme of meetings and engagements with stakeholders was very much an information-gathering exercise for the Commission, rather than an opportunity for the community to engage and deliberate in a meaningful fashion (Arnstein, 1969). In its Final Report, the Commission thus characterised its consultation on the three short-listed schemes as a way to 'test the evidence base, to identify any concerns stakeholders may have as to the accuracy, relevance or breadth of the assessments undertaken, and to seek views on the potential conclusions that might be drawn' (AC, 2015a: 92).

It is striking that, in line with its terms of reference, much of this 'testing out' was directed at forging a political settlement. A survey of the Commission's published programme of meetings and visits reveals considerable efforts dedicated to meetings with ministers and senior politicians, devolved administrations, parliamentary committees and senior civil servants. The local resident-run Heathrow Association for the Control of Aircraft Noise (HACAN) formally met with the Commission only twice, as well as accompanying the Commission on an early morning visit to Heathrow to assess aircraft noise (a visit with local MP Zac Goldsmith and representatives of the airport).[3]

As an exemplary case, the public discussion event at Heathrow on 3 December, 2014 was a staged performance, which was dominated by interventions from invited speakers. The event began with presentations from the promoters of the two Heathrow schemes and local MPs, prompting one audience member to remind Howard Davies that 'this is a public consultation', before asking 'when is the public going to speak?' (AC, 2014b: 28). Other sessions on the day revolved around presentations from local authority leaders and business representatives, followed again by responses from promoters and Howard Davies. Nevertheless, the community sessions did finally give the floor to three community organisations – HACAN, Back Heathrow and Stop Heathrow Expansion (SHE) – with interventions from the public. In total, however, less than 30 local community members intervened during the event. In her intervention, Natasha Fletcher (Teddington Action Group) criticised the closed nature of the dialogue, stating:

> I just want to get the message across that this is meant to be a public consultation. I feel that a lot of people in Teddington did not even know about this today. They could not even get a ticket. They are empty now, these seats. There is no press here. We do not have a voice. (AC, 2014b: 86)

At the same time, the Commission's formal consultations replicated the imbalances of resources between the industry and local communities. For example, the consultation on the appraisal for the three short-listed options, which ran from mid-November 2014 to early February 2015, generated approximately 72,000 responses (SYSTRA, 2015: 8). Local job creation and job security, particularly around Heathrow, were the most frequently cited reasons for supporting expansion, while noise and air quality were the most frequently voiced reasons for opposition to expansion, with relatively few responses engaging with the issue of carbon emissions (SYSTRA, 2015: 9, 109). However, 86 per cent of responses were generated by or came through campaign groups, with one single campaign, Back Heathrow, generating over 53,000 responses (SYSTRA, 2015: 21). During the consultation, Back Heathrow undertook a postal campaign to drum up support, sending out a letter and a leaflet with a tear-off slip calling for expansion that could be submitted to the consultation (SYSTRA, 2015: 23). In similar ways, SHE provided its supporters with a standard letter of its arguments and concerns against expansion, but ultimately its letter informed only

161 responses to the consultation (SYSTRA, 2015: 21). Significantly for our analysis, approximately 63,000 responses that expressed a preference for one or more of the shortlisted options did not refer directly to the evidence of the Commission or indicate that they had considered it. Equally, almost 10,000 responses that rejected one or more of the shortlisted options also made no reference to the evidence nor indicated that they had considered it (SYSTRA, 2015: 38, 42). In short, therefore, at least at this stage of the inquiry, a strong case can be made that the Commission was simply reasserting existing positions and providing opportunities for them to be voiced, rather than transforming them and building its desired 'broad consensus'.

In order to remedy such deficiencies, and in an effort to incorporate 'voices' against expansion – and perhaps also to pacify local opposition – the Commission claimed that the construction of a third runway was a way of mitigating the impacts of noise and air pollution on local communities. The proposal for a Northwest Runway was presented as a 'fundamentally different proposition' from previous proposals for a third runway at Heathrow. Its positioning to the west of current runways, the Commission stated, would 'reduce the number of people affected by noise' and would this time around be 'accompanied by strong measures' that would 'limit the impacts on those living nearby' (AC, 2015a: 11).

Reframed in this way, the rhetoric of the Commission implied that expansion would enable Heathrow to be 'a better neighbour' (AC, 2015a: 11, 30, 34, 274). Rather than posing a threat to the quality of life for local residents, expansion offered a 'unique opportunity to change the way the airport operates' (AC, 2015a: 31). But such tropes also articulated an implicit threat that opposition to expansion from local communities would result in the worsening of local noise and air quality impacts, or at least the maintenance of its existing levels. Persistent local demands for predictable respite and restrictions on night flights were thus presented as being either 'more reliably maintained' with a third runway, or more pointedly 'only possible with expansion' (AC, 2015a: 31).

The Commission also endeavoured to channel local opposition and future grievances and demands into more depoliticised sites of information and trust-building. It accepted the legacy of 'promises not fulfilled', recognising that for some local communities in and around Heathrow 'airport expansion will be unwanted' (AC, 2015a: 276). But here the political conflicts over the failures of accountability, which drove much of the resistance to expansion among local residents, were redescribed as a lack of trust, blame for which was primarily laid with Heathrow for not being a 'good neighbour', and with residents for 'often treat[ing] with suspicion' information from airport operators and the 'independent regulator', the Civil Aviation Authority (CAA) (AC, 2015a: 303).

In response, the Commission sought to move contentious issues like airspace, noise and the local impacts of airports out of the political domain. For example, it noted with regret that arrangements for airspace changes left the final decisions with the Secretary of State, thereby exposing decisions 'to being politicised, risking delay or, at the extreme, failure' (AC, 2015a: 305). Drawing on arrangements at Frankfurt and Schiphol airports, it thus advocated the creation of a funded Community Engagement Board at Heathrow, with a 'strong independent chair', 'oversight' of mitigation and compensation packages and the power to arbitrate in conflicts over compensation between communities and the airport (AC, 2015a: 299–303).

Expressed in the words of the Commission, the Board would act to 'ensure that the views of all stakeholders, but especially those living around the airport, are carefully considered' (AC, 2015a: 300). However, this role was mostly attached to the function of information giving and community facilitation, so that the Board would act as a 'trusted repository of information', 'develop awareness throughout the community' and 'provide advice and support' (AC, 2015a: 303). All in all, it amounted to a strategy of incorporation and depoliticisation – a strategy that was also embraced in the Commission's plans to deal with the issue of aircraft noise, to which we now turn.

Muting noise

In its early stages, the Commission quickly identified noise pollution as a key obstacle to the formation of an 'evidence-based consensus' in aviation policy. Much of its subsequent work was thus designed 'to rule noise out', because, in the words of one campaigner, noise is a 'big political trigger' and 'unless you deal with noise, there is no third runway at Heathrow' (personal communication with campaigner, 2014). Strategically, the Commission thus integrated into its *modus operandi* and rhetoric the longstanding demands of residents to increase the regulation of aircraft noise, accepting that the problem of aircraft noise was responsible for much of the breakdown of trust between local communities and airports, and between communities and government (AC, 2013a: 154). At the same time, it pinned opposition to expansion to the increasing frequency of aircraft flying over communities, thus acknowledging a central complaint of residents: that noise disturbance owed as much to the number of aircraft flying over communities as to the average noise disturbance experienced over several hours.

Framed in these terms, aircraft noise became a policy 'impasse', with the Commission publicly asserting that airports and government could no longer hide behind the promise of technological 'fixes' and quieter aircraft, for, in its words, 'if anything, [noise] concerns appear to have deepened even as aircraft have become progressively quieter, probably due to the increasing frequency of flights at the UK's busiest airports' (AC, 2013e: 4). This said, the Commission also pointed out that levels of noise from aircraft had declined, and would continue to do so, underlining the importance of ensuring communities received adequate information, as it had stressed in its discussion of its proposals for an independent aviation noise authority.

Like its approach to the forecasting of passenger numbers, the Commission embraced plurality. It generated a noise scorecard, which brought together different measures for day and night noise, as well as introducing 'number above' metrics to take into consideration how many times a location was overflown with noise impacts above designated levels (AC, 2015a: 170) – further recognition of the persistent complaints by residents about the frequency of planes overhead. Shortlisted schemes were also tested against multiple scenarios, with noise contours established for the current situation, the future with no expansion and the future with expansion, including the creation of contours for 2030, 2040 and 2050, as well as high-end and low-end projections, using the carbon-traded 'low-cost is king' and global growth scenarios and the carbon-capped assessment of need forecast. But, importantly, in a further incorporation of the demands of residents, the Commission accepted the limits to forecasting. It foregrounded the subjective nature of noise, acknowledging that 'quantitative results alone cannot completely capture how noise is experienced by local communities' (2015a: 171). It also called into question the continued relevance of average noise contours in measuring demands for respite and restrictions on night flights, accepting that such demands were related to the time when noise was experienced (2015a: 172).

Concessions pertaining to the measurement of noise were married to a series of noise mitigation strategies. The Commission endorsed the creation of a noise cap at Heathrow within which the airport would be legally bound to remain, holding out for residents the prospect of a noise envelope, which specified that 'daytime noise does not exceed current levels, and that an overall reduction in night noise is delivered', although this measure accepted the existing level of daytime noise pollution at Heathrow (AC, 2015a: 266–7). It also argued that following the construction of the proposed third runway there should be a ban on scheduled night flights between 11.30pm and 6am, though it reiterated throughout its warning that such a ban was 'only possible with expansion', while the construction of the third runway would also allow 'predictable respite to be more reliably maintained' (AC, 2015a: 31, 85, 246, 284, 336).

Running alongside these mitigations, as we have noted, it also offered compensation to those losing homes, some 25 per cent above 'unblighted market value', with more than £1 billion community compensation, including £700 million on noise insulation with support for schools a priority, apprenticeships and training for local people and more than

£100 million from Heathrow Airport to local areas through community infrastructure levy payments and Section 106 agreements to support local sustainable development (AC, 2015a: 31–2, 286). Further operations were also made contingent on acceptable compliance with EU air quality regulations, and finally, in time-honoured fashion, future expansion in the form of a fourth runway was ruled out (AC, 2015a: 9–10).

But equally, the Commission sought various long-term institutional and governance remedies to cure and muffle the threatening import of aircraft noise. In the first instance, the Commission redescribed the issue of noise in terms of a demand for better governance, thus making possible a technocratic resolution of the problem, which could be dealt with by an independent regulator. In its own words, the Commission argued that in addressing the impact of aircraft noise, 'however objective either party [namely, the Secretary of State for Transport or the CAA] is in its behaviour, a perception will always persist that the decisions of the former are driven by political considerations and that the latter is beholden to the industry that provides its funding. These perceptions may be unfair, but they persist' (AC, 2013a: 154).

Nonetheless, seen in the round, the Commission was quietly confident in assuming that the problem of noise was thus accommodated and duly bracketed out of the political debates surrounding the expansion of airport capacity. In effect, its strategies had sought to mute the question of noise as a potential impediment to expansion, thereby depoliticising the issue by shifting it into the domain of professional expertise and independent authoritative judgement. The intention was to make noise a tractable issue that was amenable to objective, technocratic means of adjudication and resolution (AC, 2013a: 154–6). But, significantly, the prospect of an Independent Aviation Noise Authority also endorsed a strategy of pushing contested decisions beyond the remit of the Commission itself (as with the proposed Community Engagement Board). In this way, local opposition to expansion was displaced spatially and temporally, and any grievances and disputes were to be resolved by another authority in a future time after the Commission had reported. Howard Davies and his fellow Commissioners had thus deferred and relinquished responsibility – and even accountability – over the question of noise. In its Final Report, the Commission was even able to lament the limited progress on the recommendations it put forward in its interim report, blaming the government for the 'disappointing' progress on the creation of an independent aviation noise authority (AC, 2015a: 41).

Displacing climate change

Strategies of displacement were also to characterise the Commission's approach to the deleterious impacts of aviation's rising carbon emissions on climate change. Publicly, the Commission declared that its methods of forecasting and assessment of capacity 'incorporated' and 'put at the centre' of its analysis the advice of the CCC that aviation emissions in 2050 should not exceed 37.5 $MtCO_2$ by 2050. This was a target that relied on sectors beyond aviation making 85 per cent cuts in their emissions: a factor that was recognised by the Commission but often ignored in debates over aviation expansion (AC, 2015a: 66). The Commission argued that its forecasts accepted climate change as a 'constraint', rather than as 'an output of' aviation, running carbon-trading and carbon-capped forecasts of aviation demand to inform its assessment of the need for additional capacity (AC, 2015a: 138). Such forecasts updated the work of the CCC, suggesting that its 2050 target of 37.5 $MtCO_2$ was compatible with a 67 per cent increase in passenger growth and a 38 per cent increase in air traffic movements (whereas the CCC had calculated 60 per cent and 55 per cent increases respectively) (AC, 2013a: 109–10; AEF, 2015b). But the Commission carefully concluded that any difference between its own figures and the forecasts of the CCC were explained through disparate assumptions over load factors and fuel efficiency (AC, 2013a: 110).

Yet, on closer inspection, the Commission made questionable assumptions about the relationships between aviation and carbon emissions, sliding towards what might be seen as the manipulation of inputs and weightings in its calculations to ensure that its carbon capped forecasts achieved the 2050 CCC target. For one thing, it did not 'count' non-CO_2 emissions from aviation and their impacts on climate change in its forecasts, for lack of evidence. Secondly, the carbon capped forecasts of the Commission used carbon prices as a proxy for policy measures, for international cap and trade practices, carbon taxes, or a mixture of both. However, to meet the carbon budgets designated by the CCC, the price of carbon was inflated in forecasts to £334 per tonne of CO_2 (AEF, 2015c: 2) which was over 50 per cent above the price used in forecasts by the Department of the Environment and Climate Change, with no guidance on how this inflated price would be delivered (current prices at the time of the interim report were around £3 per tonne) (AC, 2013a: 114). Moreover, it doubled DfT predictions for the use of biofuels by 2050, while mandatory carbon-saving operational measures across airports were assumed, all without any explanation about how these changes would be brought about (AEF, 2015c: 2–3). Animated by the end goal of limiting aviation emissions to 37 $MtCO_2$ in 2050, it was as though forecasts of predicted evolutions in the industry were remodelled to 'fit' with the desired outcome (AEF, 2015b: 7–8).

At the same time, the Commission persistently steered the issue of rising aviation carbon emissions into the background. In the first instance, although it recognised aviation as a carbon-intensive industry and accepted rising carbon emissions in aviation, such admissions were often made alongside strategies and arguments that downplayed increases in carbon emissions, including the making of statements that claimed, for example, that air travel was responsible for 'less than 7 per cent of UK's overall CO_2 emissions' (AC, 2015a: 7). The Commission also shied away from making any policy recommendations on instruments to reduce carbon emissions in aviation, arguing that was this was the responsibility of government (AC, 2013a: 113–14). And it failed to include the impact of aviation emissions on climate change in the final designated sift criteria for the appraisal of different options for expansion, stating that there was little difference in the carbon impacts of any of the three shortlisted sites. Finally, as we have shown, the costs of meeting the 37.5 $MtCO_2$ target in 2050 were not fully integrated into the CBA of shortlisted proposals, and its own economic experts labelled the treatment of carbon emissions as at best 'problematic' (Mackie and Pearce, 2015: 1).

Such strategies displaced responsibility for addressing the environmental challenges that accompanied airport expansion onto the CCC. The Commission itself made little or no reference to the scientific and institutional calls for demand management in aviation, calls that had ultimately brought Labour's policy of sustainable aviation to its knees. It ignored, for example, the thorny question of the 'special status' that was attributed to air travel, failing to question the legitimacy and feasibility of other industries taking an additional burden of cuts to emissions so that aviation could continue to expand. Rather, it deferred repeatedly to the judgement of the CCC, which served as a rhetorical safety net for its own statements and positionings. More fully, using our theoretical terms, the AC drew upon a highly contested assessment of aviation emissions by the CCC (2009) to embark upon a subtle 'logic of difference', which simultaneously acknowledged and downplayed carbon emissions from aviation, so that it could domesticate climate change demands against airport expansion within its recommendations.

Importantly, the Commission's deferral to the 'advice' of the CCC was mirrored in its acceptance that aviation emissions were best addressed in the international arena using the market mechanisms of emissions trading, claiming for good measure that this was the 'view of the CCC' and 'also the policy of the UK government' (AC, 2015a: 67). Pushing the management of carbon emissions into the international arena and into the market mechanisms of cap and trade regimes held out the 'promise' of a resolution to the climate change impacts of flying, while enabling continued expansion and framing rising carbon emissions outside the boundaries of the remit of the Commission. But these regimes were similarly contested and facing significant political obstacles. Indeed, aviation's participation in the EU ETS was partially suspended during the deliberations of the AC, as the EU waited on the International Civil Aviation Organisation (ICAO) to deliver agreement on a global offsetting scheme for aviation. Once again, the Commission came to rely on a ready-made solution to the negative impacts of flying, which had yet to be implemented.

As with the issue of aircraft noise, the climate change impacts of aviation were thus incorporated into a domain of tractable issues, which could then be tackled and resolved by the Commission. But it is notable that the construction of aircraft noise as an 'impasse' further relegated what was once seen as a key barrier to expansion – the climate change impacts of aviation – to a secondary and separate constraint. As part of its strategy of 'divide and rule', the Commission sought to separate demands for less noise pollution from demands for carbon reduction, so it could open up the possibility of engineering divisions between local residents, who were concerned about quality of life issues, and environmental groups, who were more focused on carbon emissions. In practice, such moves to split the problems of noise and carbon emissions exploited the potential future 'trade-offs' in policy between tackling noise pollution and lowering carbon emissions. For example, it was noted that although 'low-carbon designs' for future planes 'may be quieter than existing aircraft, they might not be as quiet as low noise designs' (CAA, 2014: 30).

Conclusion: The politics and ideology of the Airports Commission

Politically, at least until the publication of its Final Report in July 2015, the AC appears to have successfully reinforced the conditions for a policy reversal by the Cameron government. It had kept the aviation issue off the national political agenda in the run-up to the 2015 general election during which time a cross-party consensus on airport expansion did appear to be forming, at least across party leaderships (see Murphy, 2014; Murray, 2014; Watt and Wintour, 2014). The national election manifestos of the Conservative and Labour parties pledged merely to review and respond to the recommendations of the AC when they were to be published after the election. As such, the Commission provided the requisite ideological cover for the Cameron government to reverse its commitments against expansion, while satisfying the demands of the pro-expansion Heathrow lobby, which in itself was arguably a political win for the Cameron government.

Throughout its deliberations, the Commission had in fact persistently rearticulated the dominant discourses and fantasmatic narratives of aviation policy, appealing time and again to the economic boosterism of aviation, the competitive advantage of increased connectivity and the negative consequences of capacity overload – fantasmatic appeals that resonated in the economic context of austerity following the GFC. Through a carefully calibrated logic of difference, it had incorporated demands to lower carbon emissions into plans for expansion, singing the praises of emissions trading and capping regimes. The latter were especially evident in its Final Report where it both acknowledged and sidelined the widespread concerns over climate change, which had mobilised considerable opposition to expansion under New Labour. At the same time, it had purposively transformed aviation noise into the most significant obstacle to expansion, incorporating and reframing demands to regulate aircraft noise pollution into questions of trust and information. Taken together, in the words of the Secretary of State (McLoughlin, 2015a), these strategies had returned the challenge facing government back to that of 'balanc[ing] local interests against the wider, longer-term benefits for the UK'. It resulted in a reframing of the policy challenges in aviation by presenting arguments, which stood in marked opposition to the Coalition government's rejection of aviation expansion in 2010, and retreated in the final instance to the politics of 'predict and provide'.

At the heart of these political and ideological strategies were the concerted efforts of the Commission to depoliticise aviation policy. Howard Davies and his fellow Commissioners were at pains to construct the Commission as an arena beyond politics, as they appealed to the independence of its work, the generation of objective evidence and their reliance on methodological vigour. An integral element of this strategy was to displace the obstacles to expansion, such as noise and climate change, 'beyond politics', so that they were transported into a space of technocratic expertise and markets. Potential and actual political opposition was negotiated and at times negated by information, compensation or 'independent' arbitration, coupled with intermittent practices of therapeutic consultation. Indeed, for the Commission, political involvement or ministerial responsibility was deemed to be at the origin of the disputes in aviation; political values or readings went against the grain of empirical evidence and impartial data.

With respect to the public-facing aspect of the Commission's activities, these strategic framings were augmented by rhetorical appeals that celebrated the character, judgement and reliability of the new body. The need for rational and impartial deliberation was lauded by government and politicians, and echoed across different policy arenas by the leadership of the pro-expansion campaign. For example, in her opening address to delegates at the Westminster Energy, Environment and Transport Forum at the end of January 2013, Baroness Valentine, chief executive of the pro-expansion London First lobby, declared that 'we need a rational head to look at the options, which as far as I know, Howard Davies has' (Valentine, 2013: 6). And speaking on the first panel, Colin Matthews, chief executive officer at Heathrow airport, reinforced this demand for a rational dialogue, arguing that 'we do welcome the Davies Commission … If that's what it takes to have a reasonably broad agreement outside the world of politics, then surely it's worth it, because we have made decisions in the past, only we promptly undo them again with the next change in the political cycle, and that doesn't do the country any good whatsoever' (Matthews, 2013: 11). Indeed, in opening the session in January 2014, at which Howard Davies gave evidence to the Transport Committee (TC), the committee chair further legitimised the work of the Commission by announcing: 'Sir Howard, you have been asked to secure an evidence-based consensus' (TC, 2014).

As we have argued, the work of the Commission cannot be dissociated from how its chair, Howard Davies, came to 'perform authority'. Davies was immersed in the discourse and genre of science and scientific expertise, displaying a dispassionate and reasoned mode of operation. Moreover, as the work of the Commission took shape, Davies himself came in many ways to operate as an empty signifier, whose ideological appeal and performance of 'reasonable authority' functioned to conceal the differences between the competing demands for expansion and environmental protection, which were directed at the Commission, thus displacing conflict and politicisation. His 'reasoned' performance of authority was juxtaposed with the threat of a return to the 'pub politics' of previous aviation debates, that is to say, a politics which, in the aftermath of the 2010 Moratorium, the former Conservative Secretary of State for Transport, Justine Greening, an opponent of Heathrow expansion, had associated with the persistent failures to reach anything more than a temporary settlement in aviation policy from the ATWP (2003) onwards (Griggs and Howarth, 2013: 325–7). But, more importantly, Davies' performance of leadership and authority carefully constructed a space for agency outside the logics of calculation and quantification. Appealing to the faculty of judgement, Davies rested his authority not solely on the methodology of the Commission, but on his personality and his capacity to generate a 'reasonable case'. Paradoxically, given the terms of reference of the Commission, his case did not need a rational consensus, but simply the recognition that the Commission had done its best to take account of the different positions across the aviation sector.

But the limits of the depoliticising strategies and tactics were also exposed. Take, for example, the issue of aircraft noise. Shortly after the publication of the Interim Report, pro-expansion lobbies, London First and Let Britain Fly, worked to put pressure on government to institute the Commission's recommendation of an independent noise authority. In March 2014, Let Britain Fly, in collaboration with London First and HACAN – one of the main opponents to Heathrow expansion – organised a joint aviation noise summit, which was addressed by Howard Davies, as well as a public letter to *The Guardian* newspaper supporting the proposals to create an independent noise authority (Wintour, 2014). Although HACAN ran the risk of being incorporated into the expansionist agenda of the Commission and its sponsors, the aviation noise summit was itself transfigured into a new space of contestation and debate, which in many ways stifled the strategies and tactics of Let Britain Fly. With HACAN actively participating in the summit, its demands about the problem of aircraft noise were legitimised by those defending expansion, if not advanced. Speaking at the Aviation Noise Summit, Iain Osborne, the CAA's Director of Regulatory Policy, thus warned that it was 'not realistic to think that institutional reform can de-politicise noise', fearing that any authority would 'end up as being seen as just another bunch of men … aviation-focused technocrats, accused of partiality by those who don't like the outcomes' (Osborne, 2014: 3).

In short, the attempts to deal with noise in terms of a technical problem that could be managed in an administrative fashion ran aground, as the issue was partially transformed into a legitimate demand, which could no longer be framed politically as a purely 'negative NIMBY issue'. At the same time, the various strategies and tactics employed by the pro-expansion lobby to defuse the issue of noise disclosed yet further contestations, which in themselves risked splits in the coalition against airport expansion. Labelling the noise summit an 'unlikely alliance' of groups and forces, Jeff Gazzard (2014), one of the board members of the AEF, posted a letter in *The Guardian* newspaper comment page, which cast doubt on an independent aviation noise authority, suggesting that 'ombudsmen and other bodies simply fit and impose an airport's existing and planned noise on local communities come what may – just ask those living around Sydney or Charles de Gaulle airports'. Similarly, the Gatwick Area Conservation Committee (GACC), in an open letter to the DfT, publicly challenged the logic of the Commission and its belief that better information would deliver more consensus and agreement in the field of aviation noise (GACC, 2014: 2). In fact, in the lead up to the 2015 general election, HACAN called upon local residents to question parliamentary candidates about their views on the proposed third runway, shifting flights paths and noise (*HACAN News*, 6 March, 2015). It is striking that the majority of candidates standing for election in and around Heathrow and Gatwick publicly declared themselves against expansion (AirportWatch, 2015b; Topham, 2015). Hence if Howard Davies had thus endeavoured to depoliticise aviation, the limits of such depoliticisation were emerging before the Commission had completed its investigations. With the publication of its Final Report, the simmering discontent was to explode, as we shall discuss in the next chapter.

4

Repoliticising aviation policy: law, planning and persistent activism

In presenting the findings of the AC to the public at the beginning of July 2015, Howard Davies expressed his 'hope that within weeks, if not months, [ministers would] decide to go ahead [with expansion]' (Davies, 2015a). But these hopes were soon dashed. Over four and a half years, two Prime Ministers and four governments later, his efforts to deliver an 'evidence-based consensus' were still being challenged in the courts. In February 2020, in a landmark judgement, the Court of Appeal ruled that the ANPS and its plans for a third runway at Heathrow were 'illegal' because the government had failed to take adequate account of the impact of aviation emissions from expansion on its commitments under the 2015 Paris Agreement and the UK target of net zero carbon emissions by 2050 (Carrington, 2020). The Conservative government, led by Boris Johnson, who was a strong opponent of Heathrow expansion when Mayor of London, made it clear that it would not appeal the ruling, and so it was left to Heathrow Airport Limited (HAL) to challenge the verdict (Xie and Baynes, 2020). The proposed third runway was effectively stalled.

This chapter analyses the complex and messy dynamics of politicisation, depoliticisation and repoliticisation, which punctuated the aftermath of the AC, as rival discourse coalitions competed for policy hegemony. In the post-Brexit context, we argue that successive Conservative governments struggled to perpetuate the dominant social logic of 'predict and provide', as they sought in the face of sustained political opposition to deliver airport expansion by depoliticising aviation's contribution to climate change, air pollution and noise. The chapter also shows how the opponents of expansion exploited and re-politicised the novel arenas and technologies, which were designed and developed by government to remove the issue of aviation expansion from the political domain. Here we explore how the February 2020 ruling of the Court of Appeal, and the successful legal challenge to the third runway, transformed the Planning Act (PA) (2008) and Climate Change Act (CCA) (2008) and the 2015 Paris Agreement into 'counter-technologies', effectively redefining the courts as a sphere of resistance. In exploiting the new technologies and spaces of planning and climate change policy, campaigners were able to use the law courts and the process of judicial review to challenge government and open up new spaces for citizen protest and political resistance. We conclude by exposing the messy dialectics of politicisation and depoliticisation in this case, while underlining the role of strategic agency in seizing such opportunities.

Repoliticising the Airports Commission

Initially, the Conservative government was quick to praise and support Howard Davies and his fellow Commissioners for the delivery of a 'clear and reasoned report [which was] based on evidence [and which] deserves respect and consideration' (McLoughlin, 2015a). It welcomed the case for expansion, but delayed any formal announcement or decision over whether to support a third runway at Heathrow or a second runway at Gatwick. Yet it did accept Davies's urgent call for a quick decision. In presenting the Final Report to the House of Commons, Patrick McLoughlin, the Secretary of State for Transport, declared to his fellow MPs that 'all those with an interest in this important question [aviation expansion] are expecting us to act decisively. And we must act' (McLoughlin, 2015a).

Final reports or legislative blueprints are constitutive artefacts of policy, embodying the rhetoric of 'authoritative choice' that structures much of the policymaking process (Colebatch, 2014: 313; see also Freeman and Maybin, 2011; Freeman, 2019). They are moments of naming, which punctuate the policy process by identifying and temporarily 'fixing' policy discourse, and their function is to establish an ownership of policy problems, which can influence and shape how issues are framed, while also establishing lines of causality and responsibility (Gusfield, 1981). But, in so doing, policy reports or empirical findings also carry the potential of hyper-politicisation (Moran, 2003). For example, the release of a report invariably sparks off a chain of events across multiple spaces of contestation, such as press launches, presentations, summaries, responses and so on. This was the case with the AC. After months of respite, and then a 'phoney war', as its expert membership deliberated, the release of the Commission's Final Report signalled the beginning of a new bout of 'trench-warfare' (to use Claus Offe's words). It was soon evident that the government, senior politicians and policy actors had used the time of the Commission to 'prepare themselves for' the ensuing battle (Offe, 1984: 113).

Senior Conservative Ministers, including Justine Greening, Theresa May and Philip Hammond, as well as Zac Goldsmith, MP for Richmond, and the then London Mayor, Boris Johnson, had made their opposition to a third runway at Heathrow well known. Johnson immediately challenged the legitimacy of the AC, dismissing its support for the third runway at Heathrow as an 'outcome [that] I thought was inevitable because the mandate was to provide a political fig leaf for an establishment U-turn' (Mason and Watt, 2015). Goldsmith, who had made it known that he would resign and force a by-election if the third runway was given the go-ahead (Moreton, 2015; Helm, 2015), condemned the Final Report for advancing an 'obsolete' model of aviation (Bradshaw et al, 2015).

Anti-expansion residents and protesters had been divided about whether to engage with the AC. Some feared that any involvement in the work of Howard Davies and his team ran the risk of incorporation into a decision-making process designed to legitimise aviation expansion and divide campaigners at different airport locations from one another. Others saw the Commission as a moment for campaigners to advance the demands of local residents for concessions around noise, respite and night flights. These tensions were particularly heightened in the campaign against the proposed third runway at Heathrow. For the members of HACAN, the local resident group which had been at the front of the campaign against Labour's 2003 ATWP, the efforts of Davies to tackle aircraft noise, an issue its members saw as their 'big concern!', presented the organisation with a 'real opportunity to push a number of ... strategic objectives at the highest level' (Stewart, 2021: 18). Its Chair, John Stewart, who was to have three face-to-face meetings with Davies, and more with members of the Secretariat, concluded that 'by failing to engage, we [HACAN] would have failed ... communities' around Heathrow and under flight paths. Ultimately, it was a strategy that he believed had delivered significant concessions as the AC came out in support of alternative noise metrics, a noise envelope, backed respite and a ban on scheduled night flights between 11:30 at night and 6 o'clock in the morning, and also supported the creation of an Independent Aviation Noise Authority. Stewart firmly believed and argued publicly that 'historic progress was being made' (Stewart, 2021: 22).

Yet this strategy of engagement was not without its political costs. In his personal account of his participation in the AC, Stewart acknowledges that the recommendations on aircraft noise were interpreted by others within the campaign as a means of legitimising a new runway. Perhaps reflecting the strident debates between campaigners, he even questioned why climate change campaigners did not take up the opportunity to engage with the AC: 'I'm not suggesting [climate change campaigners should have] dropped their opposition to the runway but that Davies could have been used more effectively' (Stewart, 2021: 22). Over time, however, HACAN's dual strategy, which progressively combined its long-standing opposition to a proposed third runway alongside a constructive dialogue with the AC and Heathrow Airport in an effort to reduce airport noise and involve local communities in the airport's governance, came unstuck.

To begin with, following the Final Report of the AC, and in preparation of its case for planning permission, Heathrow Airport worked to implement the Commission's recommendations. In particular, it established the

Heathrow Community Noise Forum and the Heathrow Community Engagement Board (HCEB). As it did so, splits emerged in the campaign against the third runway as some campaigners and residents argued that HACAN was positioning itself 'too close to what some regarded as "the enemy"' (Stewart, 2021: 28). Sharp clashes and antagonisms thus emerged about the strategic priorities of noise mitigation and the fight against climate change. Ultimately, HACAN was to take its distance from the broader campaign against the proposed third runway. It decided not to join the No 3rd Runway Coalition of MPs, local authorities, resident groups, trade unions and environmental organisations opposed to Heathrow expansion, choosing instead to focus its resources on noise and flight path issues. Stewart himself observed that he 'continued to be disappointed by the indifference shown by a handful of environmentalists to the interests of local communities', drawing attention to the potential fault lines between campaigners' demands to reduce noise pollution and lower carbon emissions from aviation (Stewart, 2021: 28).

However, in the final days and immediate aftermath of the AC, and with a 'common' opposition to the proposed third runway still more or less intact, both local residents and campaigners moved to attack the political independence of the AC. For one thing, they targeted and discredited the personal reputation of Howard Davies. In a scathing assessment timed to undermine the recommendations of the Final Report, AirportWatch (2015a: 3) characterised the 'history and analysis' of the Commission as a 'stitch up', and it dismissed Davies as an 'establishment figure', working with 'virtually silent part-time commissioners', and a 'secretariat drawn mainly from the Department for Transport', who 'will return to their roles … to implement the policies of their political masters' (2015: 1). Ultimately, AirportWatch disparaged the conclusions of the Commission as little more than an ideological smokescreen for the Cameron government, accusing it of having omitted 'inconvenient truths' over climate change and air quality, while pouring scorn on its economic and social modelling of the impacts of aviation. There was no surprise, in their words, that the AC had 'duly c[o]me up with the result the government wanted – airport expansion justified by economic benefits' (2015a: 3).

Attacks of this sort challenged the very strategies and tactics of depoliticisation employed by Howard Davies and his fellow Commissioners, namely, the appeal to the use of rigorous scientific methods and the alleged independence of both the Commission and Davies himself, and they were repeated across the multiple arenas of airport policy and politics. In July 2015, reports emerged that the Local Authorities Aircraft Noise Council was considering legal action against the 'biased and flawed' report of the AC.[1] In early August, the Teddington Action Group threw doubt on the independence of Howard Davies, alleging that, while chair of the Commission, he worked as a board member of Prudential insurance company, which spent some £300 million on properties around Heathrow in the run-up to the publication of the Final Report (Davies, 2015b). By the end of August, local councils in south London were publicly claiming that the AC 'buried' economic evidence that challenged its forecasts.[2]

Such accusations resonated throughout the policy arena, as Gatwick Airport added its voice to the intensifying policy debate by publishing its own riposte to the findings of the Commission (Gatwick Airport, 2015a). Stewart Wingate, its Chief Executive, argued that 'the Final Report contains so many omissions and basic errors that its reliability as the basis of aviation policy must be called into question. The findings of this report simply do not add up' (Gatwick Airport, 2015b). The owners of Gatwick Airport refused to concede defeat to Heathrow, while Wingate repeatedly insisted that 'Gatwick is still very much in the race. The Commission's report makes clear that expansion at Gatwick is deliverable' (Gatwick Airport, 2015c).

During the summer of 2015, anti-expansion groups and local residents surrounding Heathrow also questioned the political legitimacy and personal integrity of David Cameron, focusing on his earlier pre-2010 election commitments to a 'no ifs no buts' pledge against expansion at the London airport. On 13 July 2015, 13 activists from Plane Stupid occupied the northern runway at Heathrow Airport for 6 hours, unfurling banners declaring 'no third runway, no ifs, no buts' (Dearden, 2015). On the day after the release of the Final Report, local residents blocked the Heathrow Airport tunnel (Clementine, 2015). Protests also took place at the Conservative party conference in October 2015, as residents and campaigners demonstrated outside the conference hall behind a model plane emblazoned with the words 'no third runway, no ifs, no buts', while piping aircraft noises in the early morning into the Midland Hotel where delegates were staying (Cumber, 2015). In fact, the slogan 'no ifs, no buts' began to operate as an empty signifier, which was used by activists and groups to make possible the construction of equivalences between their different demands for noise controls, carbon emissions reductions, stronger political leadership and increased corporate regulation. Such equivalences enabled the movement to garner wider public support, while articulating the threat of the third runway at Heathrow to local communities and their well-being.

Following the logic of this strategy, campaigners endeavoured to shift public attention on to the Commission's analysis of air quality and the capacity of an expanded Heathrow airport to meet EU limits on air pollution, thus politicising this dimension of the issue. In the run-up to the publication of the Final Report of the AC, ClientEarth won an appeal in the Supreme Court against the government for failing to meet EU air quality directives (Harvey, 2015). And as rounds of court challenges unfolded over the next 3 years, Heathrow expansion was successfully included in this increasingly salient issue, as a range of groups drew equivalences between demands for clean air and opposition to airport expansion. ClientEarth subsequently called for a 'detailed analysis' of Heathrow Airport's May 2016 plans to tackle air pollution. Its lawyer, Alan Andrews, argued that 'air pollution around the airport needs to be cut drastically before we can think about expansion. It's difficult to see how that would happen without something far more radical than what's currently on the table' (Date, 2016).

In this shifting political context, a group of six local council leaders, eight MPs, environmental pressure groups such as Greenpeace, FoE and the AEF, as well as HACAN and other local resident groups, wrote an open letter to the Prime Minister at the end of July 2015 arguing that Heathrow expansion would not meet air quality limits and casting doubt on the consultation on air quality undertaken by the AC. The signatories of the letter stated that air quality was not taken 'seriously' by the Commission, and they criticised the 'exceptional consultation' on air quality, which had begun on 8 May only to end 3 weeks later on 29 May, 1 month before the publication of the report. They also broadened their attack on the alleged 'open' approach of the AC, suggesting that the 'Commission effectively treated the consultation as a tick box exercise and one that was immaterial to the overall report'.[3]

At the same time, the Commission's downplaying of aviation's impact on climate change came under sustained attack. Plane Stupid decried the Davies Commission when its activists occupied the North Runway at Heathrow, proclaiming that 'building more runways goes against everything we're being told by scientists and experts' (Plane Stupid, 2015). In equal measure, James Lees (2015) of the AEF condemned the Commission for failing to take full account of aviation's carbon emissions. He claimed that 'Sir Howard's lack of interest in all things climate-related also appears to represent the AC's approach to this issue'. Typically, these attacks again challenged the alleged rational and reasonable approach of the Commission, and indeed the previous appeals to the reputational power and personal style of Howard Davies. Greenpeace for its part belittled the environmental case for expansion in the Final Report, stating that it was so 'riddled with holes that you could fly an Airbus through [it]', and they challenged the very foundations of the work of the Commission, when they argued that the Final Report exhibited a 'tendency to assume that all sorts of wonderful and unexpected things will happen and relies on this procession of political implausibilities to make the third runway plausible. It is really only one step away from saying "so long as someone solves all the problems, there'll be no problems"' (Greenpeace, 2015).

By the end of the summer, campaigners and affected parties were reactivating and reassembling the various demands that had been bolted together in the successful struggle against Labour's proposals for a third runway at Heathrow in the 2000s. In September 2015, the cross-party No Third Runway campaign was launched, the London Assembly voted against the third runway proposal, and all the main candidates for the London mayoral elections came out against expansion at Heathrow (AirportWatch 2015c; Dyer, 2015; HACAN, 2015). In addition, Labour's new leader, Jeremy Corbyn, who had opposed the third runway during his leadership campaign (Grice, 2015), appointed John McDonnell as Shadow Chancellor, a long-time vocal opponent of Heathrow expansion and MP for Hayes and Harlington near the airport. His appointment and the election of Corbyn signalled a change in the approach of the Labour leadership towards the aviation industry. McDonnell was quick to amplify the issue of air quality, while drawing equivalences between air quality, social injustice and struggles against Heathrow expansion. At a rally in October 2015, for example, he informed campaigners that '[i]n my constituency ... people are literally dying. They're dying because the air has already been poisoned by the aviation industry.'[4]

In fact, in a rerun of the discrediting of the ATWP (2003) and its discourse of 'sustainable aviation', attacks from campaigners gained institutional support from the EAC. In July 2015, the EAC launched an inquiry into the findings of the AC, focusing its attention in particular on whether the 'indicative policies' and 'proposed mitigations' of the AC were 'realistic and achievable', and the 'steps' government should take to ensure its decision on the AC's Final Report was 'consistent with its commitments on sustainable development' (EAC, 2015a). In general, the EAC attacked the analytical underpinnings of the AC's conclusions, foregrounding limitations within its data, as well as its interpretations, notably in the realm of carbon emissions and air quality, as it sought to pressurise government to re-own the issue of airport expansion. To begin with, it called on the alternative expertise of the CCC to 'comment' on the forecasts of the Commission, exposing what it saw as 'a significant gap between [the theoretical approach] of the AC towards emissions and the current policy environment' (EAC, 2015b: 3). Moreover, it demanded that government then 'act on any recommendations' from this additional scrutiny of the work of the Commission (EAC, 2015b: 6). Similarly, its forceful criticisms of the AC's work on air quality called for government to position itself clearly in relation to the Commission's interpretation of the Air Quality Directive, while setting out how its national air quality strategy could meet legal pollution limits and establish effective monitoring and binding air quality measures that separated air pollution from transport in general from that caused by aviation (EAC, 2015b: 13–16).

The Conservative government deferred the challenges of the EAC and others, as they sought to evade the political battlefield of aviation policy, retreating behind calls for further evidence and analysis, while delaying any decision over expansion. A week after the publication in December 2015 of the EAC Report on the work of the AC, Patrick McLoughlin, Secretary of State for Transport, put back any government decision on expansion until the summer of 2016. McLoughlin noted that the government 'accepts the case for expansion', arguing that the Commission made a 'strong case for expansion in the south-east'. Yet, after almost 3 years of investigation by the Commission, the Secretary of State still argued that there was a need for further information and clarification. In fact, the government openly acknowledged the EAC's reservations over the impact of airport expansion on air quality, noise mitigation and carbon emissions, as McLoughlin informed Parliament that 'I want to get this decision right', which 'means getting the environmental response right' (McLoughlin, 2015b).

McLoughlin's intervention showed that in the short period since the publication of the AC's Final Report there had been an effective repoliticisation of aviation policy, dismantling the presumption that an 'evidence-based consensus' had emerged from the work of the AC. Nonetheless, the work of the AC had facilitated the Conservative Party's policy reversal on airport expansion in South East England without apparent costs to the political reputation of Cameron and his efforts to detoxify his party, and it had put expansion at Heathrow firmly back on the political agenda. Still, for the Cameron government, the carefully engineered ideological cover for these transitions quickly evaporated as responsibility for decision-making was publicly returned to government and the domain of politics. For one thing, Howard Davies had had to publicly defend the Commission's methods of working and his personal reputation.[5] In equal measure, the 'science of airport expansion' – the methods and data analysis underpinning the work of the Commission – was once again being contested by many of the same actors who delegitimised the ATWP (2003). But, more importantly, while reports circulated that Cameron was taking 'personal responsibility' for the decision on expansion in a Cabinet Committee, which did not include senior ministers opposed to the third runway at Heathrow (Chorley, 2015), the Chancellor George Osborne was acknowledging on the BBC news programme, *Today*, that 'we now have an independent report that has forced the choice on government ... and said "here if you want to build a runway, and by the way you need to, you can either put one at Gatwick or you can put one at Heathrow, and now you decide"'.[6]

More fully, then, local residents and campaigners had sought to re-politicise climate change, as they challenged the efforts by the Commission to push the impact of rising carbon emissions from aviation to the margins of political debate, while adding climate change to the issue of noise pollution as a recognised barrier to expansion at Heathrow airport. At the same time, they had solidified the equivalences between demands for cleaner air and opposition to Heathrow expansion, adding the manipulation of existing air quality data and requirements to the charge list facing the government as it moved to implement the recommendations of Howard Davies. If Davies had endeavoured to abbreviate the focus of the inquiry to the problem of aviation noise as the main obstacle to expansion, campaigners and local residents had quickly added the issues of climate change and air quality to the list of items in need of depoliticisation.

'Predict and provide' redux: the Conservative government's 'go for growth'

It was not until 25 October 2016 that the Conservative government formally accepted the case for a planned third runway at Heathrow airport, almost 18 months after the publication of the Final Report of the AC (DfT and Grayling, 2016). In these 18 months, the shock result of the Brexit referendum in June 2016 had radically transformed the political status quo. The vote to leave the EU triggered the resignation of David Cameron as Prime Minister, who was replaced by Theresa May, the former Home Secretary. In the wake of the referendum, the fate of her premiership was to be determined by her ability to navigate and negotiate, not least within her own party, the political twists and turns of an acceptable and workable 'exit' agreement with the EU. Sensing division and weakness within the Labour ranks, May called a snap election in June 2017, as she sought to strengthen her parliamentary majority in Brexit negotiations, though the decision ultimately backfired as her party lost its overall majority in the Commons.

Ideological reframing and the new planning technology

As the politics of Brexit dominated the parliamentary agenda and the public imagination, it might have been expected that aviation expansion would slowly slip further into the political 'long grass', especially with the opposition to Heathrow expansion within and outside the House of Commons. However, as the May government increasingly framed its policy agenda through the construction of a new post-Brexit imaginary – the promise 'to forge a bold new positive role for ourselves in the world' (May, 2018) – the potential expansion of Heathrow was invested with a new urgency. The government continued to use and embellish the sedimented tropes of the economic and social benefits of Heathrow expansion and aviation in general, which were invariably threatened by an airport 'capacity crunch' and expansion at European and international competitors.

But the international connectivity of air travel was also reframed as a vital ingredient of the generation of new post-Brexit trade deals, and a key mechanism for delivering the 'shared society' that was promised by the May premiership (May, 2017). In announcing the government's support for a third runway to the House of Commons, Chris Grayling, the Secretary of State for Transport, argued that Heathrow expansion would 'send a very clear message that this country is open for business', rehashing the 'open for business' post-Brexit imaginary of the May government (Hansard, 2016). Called upon to justify its decision to expand, the government employed and reworked elements of this imaginary, even repeating arguments that the third runway at Heathrow provided much needed long-haul flights, which 'will be crucial as we leave the EU so that we can get out into the world and do business with old allies and new partners alike'. The British government's rhetoric thus rearticulated Heathrow Airport as a post-Brexit 'growth engine for the whole of the UK', with its increased connectivity to regional airports 'ensuring we have an economy that works for everyone' (DfT, 2017a: 5).

The May government also confirmed that planning permission for the new project would fall under the auspices of the 2008 Planning Act for 'nationally significant' infrastructure projects. The New Labour government had introduced the 2008 Act because it was keen to attract 'footloose capital' in an increasingly financialised global market for infrastructure (Marshall, 2011: 461; see also Newman, 2009: 460–1). Sponsored by the Treasury, it sought to minimise the uncertainty and costs associated with planning delays, symbolised by the Terminal Five 'debacle' at Heathrow, the longest public inquiry in UK history (Cowell and Marshall, 2016). In practice, it took infrastructure planning outside the domain of 'normal' planning through the granting of Development Consent Orders (DCOs) by a newly-established independent Infrastructure Planning Commission (IPC) on the back of National Policy Statements (NPS). The idea of an NPS was designed to determine infrastructure needs in specific areas and was led by individual ministries, but was subject to public consultation and ultimately approved in Parliament. However, this strategy of reforming infrastructure planning also sought to depoliticise this critical practice by removing the final approval of large infrastructure projects from the Secretary of State; constraining the modes and spaces of contestation; and developing a new 'ordering' of time through the tighter temporal regulation of the public-led elements of the planning process (Marshall, 2011, 2012; Cowell and Marshall, 2016).

The state was effectively recast into a policy setting role. The NPS would set out the government's objectives for national infrastructure, detailing projected capacity demands and locations for development, as well as establishing how new proposals would meet commitments to sustainable development and coordinate with policies across government. It was left to the promoters of particular infrastructure projects to manage the consultation process, while campaigners became increasingly dependent on the processes of judicial review after the planning decision had been either approved or not (Newman, 2009). Importantly, however, the Localism Act (2011) pulled back on the efforts to remove final approval for schemes from the hands of the Secretary of State, replacing the IPC with the Major Infrastructures Planning Unit within the Planning Inspectorate and returning the final say over the approval of schemes to Ministers.[7]

Nonetheless, it remained the case that stakeholder consultation was effectively limited to the pre-application stage of the DCO, with responsibility for consultation passing from the state to the developers, who reported on the outcomes of consultation in their DCO application. In practice, the Act imposed narrow time limitations on the planning process, so that the review of an application for development was restricted to 1 year (6 months of examination by five inspectors appointed by the Secretary of State, followed by 3 months for Inspectors to formulate recommendations, and 3 months for the Secretary of State to make a final decision on the project). Opponents to developments had to 'register' their interest so as to have the opportunity to provide evidence in writing to the Inspectors, though the privileging of written representations constituted another constraint on public participation and representation. Following the decision by the Secretary of State, there was then a 6-week window for opponents to lodge a legal challenge to the process through judicial review in the High Court. Ultimately, planning approval for any infrastructural projects by the Secretary of State rested on the scheme meeting the pre-approved conditions of the NPS, which had already obtained parliamentary approval (Marshall, 2011).

As a new and emergent technology of government, therefore, the Planning Act (2008) brought into being a truncated form of public consultation, whereby communities and campaigners were able to voice some opposition to proposed developments, but with little obligation on the behalf of authorities to listen or capacity for communities and campaigners to effectively challenge decisions. The DfT (2017a) began to roll out such measures in February 2017, beginning the planning process with the release for consultation of a draft ANPS. It was accompanied by the opening of consultation on night flights (2017b), national airspace reform (2017c) and a revised aviation strategy for government (2017d). The consultation around the ANPS ended in May 2017, before the release of a revised draft ANPS after the June election in October (2017e). Consultation on the revised ANPS opened in October and ended in December 2017 (Le Blond, 2019), which laid the ground for Heathrow Airport (2018a) to begin its consultations in preparation of its application for a DCO.

The airport initially consulted between January and March 2018 on the design, operations and mitigation of the impacts of an expanded airport. In the run-up to the consultation, it also announced the putting in place of the HCEB – one of the recommendations of the AC – which was aimed at depoliticising noise and the expansion of the airport: a logic of difference that explicitly endeavoured to incorporate the community in the planning and decision-making of the airport. The newly created Board was at pains to declare its independence from Heathrow Airport and the government, highlighting its values of 'independence, impartiality, inclusivity, transparency and integrity'. Rachael Cerfontyne, who was previously deputy chair of the Independent Police Complaints Commission, was appointed as its first chair (Stewart, 2021: 38). At the same time, the government responded to another of Howard Davies's recommendations by establishing an Independent Commission on Civil Aviation Noise (ICCAN) in November 2018. However, unlike the functions envisaged by the AC for an independent aviation noise commission, ICCAN's mission was initially restricted to only 2 years, and it openly admitted in its public-facing activities that it was not a noise ombudsman, could not deal with complaints and could not stop airports expanding.[8]

Fast planning meets politics

As a technology of government, the revised planning mechanisms were directed at constraining opposition within the planning process so as to 'speed up' decision-making. However, skirting around such arenas, opponents of expansion simply invested in alternative spaces of protest and contestation. The October 2016 decision to grant approval for the third runway had intensified once again the politicisation of aviation debates. Zac Goldsmith, Conservative MP for Richmond, one of the constituencies under Heathrow flightpaths, honoured his promise to resign and force a by-election. Leading Cabinet Ministers continued to decry the decision. Boris Johnson, who had been appointed Foreign Secretary in the May Cabinet, described the third runway as 'undeliverable', while Justine Greening, the Education Secretary, said that she was 'extremely disappointed' (Siddique and Phipps, 2016). It was reported that up to 60 Conservative MPs were prepared to vote against any expansion in the Commons, and the Labour leadership was known to be opposed to expansion (Riley-Smith, 2016). Indeed, Cabinet ministers such as Johnson and Greening were given leave to voice opposition to the runway as long as they did not campaign against it (Keate, 2016). As anti-expansion campaigners were quick to point out, Theresa May herself had voiced her opposition to Heathrow expansion in 2008 on the grounds of climate change (Howard, 2016).

Across the aviation policy arena, attacks on the decision continued to come from both supporters and opponents of expansion. Gatwick airport declared again that the decision was 'not the right answer for Britain', while Willie Walsh, head of the International Airlines Group (IAG), the parent company of BA, raised fears of increased landing charges for airlines as Heathrow sought to fund expansion, going on to call the airport operators 'fat, dumb and happy'.[9] The CAA wrote to Heathrow in October 2016 expressing its concerns that the airport keep its landing charges down, an issue that was to gather momentum as the divisions between the business models of airlines and airport operators became increasingly contentious.[10] In fact, when the DfT reduced the projected monetised benefits of expansion at Heathrow by some £80 billion compared with the AC's estimates, the business case for expansion at Heathrow was openly questioned (HACAN, 2017). This reduction in predicted benefits merely added to earlier criticisms, which were levelled by the AC's own advisors, namely that the Commissioners had overblown the economic case for expansion (Mackie and Pearce, 2015). Indeed, from July 2016 onwards, Andrew Tyrie, the chair of the Treasury Select Committee and MP for Chichester near Gatwick, called for the government to publish its revised CBA of Heathrow expansion, and he challenged the weight given to 'the seldom used' Net Public Value measure in the economic case for Heathrow.[11] At the same time, the TC continued to question the financial costs of the third runway. In its March 2018 report on the draft ANPS it called on the government to deliver 'evidence' that the third runway was 'both affordable and deliverable', and to assuage the fear of airlines that landing charges would rise to fund expansion (Transport Committee, 2018: 7, 28–9).

Local residents met the October 2016 decision to go ahead with the third runway at Heathrow with equal dismay. Teddington Action Group began a process of judicial review for 'apparent bias', arguing that Howard Davies undertook work for the Government of Singapore Investment Corporation (GIC), the Singaporean sovereign fund and one of the main shareholders of Heathrow Airport, a role he occupied until his appointment as chair of the AC and which he allegedly did not disclose in the AC's register of interests.[12] HACAN and other resident groups also expressed their continued opposition to the proposed runway. John Stewart, chair of HACAN, argued that 'Heathrow will be rejoicing and seeing it as the end of the battle. For many people, including the big green organisations, it is day one' (Topham, 2016). On cue, Reclaim the Power and Plane Stupid returned firmly to the domain of aviation politics, with a spokesperson for Plane Stupid declaring in a press release that 'Obedience to this government is suicide. If they think we're going to quietly follow them over the cliff, they're dreaming.'[13] Earlier in the year, the 'Heathrow 13' – the Plane Stupid activists who had occupied the Northern runway at the airport in July 2015 – had used their high-profile trial for aggravated trespass and entering the restricted area of an aerodrome to draw public attention to the health impacts of air pollution and climate change from aviation and airport expansion. At their sentencing in February 2016, they reiterated to the assembled press that 'the science is clear … There can be no new runways in the UK if we are to take climate change seriously' (McVeigh, 2016).

Strenuous efforts were made to publicise and re-politicise climate change as campaigners denounced the negligence of the May government and the AC. Friends of the Earth, for example, argued that the decision to approve the third runway in 2016 'makes a complete mockery of government commitments to tackle climate change'.[14] John Sauven, the director of Greenpeace UK, attacked the 'incomplete and misleading information' behind the decision, questioning the rationality and legitimacy of a 'privatised' decision-making process, which descended into a competition between Heathrow and Gatwick over site location. The consequence was that climate change commitments and the challenge of rising aviation emissions had been rendered 'invisible' in the Final Report of the AC and its recommendations, where the solution to rising aviation emissions 'exist[ed] as fragments scattered through his [Howard Davies's] 600-page multi-volume report in as an obscure and obfuscatory manner as he could manage. It's designed, very effectively, not to be understood' (Sauven, 2016).

The discursive tactics of depoliticisation

More often than not, three core issues animated this broad coalition against expansion, and they were evident in the different arenas where it sought to expand its audience: noise, air quality and climate change (see, for example, the criticisms of the Airports Commission made by the AEF, 2016a, 2016b). Faced with such opposition, the May government continued stubbornly to downplay issues of climate change, while seeking to incorporate demands for controls on noise pollution and air quality. The Secretary of State for Transport made little mention of climate change and aviation emissions when he announced the decision to support Heathrow expansion to the Commons in October 2016, merely assuring MPs that the third runway could be delivered within existing carbon limits.

In contrast, the issues of noise and air quality were foregrounded as the key considerations or obstacles to expansion. However, the claims and demands arising from these issues were incorporated into the discourse of expansion. The Secretary of State thus promised a 'world class package of [£2.6 billion] compensation and mitigation', declaring that the 'government will grant development consent only if we remain satisfied that a new runway will not impact on the UK's compliance with its air quality obligations'. In this way, the problem of air quality was framed as a 'significant national health issue that the Government takes immensely seriously'. Similarly, the government recognised the demands for noise controls by confirming that the six and a half hour ban on scheduled night flights was a condition of expansion, while also affirming 'clear and legally enforceable noise performance targets'. When questioned by MPs over the creation of an independent noise commission, Chris Grayling committed the government to 'proper independent noise monitoring', arguing that he had 'not downgraded' the recommendation for a noise commission. But he did add that 'it is just a question of working out the best way to do that' and the ensuing debates about the role of the ICCAN were a testament to such tensions. Climate change was thus kept at the margins of the debate, while air quality and noise pollution were added to the major obstacles against expansion, or to the list of issues requiring 'depoliticisation' (Hansard, 2016).

In this respect, the Further Review and Sensitivities Report (DfT, 2016), which accompanied the decision to construct the new runway, appeared to move the May government away from the commitment to keep CO_2 emissions from flights departing UK airports to 2005 levels of 37.5 $MtCO_2$ by 2050, thus according with the recommendations of the CCC. Describing the AC as a 'sound and robust piece of evidence' (2016: 5), the DfT declared its preference for the Commission's carbon-traded scenario, which it saw as 'consistent with cross-government guidance' (2016: 26), rather than the 'carbon-capped scenario, which aligned emissions from flights leaving UK airports with the CCC's recommendation to keep aviation emissions at 2005 levels (2016: 47). Carbon trading, the DfT argued, enabled emissions from UK flights to increase without an increase in emissions at the international level. In effect, it removed aviation emissions from any assessment of proposed schemes for expansion, concluding that carbon trading meant that 'increases in aircraft CO_2 emissions from expansion were therefore not treated as additional (as they would be offset by emissions reductions in other sectors, paid for by the aviation sector) and were not included in the monetised assessment of costs and benefits' (2016: 26). Such arguments were emboldened by the appeals to the UK's role in the development of the Carbon Offsetting and Reduction Scheme for International Aviation (CORSIA) – the planned global offsetting scheme in aviation – which was agreed by the ICAO in 2016.

As the consultation on the ANPS unfolded, such discursive tactics were rearticulated and put to work. In the Foreword to the consultation document on the draft ANPS in 2017, Chris Grayling, the Secretary of State, designated the meeting of air quality limits to be a condition of expansion, noting again how 'poor air quality is a national health issue which this Government takes very seriously.' The Secretary of State also argued that the mitigation of noise impacts, including predictable periods of respite on local communities, were to be subject to 'binding planning requirements' for development consent to be granted. In stark contrast, while climate change was identified as 'one of the most serious risks to our economic and national security', Grayling merely declared himself to be 'confident that the Heathrow Northwest Runway scheme can be delivered within [climate change] limits' (DfT, 2017a: 6). So, by the time the revised draft ANPS was published in October, the government was arguing that 'any increase in carbon emissions alone is not a reason to refuse development consent, unless the increase in carbon emissions resulting from the project is so significant that it would have a material impact on the ability of Government to meet its carbon reduction targets, including carbon budgets' (DfT, 2017e: 58). In the subsequent judicial review of the ANPS, opponents to expansion were to point out that it was unclear what the Secretary of State and the DfT meant by a 'material impact'.

The final version of the ANPS put before the Commons in June 2018 reiterated this framing and balancing of climate change, noise and air quality. Much of the strategy to depoliticise Heathrow expansion rested on the rhetorical work of the AC. At crucial points, the ANPS mimicked the language of the AC, arguing that the 'do nothing' scenario was 'detrimental to the UK economy', while extolling the economic contribution of aviation, which had 'only increased following the country's decision to leave the European Union' (DfT, 2018a: 14–15). Time and again, the ANPS confirmed the confidence of the government in the 'AC's arguments and reasoning [which] are clear and thorough' and based on a 'sound' use of evidence (DfT, 2018a: 18) In a nutshell, the AC acted as a shield for government to dismiss environmental demands against expansion, and the government did little more than 'agree' with its conclusions that expansion could take place under the obligations of the CCA (2008). More precisely, it recognised that 'expansion must be deliverable within national targets on greenhouse gas emissions *and* in accordance with legal obligations on air quality' (DfT, 2018a: 16). However, there was little or no detail on how these targets and legal obligations would be met, except for the encouragement of carbon trading scenarios, while, as we have foregrounded, no account of rising carbon emissions was made when deciding which of the rival airport schemes to adopt – a decision that appeared to favour the Heathrow Northwest runway, which arguably produced the most emissions, but was feted for its connectivity (DfT, 2018a: 30–1).

The ANPS was duly approved in the Commons by a majority of 296 on 25 June. The Corbyn leadership of the Labour Party gave its MPs a free vote, and although it opposed the approval of the third runway at Heathrow, some 119 Labour MPs supported the ANPS and 96 voted against. The Scottish National Party abstained, while Boris Johnson, the Foreign Secretary, who had made a public commitment to oppose Heathrow expansion, was on an international trip and unable to attend the vote (Buchan, 2019). Greg Hands, the sitting MP for the London Borough of Chelsea and Fulham and International Trade Minister, resigned from the government, as he was unable to vote for the ANPS, and the Conservative government had whipped its MPs into supporting the third runway.[15]

By securing parliamentary approval for the ANPS, the May government closed another stage in the implementation of the recommendations of the AC. The acceptance of the ANPS had once more inscribed the logic of 'predict and provide' at the heart of the UK government and state. In its effort to depoliticise Heathrow expansion, the government had sought to transform rising emissions from aviation into a tractable policy issue by emphasising the logics and scenarios of carbon emissions trading as the realistic 'solution' to the sustainability of aviation and the enabler of expansion. At the same time, the issues of air quality and noise pollution were incorporated into the discourse of expansion, now reframed in ways that could be mitigated by 'world-leading' benefits, compensation and improved governance. In this process, the arguments of the AC were recycled as 'acts of faith' to negate and undermine opposition against expansion: the government simply confirmed that expansion could meet the targets of the CCC without setting out any strategic plans to meet them.

It is important to stress that as the May government tied aviation more closely to its vision of a new global Britain, so the discourse of government increasingly reinforced the logic and rhetoric of 'predict and provide', which had been integral to the ATWP (2003). Its strategic consultation document, *Aviation 2050*, which was published in December 2018, returned to the fundamental pillars of a partnership approach with industry: the avoidance of market distortion; international action to bring about emissions trading in aviation; and the buy-in to technological fixes. In the Foreword, the Aviation Minister, Baroness Sugg, underlined how 'this consultation makes clear the government supports aviation industry growth', describing 'a thriving aviation sector [as] tangible evidence of economic confidence, growing tourism, increased trade and business investment' (DfT, 2018b: 6–7). Significantly, also, the Planning Act (2008) had shifted political attention to the approval of the ANPS. As a technology of government, its truncated practices of consultation led local residents and campaigners against airport expansion to exploit alternative venues and spaces of contestation. One such space was that of the courts and the logic of legal challenge, which we now discuss.

Legal challenges, the Climate Change Act and the Climate Change Committee

Legal spaces like the High Court and the practices of judicial review are best viewed as relatively open-textured arenas that enable campaigners and groups to challenge, publicise, politicise and organise their protest and resistance against proposed projects and plans. Although they are no guarantee of victory, as they embody particular institutional biases and relations of power, legally enshrined rights and claims can provide the means and opportunity to challenge illegal or unwarranted actions and unjust state practices, while potentially overturning unlawful decisions and policies. Indeed, in providing a normative counterpoint to executive power and public policy, the decisions and forms of legal reasoning that emerge also furnish significant discursive and rhetorical resources for protesters to continue their struggles and campaigns in adjacent spaces and social sites.

Local councils and campaigners against Heathrow expansion had launched legal action against government in the wake of the AC and the go-head for the third runway at Heathrow. In January 2017, the councils of Hillingdon, Richmond, Wandsworth, Windsor and Maidenhead, with Greenpeace and a local resident, filed a request for judicial review on the grounds that the approval of the proposed third runway failed to meet air quality standards and broke the legitimate expectations of residents that there would not be further expansion at Heathrow airport. Their challenge echoed a long-standing narrative of 'broken promises', which had been deployed by local residents against Labour's plans for expansion in 2003, and listed no less than 19 'promises' that politicians made not to expand airports, including David Cameron's 'no ifs, no buts' pledge and Theresa May's commitment to her constituents to campaign against the expansion of the airport.[16] However, the High Court ruled that the legal challenge could not be heard until the end of the consultation on the ANPS, delaying in the short to medium term any legal challenge against Heathrow expansion (Simpson, 2017). Commenting on the ruling, Ravi Govindia, leader of Wandsworth Council, argued that 'The Government has taken a colossal gamble by delaying this legal action for at least a year. The country is now going to waste more time developing a scheme that will never pass a simple legal test on air quality.'[17]

Following the approval of the ANPS in June 2018, councils and campaigners reignited their legal challenges against the third runway. In July 2018 the councils of Hillingdon, Richmond, Wandsworth, Windsor and Maidenhead, joined by Hammersmith and Fulham Council, Greenpeace and the Mayor of London, Sadiq Khan, announced their intention to call for a judicial review of the decision to approve the third runway (London Borough of Richmond-upon-Thames, 2018). Their appeal challenged the 'unlawful' designation of the ANPS by the Secretary of State, and the grounds of the challenge targeted air quality, noise, climate change and the limits of strategic environmental assessment, surface access, the alleged breach of the habitats directive and what was seen as a flawed consultation process.[18] The councils and campaigners were joined by Plan B Earth, the climate change charity. Plan B Earth and 11 claimants had unsuccessfully launched a claim for judicial review of the UK's 2050 Carbon Target in December 2017, calling upon government to bring its domestic targets in line with the commitments of the Paris Agreement to pursue efforts to keep global rises in temperature to 1.5 °C (Hicks, 2022: 93). Here it began another round of legal action against the Secretary of State for the failure of the ANPS to take account of the impact of aviation emissions on the UK's commitments to address climate change.[19] The failure of the ANPS to address sustainable development was also the focus of a further appeal brought by FoE.[20] In fact, five judicial appeals, totalling 26 challenges, were launched against the ANPS and the decision to expand Heathrow (including an appeal by Neil Spurrier, a member of the Teddington Action Group, on the grounds of air pollution, and an appeal against the selected scheme by developers, Heathrow Hub, whose plans to extend the existing runway had been rejected (see Hicks, 2022: 105–6)). At the heart of these challenges were contested readings of government policy towards climate change, the government's obligations under the Climate Change Act (2008) and the Paris Agreement (2015), and the duties of the Secretary of State under the Planning Act (2008). However, before analysing such legal challenges, we first investigate the different logics of politicisation and depoliticisation surrounding the CCA and the PA, two pieces of legislation that were published in tandem on the same day in 2008.

The paradoxes of politicisation and depoliticisation

The CCA, which became law during Gordon Brown's Labour government, committed the British government to a legally-binding cut of 80 per cent reductions in 1990 levels of carbon emissions by 2050. Like the PA, the CCA sought to stabilise the investment environment for low carbon infrastructure, providing confidence to investors by binding future governments into long-term emissions targets (McGregor et al, 2012; Lockwood, 2013). The Labour government established an independent expert body, the CCC, to act as an institutional agent of this process of carbon reduction. Its work was to advise on carbon emission targets, setting 5-year carbon budgets and reporting annually on progress to Parliament to which the government was obliged to respond (McGregor et al, 2012). But it is striking that emissions from international aviation and shipping were not included in the carbon budgets set by the CCC, even though the CCC declared in 2009 that levels of aviation emissions should be reduced to 2005 levels by 2050.

If we position the PA and the CCA in terms of the overall sweep of our genealogical narrative, we can track the operation of two different and competing logics. On the one hand, the Planning Act sought to depoliticise the planning processes surrounding large infrastructure projects. On the other hand, the CCA locked in an institutional politicisation of climate change through the CCC. As Lockwood (2013: 1342) points out, the CCC, with no formal powers per se, exercised a critical role of analysis and monitoring, 'not so much binding the hands of government as standing over it watching carefully'. The state retained responsibility for, and much of the ownership of, climate change mitigation and adaptation. But the interventions of the CCC, combined with its role in setting and adopting carbon budgets, as well as its annual assessment of progress in specific areas, promised a continual cycle of periods of hyper-politicisation.

Against this background, the CCC was called upon regularly to intervene in the decision to approve the third runway at Heathrow, which it did, posing as a form of counter-expertise to the AC and the DfT. When the go-ahead for expansion at Heathrow was publicly announced, it published a statement calling for the May government to develop a strategic policy framework for UK aviation emissions, demonstrating its plans to keep aviation emissions at 2005 levels by 2050. More fully, the CCC called on government to go further than this, as it set out deeper cuts to aviation in light of the 2015 Paris Agreement and its commitment for moves towards net zero in the second half of the century.[21] Typically, in a public letter to the Secretary of Business, Energy and Industrial Strategy at the end of November 2016, Lord Deben, the chair of the CCC, questioned the business case behind Heathrow expansion, which suggested that aviation emissions from the airport would potentially break the Committee's 2009 planning assumption for aviation emissions to be at 2005 levels in 2050. If this was to be the case, the Committee cautioned, then other sectors would have to go beyond the planned 85 per cent reductions to their emissions by 2050 to compensate for the higher emissions from aviation. The Committee also shed doubt on the capacity of all other sectors to do so.[22]

Such arguments were amplified by the EAC. At the end of February 2017, the parliamentary select committee released its follow-up report on the recommendations of the AC. The report decried the absence of a 'step change' in the approach to environmental mitigation by the government and called for new modelling and approaches to air quality, as well as effective and more ambitious noise mitigation measures enforced by an Independent Aviation Noise Authority. Importantly, it buttressed the demands of the CCC, berating the lack of clarity from government on how it would ensure that Heathrow expansion would meet carbon emission limits. It expressed dissatisfaction with the fact that the government was 'considering rejecting the CCC's advice', arguing that government should 'set out clearly the resulting additional emissions reduction requirements from aviation expansion on other sectors of the economy and the resulting costs to those sectors'. In fact, it called for any strategy to be 'subjected to independent scrutiny by the CCC' (EAC, 2017: 3–4).

With respect to the judicial review of the ANPS, the work of the CCC, the CCA and the PA were interwoven. The PA was aligned with the demands of sustainable development and climate change, as set down in the CCA. First, Section 5, clause 8 of the PA stipulated that the assessment and rationale for the infrastructure policies in an NPS 'must (in particular) include an explanation of how the policy ... takes account of Government policy relating to the mitigation of, and adaptation to, climate change'. Secondly, Section 10 states that in designating and reviewing national policy statements the Secretary of State 'must, in exercising those functions, do so with the objective of contributing to the achievement of sustainable development' and with 'regard to the desirability of mitigating, and adapting, to climate change'.[23] It was the interpretation of these two clauses and how they were fulfilled by the May government that were to become the central planks of a judicial challenge to the ANPS, not least because at the end of June 2018 the CCC announced its intention to review its targets for the reduction of aviation emissions up to 2050 and beyond in an effort to set out 'the overall policy approach' that government should pursue (CCC, 2018: 172).

Contesting aviation expansion and climate change in the courts

Returning explicitly to the logic of legal challenge, we now analyse the judicial reviews, which were brought to the High Court in March 2019, paying particular attention to the climate change challenges brought by Plan B Earth and FoE. Plan B Earth argued that the Secretary of State in designating the ANPS had ultimately failed to adequately take into account the CCA and the advice of the CCC, and importantly, the obligations of the 2015 Paris Agreement and the April 2018 commitment of government to review existing climate change targets (Plan B Earth, 2018). Hence, the legal challenge of Plan B Earth rested on the definition of 'government policy' under Section 5(8) of the Planning Act (2008). It claimed that in June 2018, at the time of the designation of the ANPS, 'government policy' incorporated the Paris Agreement and its limits on the rise in global temperature to 1.5 °C, not the 2 °C rise predicated in the carbon budgets of the CCA and the work of the AC. In support of its argument, and signalling its claim for judicial review, Plan B Earth cited a letter (dated 14 June, 2018) from Lord Deben and Baroness Brown of Cambridge, the Chair and Deputy Chair of the CCC respectively, which had expressed their joint 'surprise' that the statement of the Secretary of State to the House of Commons on the ANPS 'made no mention' of the legally binding commitments of the Climate Change Act nor of the Paris Agreement.[24]

In court, Tim Crosland, lead counsel for Plan B, thus dismissed references to a 2 °C target in the ANPS as an 'irrelevant condition' and 'historic discredited target', which was 'rejected as inadequate by 195 governments'. He argued further that there was no discussion in the ANPS as to why 2 °C was taken as a 'benchmark' or how in 2018 it was a relevant indicator of government policy (High Court, 2020: 98, 113). Indeed, he was also to cite statements that were made by Andrea Leadsom in 2016, the Minister of State for Energy, and Amber Rudd, the Secretary of State for Energy and Climate Change, which acknowledged the need for government to enshrine net zero in UK law (Hicks, 2022: 111–12). He also drew attention to government policy documents prior to the designation of the ANPS, notably the October 2017 Clean Growth Strategy, which recognised the need to update policy in line with the 1.5 °C commitment enshrined in the Paris Agreement. Here he claimed that ahead of the June designation of the ANPS the government had even seen a draft version of the October 2018 Intergovernmental Panel on Climate Change (IPCC) report on the different climate impacts of a rise in global temperature of 1.5 and 2.0 °C (High Court, 2020: 96, 128–30, 156, 164; Hicks, 2022: 112–13; see also IPCC, 2018).

The climate change and sustainable development obligations on the Secretary of State under the PA were also targeted by FoE. However, it took a different tack to Plan B Earth, focusing attention on the demands of Section 10 of the 2008 Act. FoE lawyers claimed that in not considering the Paris Agreement and the developing scientific knowledge of climate change, the Secretary of State had not sufficiently fulfilled their sustainable development obligations and the mitigation of, and adaption to, climate change (Hicks, 2022: 114–16). Moreover, FoE argued that the demands of sustainable development went further than simply meeting the carbon budgets of the CCA, requiring the Secretary of State to consider the needs of future generations and the non-carbon emissions of aviation as part of the precautionary principle towards climate change, as well as calculating the emissions from expansion at Heathrow beyond 2050 and considering the Paris Agreement as part of any Strategic Environmental Assessment. Here FoE claimed that the Secretary of State had to take into account the Paris Agreement in the designation of the ANPS, underlining its material relevance for the ANPS, such that 'one way or another those matters (the Paris Agreement and post-Paris) needed to be part of the evaluation that led into this ANPS and they wrongly weren't' (High Court, 2020: 7–8). In court, David Wolfe QC, leading the case for the FoE, challenged claims that the Secretary of State was unable to act on the Paris Agreement until the CCC had translated new commitments of 1.5 °C into domestic law. He declared in court that it was not right to argue that the CCC was instructing the government to 'sit back' (High Court, 2020: 23), and (like the counsel for Plan B Earth) bolstered such claims with allegations that the government had even had access to a draft IPCC report in January 2018, which set out how to meet the 1.5 °C target, before the publication of the ANPS and its approval in Parliament (High Court, 2020: 24–5).

The High Court dismissed all 26 legal challenges to the ANPS in its May 2019 ruling (Hicks, 2022: 131–5). In rejecting the grounds of the challenges of Plan B Earth and FoE, the Court ruled that as an international treaty the Paris Agreement had no domestic legal force until it was translated into national statute, adding that beyond its commitment to 1.5 °C rises in global temperature, it imposed no specific policy responses on any nation-state. Hence, the High Court concluded that at the time of the designation of the ANPS, the CCA, with its Section 1 commitment to 80 per cent reductions in carbon emissions by 2050 compared to 1990, was the 'entrenched policy' of government (High Court, 2019: paragraph 608). It declared that this target could not be changed without parliamentary agreement and, moreover, that Section 1 of the CCA was potentially compatible with the 1.5 °C global temperature rise of the Paris Agreement, such that it was arguably a 'rational response' to maintain the CCA target 'at least for the time being' (High Court, 2019: paragraph 610). Policy and international treaties could not, the High Court determined, over-ride statute in the form of the CCA (High Court, 2019, paragraph 615). Indeed, government lawyers had argued in court that legal advice to the Secretary of State implied that the Planning Act required him *not* to consider international treaties unless it was explicitly instructed to do so in the Act itself.

The High Court also rejected the argument of FoE that the ANPS provided no explanation of how it took account of government policy towards climate change adaptation and mitigation. The High Court reasoned that planning policies 'are full of broad statements of policy' (High Court, 2019: paragraph 629) to be applied at a later date, concluding that the ANPS did not breach the provisions of Section 5 of the Planning Act. Moreover, it argued that in fulfilling the duty to contribute to sustainable development under Section 10 of the Planning Act, it was at the discretion of the Secretary of State as to whether he took international agreements into account. It was thus down to his political judgement whether or not to review the ANPS if scientific evidence changed. Similarly, the failure to include the Paris Agreement in the Appraisal of Sustainability could not be deemed 'irrational' when 'plainly work on that matter [was] currently in hand and decisions [had] yet to be reached' (2019: paragraph 654). Finally, the Court added that 'in any event' any future DCO would be assessed against the scientific evidence at the time of the application (2019: paragraph 648), and that the DCO would 'clearly include' emissions from aircraft using Heathrow (2019: paragraph 631). On the whole, this was a strategic clarification that related to the grounds of future campaigning, which had come from FoE's questioning of which targets would apply at the time of the DCO, what they would include and what was meant by 'material impact on the ability of the Government to meet its carbon reduction targets' (2019: paragraph 11; see Hicks, 2022: 135).

The May government welcomed the judgement of the High Court, as did Grayling, the Secretary of State, who stated in Parliament that 'Heathrow expansion is more important than ever as we plan to exit the EU'. Grayling even went on to criticise the use of 'scarce taxpayers' resources' to defend the ANPS in courts, 'urg[ing] all parties, particularly local authorities and community groups affected by the proposals to move forward and engage closely with the planning process', while concluding that 'this government has taken the right decision, endorsed by a large majority of MPs, which had been ducked by other governments for decades'.[25] Campaigners against the third runway disagreed. All parties to the failed judicial review announced their decision to appeal the judgement. The right to appeal was granted in July.

Ironically, the judgement of the High Court was delivered on the day that the House of Commons voted to declare a climate emergency. It thus appeared to clash with the shifting political context, which had in turn been partly induced by the actions of Extinction Rebellion and the international climate change campaign led by Greta Thunberg, which began with her coming out of school in a 'strike' against climate change. Thunberg addressed the UK Parliament in April 2019, while Extinction Rebellion blocked key routes across the capital over 11 days in the same month (BBC News, 2019; Taylor and Gayle, 2019). Launched in 2018, Extinction Rebellion, the activist civil disobedience climate change movement, engaged in a series of high-profile media demonstrations designed to force government to declare a climate emergency, commit to the reduction of carbon emissions to net zero by 2025 and form a citizens' assembly to determine such a transition. Its activists targeted the plans to expand Heathrow and the issue of rising aviation emissions, with drone attacks on the airport as well as mass sit-ins against plans for expansion (PA Media, 2015; Somerville, 2019).

Indeed, as councils and campaigners brought their appeal to the courts, the Shadow Chancellor, John McDonnell, was emboldened to state: 'I think legislatively things have moved and politically, with the current campaigning by Extinction Rebellion, the pressure is on all politicians to recognise this is a project [the third runway at Heathrow] that cannot stand' (Laville, 2019). The wider acceptance of his position beyond the courts appeared to become more likely as Boris Johnson, an opponent of Heathrow expansion, was elected Prime Minister by the Conservative Party following the resignation of Theresa May at the end of July 2019, after the defeat of her proposed Brexit agreement in the Commons. On top of this, in the wake of the High Court judgement, the CCC had published new guidance that called for government to commit to net zero emissions by 2050, arguing that the contribution of aviation to rising emissions could no longer be 'ignored' in future carbon budgets (CCC, 2019a: 175). At the end of June 2019, the government duly committed to the CCC's recommendation, setting a net zero target for UK emissions by 2050.

In this shifting political conjuncture, the hearing in the Court of Appeal opened in October 2019, just days after the chair of the CCC had written to the Secretary of State advocating further demand management in aviation and the reconsideration of airport capacity in the context of the transition to net zero, where 'current planned additional capacity in London, including the third runway at Heathrow, is likely to leave at most very limited room for growth at non-London airports' (CCC, 2019b: 14). At the appeal hearing, the cases of FoE and Plan B Earth revolved again around the interpretation of Sections 5(8) and 10 of the 2008 Planning Act. However, in its ruling at the end of February 2020, the Court of Appeal was to reverse the judgement of the High Court, agreeing that the Secretary of State, in designating the ANPS, had not adequately taken account of the Paris Agreement, while endorsing the legal challenges of Plan B Earth and FoE under Sections 5 and 10 of the Planning Act.

More fully, the Court of Appeal recognised that the Secretary of State received legal advice not to take the Paris Agreement into consideration, such that he did not question whether to do so as a matter of discretion (Court of Appeal 2020, paragraph 237). But the Court argued that if the Secretary of State had recognised his discretion, 'the only reasonable view open to him was that the Paris Agreement was so obviously material that it had to be taken into account' (2020: paragraph 237). Hence, when publishing the ANPS, the government had not, the Court concluded, 'taken into account its own firm policy commitments' under Paris, a failing which was 'legally fatal to the ANPS in its present form' (2020: paragraphs 283–4). Indeed, in delivering the judgement, Lord Justice Lindblom declared that 'the national planning statement was not produced as the law requires' (Carrington, 2020). However, the Court did not overturn the earlier dismissal of the challenges on air and noise pollution, traffic and the costs of the runway.

The victory of campaigners was widely seen to have brought Heathrow expansion to a halt. Plan B Earth and FoE argued that the judgement was 'a massive climate justice win for present and future generations'.[26] The new Conservative government, with Boris Johnson at its helm, confirmed that it would not appeal the ruling. As one Conservative MP commented, the ruling was a 'Pontius Pilate moment for Boris, because it lands a potentially killer punch to Heathrow, but the PM can say "it's nothing to do with me"' (Powely et al, 2020). Yet there was political fallout. In the immediate aftermath of the ruling, Tim Shipman opined on the BBC's *Politics Live* news show that the decision represented a 'massive collective failure of the political class over the last twenty odd years'.[27] George Osborne tweeted that the judges had 'kill[ed] off Heathrow 3rd runway and Britain getting the modern air transport infrastructure we need, despite the elected Parliament voting for it overwhelmingly' (Bell, 2020).

Strikingly, it was left to Heathrow Airport to appeal the judgement in the absence of any government desire to move the dossier forward. The airport was duly given permission at the beginning of May to appeal the ruling at the Supreme Court, with the case scheduled to open in early October 2020. It thus remained to be seen whether the courts had struck a final blow to the proposed third runway or whether, ultimately, legal challenge was little more than a successful strategy of delay. Of course, campaigners had previously stalled the third runway in the courts in 2010, only for it to return to the political agenda a few years later.

Conclusion

In the summer of 2015, the AC had in many ways already done its job: it had put aviation expansion firmly back on the political agenda and made the case for government to back Heathrow over Gatwick or other competitors. In the 'trench warfare' that followed the publication of its Final Report, successive Conservative governments did not retreat from the commitment to aviation expansion, even the government of Boris Johnson. If anything, the policy rhetoric in government circles became further attached to the logic of 'predict and provide', as the efforts to depoliticise airport expansion had appeared to constrain and dampen the negative coverage and public discussion of its impacts on climate change, air pollution and noise, rendering proposals for the further development of Heathrow or Gatwick a more tractable policy issue, while pushing aviation externalities to the margins of political debate. So, in the shifting political context of Brexit and the May government, aviation expansion was once again overtly tied to connectivity, mobility and economic growth.

Such efforts to depoliticise aviation expansion created dilemmas for opponents to the planned third runway at Heathrow, particularly as the mechanisms involved in the production of the ANPS returned to the divide and rule politics of decisions over site location, in contrast to the national consultation that informed the ATWP (2003). Following the Final Report of the AC in July 2015, local residents, environmental activists and state institutions from the EAC to the CCC moved to discredit the report, re-politicising the issues of climate change, air quality and noise. The Commission's Final Report, its way of working and also the role and character of Davies himself, were immediately contested. In fact, opposition groups engaged in a hegemonic battle with the pro-expansionist forces, exploiting and re-politicising the new technologies and techniques of government, while opening up novel spaces to contest the expansion proposals and project. Indeed, the ruling of the Court of Appeal in 2020, and the successful legal challenge to the third runway, exploited the Planning Act (2008) and the ANPS, as well as the Climate Change Act (2008) and the Paris Agreement (2015), refashioning them as counter-technologies, while also highlighting the courts as a space of resistance.

In exploiting these novel technologies of government in planning and climate change, campaigners, protesters and citizens disclosed the complicated and messy dialectics of politicisation, depoliticisation and repoliticisation. The 2008 Acts pointed in different directions: the Climate Change Act opened up further spaces for the politicisation of the environment, while the Planning Act sought to depoliticise decisions over large infrastructure projects. But it was the interweaving of these two opposed logics, each rooted in different legislative ends, which transfigured the political opportunity structures for activists and opponents of expansion, thus making possible the fashioning of a new counter-technology of government. Campaigners were thus able to use the law courts and the process of judicial review to challenge government, demonstrating the complex dynamics between politicisation and depoliticisation, and underlining the role of strategic agency in seizing such opportunities. In short, while the formal grounds for judicial review rested on the Planning Act, arguments in the courts displayed rival interpretations of the Climate Change Act, the advice of the CCC and the obligations of the Paris Agreement and their relation to the Climate Change Act.

Extreme turbulence: problematisations, multiple crises and new demands

The victory of campaigners against the planned Heathrow expansion in the Court of Appeal in February 2020 came almost a month before the UK entered its first lockdown to combat rising COVID-19 infections within its population. The collapse of international travel following the pandemic had severe repercussions across the aviation industry, with unprecedented collapses in passenger numbers, the grounding of airlines and closing of runways, bringing waves of job losses in airlines and airports. In April 2020, scheduled flights in the UK fell by 92.6 per cent compared to the same month in 2019. Airlines were still operating only an estimated 20 per cent of scheduled flights 7 months later in November 2020 (Sun et al, 2021). In June 2020, the House of Commons Transport Committee had already called for targeted measures to support the aviation industry, including 12 months of business rate relief for airlines and airports, and the suspension of APD on flights for 6 months (Transport Committee, 2020: 3–4).

As passenger numbers in the aviation industry collapsed, the case for additional capacity and the economic arguments in favour of expansion and its financing were at best faltering. Addressing MPs in May 2020, John Holland-Kaye, chief executive of Heathrow Airport, recognised that the impact of the pandemic meant that a new runway may only 'be needed in 10 to 15 years' time' (No Third Runway Coalition, 2020). He later estimated that Heathrow Airport had accumulated losses of some £3 billion during 2020 and the first half of 2021, in part due to the fixed costs of airport operations (*Finance Monthly*, 2021). Gatwick Airport fared no better, experiencing losses of approximately three-quarters of a billion pounds, as well as cutting its workforce in half. Its chief executive, Stewart Wingate, argued that the financial stability of the airport was not helped by the loss of flights to Heathrow as airlines concentrated their operations at the UK international hub (Transport Committee, 2021a).

This chapter contextualises and analyses the COVID-19 conjuncture, reprising and drawing together the multiple threads of our genealogy of the technologies and techniques that UK governments have used to tackle the problems of aviation expansion and its demands for more and efficient airport capacity. We begin by setting out the first six problematisations, which emerged in different conjunctures since 1945, focusing on the construction of the problems, the proposed solutions, the technologies and rationalities that were elaborated to tackle the problems, the outcomes, specific sites of the problems and the political struggles that ensued. Such genealogical interpretations provide the basis for an initial set of characterisations and conclusions, which evaluates the strengths and weaknesses of the various technologies and techniques that were devised and used.

Here we argue that despite the fact some technologies, such as public inquiries, were frequently deemed to be costly and inefficient, often resulting in concerted efforts to reform the entire planning system, they actually enabled an incremental, if haphazard, expansion of the UK's airport capacity. Nonetheless, as political pressures intensified, sometimes becoming nationalised, and even globalised, so airports policy and planning was transformed into an intractable policy controversy, becoming more difficult, if not impossible, to resolve. Indeed, the technologies of government designed to depoliticise the issue of aviation expansion have failed to contain the politicisation and re-politicisation of aviation as campaigners and opponents of expansion have skilfully repurposed them to expose the limitations of plans and policies for expansion.

The multiple crises that erupted after the AC delivered its Final Report in 2015 exacerbated this dilemma, unleashing a period of extreme turbulence for the aviation industry and airports, though also disclosing new possibilities for alternative forms of travel, consumption, social organisation and living: the real (if still marginal) prospect of a sustainable, post-aviation future. In these new circumstances, we argue that the global pandemic ushered in a novel seventh problematisation for the government of Boris Johnson, calling into question its sponsorship of the aviation industry in ways not experienced since the end of the Second World War. Johnson, and his Chancellor, Rishi Sunak, in particular, were quickly faced with the challenge of whether or not to respond to demands for a recovery package for aviation (Acuity Analysis, 2021; Airlines UK, 2021; Airport Operators Association, 2021; International Airport Review, 2021), and if so, whether to attach any environmental conditions to any bailout deals.

Support for the proposed recovery package was contested, as environmental campaigners framed the collapse of flying during the pandemic as a political window to advance the potential for aviation degrowth and transition (Bostrom, 2021; Hinks, 2021). The subsequent decision of the Supreme Court to reverse the Court of Appeal's judgement to block the ANPS amplified the pressures on the Johnson government, having removed the legal barriers to the expansion of Heathrow. So, in the run-up to COP26 in November 2021, and set against the backdrop of the intensifying climate crisis, new lines of antagonism were forming in the battlefield of aviation, as government itself faced contradictory pressures between support for the recovery of UK aviation, its vision of post-Brexit Britain, its climate change commitments and its response to the COVID-19 pandemic. We begin by mapping out the core problematisations, which ordered and directed the different endeavours by successive UK governments and the state in implementing the logic of 'predict and provide', before turning to the legal arena of struggle.

Problematisations and technologies of government

The character and relative strengths of the UK after the Second World War in commercial aviation led to the emergence and installation of a series of core beliefs, which guided successive policy strategies and their attendant technologies and techniques of government. Heathrow was 'chosen' by the UK state to become the leading civil airport at the end of the war, while Gatwick was designated Britain's second airport in 1950 and a refurbished airport was officially opened in 1958. Path dependency, coupled with the pathologies of the 'Concorde Fallacy', where government and airport operators defended their investment, even though the commitment cost more than its abandonment and the development of an alternative, meant that Heathrow became the *de facto* hub airport. This was the case despite its less than optimal location close to the capital city and flight paths that straddled large swathes of its suburbs. Yet such assumptions strongly influenced future decisions about the location and growth of other London and regional airports.

The core belief that guided policymakers in these initial decisions and for the rest of the century until the present day is captured in the logic of 'predict and provide', though as we have shown in previous chapters this underlying assumption has been accompanied by varying strategies, governmental technologies and ideological justifications. Table 5.1 represents this complex picture, and our discussion in this chapter focuses initially on its contents. A first sociological observation to be made is that over time the issue of aviation and airport capacity has become increasingly complex. In a context of rapid expansion, as global travel and demands for economic and social connectivity have expanded exponentially, issues about local environmental impacts, such as noise, air pollution, the compensation of affected residents and concerns about the countryside, have been complicated by growing concerns about large-scale mass ground transportation, the financing of large infrastructure projects, fluctuations in global passenger demand and energy costs, debates about new technologies, the ability of government to deliver mega-projects and – increasingly so – climate change and carbon emissions. At the same time, the changing times have brought increasing public engagement and political contestation in many different forms. Such citizen interventions are not just evident in local disputes at particular airport sites, but are increasingly national and even global in their scope. Moreover, the nature of such contestations has also accrued greater sophistication, density and intensity, as campaigners have not only proved dogged and persistent,

Table 5.1: A genealogy of the politics of 'predict and provide' in UK aviation policy

	Problems	Solutions	Technologies and techniques of government	Discursive framing	Policy and political outcomes	Critical conjunctures
P1	Building an aviation industry in post-war Britain	State ownership of and investment in London airports Public and private ownership of regional airports	State-led modelling and forecasting Market forces	Maintaining global economic and political power against US (and other) foreign competition	Heathrow and Gatwick installed and enshrined as main London (and UK) airports	1946–1958
P2	Dealing with growing consumer demand in South East England	Third London Airport	Roskill Commission Cost-benefit analysis	Optimum site location	Major political battles Stansted becomes de facto third London airport	1968–1973
P3	Enhancing competitiveness and meeting growing consumer demand in progressively deregulated skies	Piecemeal expansion Privatisation, liberalisation and deregulation	Public inquiries	Noise and quality of life for local residents	Fourth and Fifth Terminals at Heathrow Second runway at Manchester	1986–1992
P4	Balancing demands for expansion with environmental constraints	Develop a national aviation plan for 30 years	National public consultation and deliberation Reform of planning system for national infrastructures Ideology of sustainable aviation	Noise, quality of life, balance between economy and climate change/environment	Plans for largest expansion of airports since WW2 Planned new runways at Heathrow and Stansted Major political contestation Formation of national discourse coalitions Plans defeated and abandoned	2000–2003

(continued)

Table 5.1: A genealogy of the politics of 'predict and provide' in UK aviation policy (continued)

	Problems	Solutions	Technologies and techniques of government	Discursive framing	Policy and political outcomes	Critical conjunctures
P5	Making aviation and airports policy sustainable in a context of unprecedented climate change	'Capacity off the agenda' – onus put onto industry More efficient use of existing capacity	State-led review Appointment of ministers Governance networks	Climate change Regional balance and efficiency Integrated transport	Moratorium on development in South East England No credible 'sustainable aviation' alternative	2010–2011
P6	Increasing airport capacity in South East England, protecting the position of London as a global city and balancing demands for expansion with environmental constraints	Support for London Heathrow and third runway 'Best solution for carbon bucks'	Airports Commission Airports National Policy statement	Need for economic growth Noise and community engagement	Heathrow expansion redux Resurgence of political protest The turn to legal challenges	2012–2015
P7	Coping with legal challenges and COVID-19 in the face of dislocations and radical critique of the aviation industry	'Business as usual' Technological fixes	State subsidies State-industry complexes	'Build Back Better' Jet Zero	Legal battles Uncertainty and policy vacillation Potential restructurings and transformations of aviation	2020–2021

but they have successfully innovated and experimented, developing new strategies and tactics, while moving nimbly between different spaces and sites of struggle.

In dealing with this increasingly multifaceted issue, evident in the growing public engagement and political contestation, our genealogical interpretations disclose the way governments and (to a lesser extent) airports, airlines, their lobbies, and their groups and representatives in civil society, evolved and tried out various technologies of government, the latter containing a series of nested techniques of acquiring and processing knowledge. The broad sweep of our genealogy suggests that in P1, our first problematisation, which stretches loosely across the 1940s and 1950s, the initial technologies that governments employed involved incremental decision-making by central government for the planning of core airports, using forecasting and traditional planning devices, while leaving the emergence and development of other airports to the play of market forces, though the latter were constrained by the emergence and consolidation of national and international regulation. In certain respects, such technologies were successful in establishing Heathrow and Gatwick as the leading UK airports, laying down a clear path for the future trajectories of development and expansion. But they bequeathed problems that made future planning and decision-making more difficult, if not impossible.

Infused with a new belief in scientific planning – resonating with Harold Wilson's extolling of 'the white heat of the technological revolution' – the Roskill Commission, which is the centrepiece of P2, intimated a new era of scientific, impartial and efficient public decision-making. Recourse to the technology of an expert Commission promised to address the demand for a third London airport that would satisfy passengers, the airline industry and the economy alike. The newly forged technique of CBA would resolve the perceived congestion and demands in South East England by laying the rational grounds for choosing the appropriate location and character of London's third airport. But the enormous time, effort and money that was invested in Roskill ended in failure, scuppered by political challenges and squabbles, and eventually the vacillations of the global economy as much as the inadequacies of the newly minted technique of government. CBA had not overcome the problem of politics, though it remained an important weapon in the arsenal of policy-makers, especially the DfT, which had in many respects pioneered the bright new technique.

For the next 30 years, as evident in P3, airport planning and policy turned to the role of public inquiries as the preferred means of decision-making, seeking to incorporate local communities in the reaching of balanced and acceptable solutions to complex dilemmas. But they were often perceived to be too costly and slow-moving by governments and corporations alike, while local communities often berated the decisions they took, as well as their grounds. Indeed, the decision to launch the Roskill Commission came after the frustrations and difficulties of government in gaining approval through the public inquiry system for expansion at Stansted Airport in the 1960s. Yet the incremental system of decision-making did deliver new projects and infrastructure. Having received the go-ahead at the public inquiry, and in the face of mounting criticism, as well as the occupation of the proposed site for expansion, Manchester Airport successfully built a second runway in the early 2000s, while Heathrow was able to build its Fourth and Fifth Terminals, despite the long 'delays' and perceived inefficiencies, especially with respect to Terminal 5.

As we show in P4, widespread concerns about debilitating delays in the public inquiry process, as well as the problems of incremental planning and fragmented policy-making, led the New Labour government to propose and develop a national and integrated policy framework, which would govern aviation and airport expansion for a generation. Here the preferred technology of government was a national public consultation, which sought to encourage the widespread involvement of affected parties across the country, while also achieving 'buy-in' for a new national consensus and settlement. Yet the new technology had to be underwritten by the tried and tested fantasies of aviation and the outcomes of the consultation still rested firmly on the techniques of forecasting and ultimately the logic of 'predict and provide'. In fact, their endeavours to develop a comprehensive and balanced policy framework, which they presented in the ATWP (2003), only opened the door to a widespread, national and increasingly unified opposition movement, which was able to connect with environmental protesters and local campaigners to demand a halt to large-scale airport expansion *tout court*. A paradox of this third technology of government, then, was the *nationalisation* of the airports issue, which had previously been more spatially and locally discussed and decided (Schattschneider, 1960).

One important consequence of this new round of intense political struggle and campaigning, as we demonstrate in P5, was that in 2010 the new Coalition government decided initially to rule out new airport expansion in South East England, condemning its predecessor for not giving 'sufficient weight' to the contribution of aviation's rising carbon emissions to climate change (DfT, 2011: 4). But it was noticeable that P5 was not a fully-fledged problematisation of aviation and airport capacity. Instead, it is better conceptualised as a proto-problematisation, which was able to pinpoint the deficiencies in the White Paper of 2003, and the subsequent efforts to expand Heathrow by building a third runway, but was not able to provide a credible alternative to airport expansion. Nor was it able to contest and remove the commitment to the logic of 'predict and provide'.

The failure of those in government and the anti-airport expansion coalition to institutionalise an alternative strategy, which was predicated on new core beliefs, made way for David Cameron to announce the AC in 2012, which once again proposed the expansion of Heathrow, as we describe in P6. More fully, this problematisation can be seen as an endeavour by the UK government to depoliticise and legitimise the increase in airport capacity in South East England by taking the issue out of the political domain, while providing a rational and technocratic solution that could secure a workable political consensus. In this way, the government eventually decided to 'franchise out' this political decision to a supposedly neutral and impartial third party, whose integrity, scientific expertise and objective method of decision-making would deliver a rationally acceptable solution for all.

Not unlike the Roskill Commission, but now in a much more complex and antagonistic environment, the government thus invested heavily in a purportedly neutral technology of government that would resolve a politically contentious issue. But the framing of the AC through its terms of reference, and the choice of Davies as its Chair prior to these processes, exposed the fact that the government was strongly predisposed to favouring the Heathrow case anyway (Le Blond, 2019: 117–18). However, apart from providing ideological cover for the policy reversal of the Conservative government, the new strategy and technology has not yet delivered the preferred outcome; for the time being at least it remains a failure on the scale of Roskill.

Moreover, the deliberations and consultations involved in P6 were complicated by the emergence and use of a new technology of government, which accompanied the reform of UK planning in 2008. As we noted in Chapter 4, the Planning Act (2008), working alongside the CCA (2008), sought to accelerate the process for approving major new infrastructure projects such as airports, roads, harbours and energy facilities, effectively placing infrastructure planning outside the domain of 'normal' planning, by requiring the granting of DCOs by the promoter based on guidelines set out in an NPS, which was prepared by the government. The purpose of the NPS was to justify the need for any development and other policy deliberations, while the proposed policy's environmental sustainability had to be considered beforehand by the Secretary of State in order to ensure its compliance with necessary standards and policy commitments. As it played out, the desire to overhaul and rationalise the previous 'outmoded' planning regime in order to save costs and increase efficiency introduced a degree of parliamentary scrutiny, limited forms of public consultation and engagement, as well as legal challenge, bringing further delay and more complexity to P6. Using this emerging space, campaigners exploited the demands upon the role of the Secretary of State in the Planning Act (2008) to hold up expansion in the courts through the strategy of judicial review and the questioning of the ANPS.

Taken as a whole, then, the various threads of our genealogy demonstrate the patterns of change and continuity in the policy conflicts surrounding the expansion of air travel in the UK. Once sedimented into the institutions and practices of the British state over time, the logic of 'predict and provide' and the endeavours to implement its imperatives, required multiple technologies and strategies, as governments and the aviation industry sought to overcome the problem of politics. Yet the results were mixed: some technologies were more successful than others, while others failed altogether. In short, there was no consistent institutional fix that was able to deliver aviation expansion. Rather, technologies of government, together with an array of techniques, rationalities and bodies of knowledge, waxed and waned as dominant policy problematisations changed over time.

In many ways, aviation policy 'failed forwards' (Jones, 2019: 16), as UK governments addressed the outcomes of the strategic decisions and technologies implemented by their predecessors or themselves. So, while passenger numbers continued to expand, and then accelerate from the 1990s, the stark fact remains that successive British governments were unable to engineer a partial or temporary policy settlement in aviation. If anything, pressures for such a settlement intensified as air travel was linked to the pressing issue of climate change and social and economic injustice. Finally, in P7, interlocking economic, environmental and social crises of the post-Brexit context, which were exacerbated by the global pandemic, dislocated the hegemonic 'grip' of air travel and mobility, provoking more political contestation and reaction. It is to such questions that we now turn. We begin with the decision of the Supreme Court to reverse the judgement of the Court of Appeal in December 2020, giving Heathrow the go-ahead to move forward with its application for a DCO for the construction of a third runway at the airport.

The return of the courts: rival interpretations and conflicting disagreements

Heathrow Airport Limited led the appeal to the Supreme Court in October 2020 (Supreme Court, 2020a). The Johnson Government, which accepted the ruling of the Court of Appeal, watched from the sidelines as the hearings began. The legal question facing the Court remained whether the Secretary of State had, in designating the ANPS, taken adequate account of the demands of the Paris Agreement and its commitment to keep global rises in temperature to as close to 1.5°C as possible. Plan B Earth had successfully argued at the Court of Appeal that the Secretary of State should have considered the obligations of the Paris Agreement. That is to say, it claimed that, at the time of the designation of the ANPS, the Paris commitments should have been covered by Section 5(8) of the Planning Act (2008), as part of the existing 'government policy' towards climate change mitigation and adaptation.

FoE had also successfully argued that by failing to account for the Paris Agreement, the ANPS breached Sections 10(2) and 10(3) of the 2008 Act, which require any NPS to demonstrate how planned infrastructure contributes to sustainable development, with particular regard to mitigating and adapting to climate change. As part of their appeal, the FoE legal team reasoned that the Secretary of State should also have taken account of the government's Paris commitments in the Strategic Environmental Assessment that accompanied the ANPS, as well as considering in the ANPS itself the impact of emissions from the use of the third runway after 2050 and non-CO_2 emissions from aviation in general. Such arguments appeared in the shifting economic, political and social context of the Johnson government and its efforts to stem the pandemic, and so resonated more strongly beyond the courts. Lord Anderson, for example, QC for HAL informed the judges of the Supreme Court that Heathrow Airport was to continue with the third runway '*despite* the pandemic' (Supreme Court, 2020b: 6, paragraph 18, our italics).

However, the Supreme Court was to reverse the decision of the Court of Appeal, siding with the initial judgement of the High Court. More fully, three interconnected and contested arguments were decisive in the ruling of the Court: what constituted government policy; what fell under the category of 'legitimate considerations' for the Secretary of State; and what determined the remit of any future DCO. First, the Supreme Court argued that government policy was to be defined as 'carefully formulated written statements', not ministerial oral statements or interventions, but a 'formal written statement of established policy', which it added 'is clear, unambiguous and devoid of relevant qualification'. No weight, it concluded, should therefore be given to arguments that advanced ministerial statements as evidence of 'government policy' (Supreme Court, 2020b: 36, paragraph 106). Hence, the Court summarily rejected the claims of Plan B Earth, which referred in part to oral statements by ministers on the need to adapt government commitments to the demands of the Paris Agreement. The Court also argued that to accept oral ministerial statements as government policy would set a 'bear trap' for civil servants who would face the difficult task of monitoring all statements as evidence of government policy (Supreme Court, 2020b: 36, paragraph 105). Moreover, in the view of the Court, the statements brought in evidence by Plan B Earth were 'not clear, did not refer to the Paris Temperature Targets at all, and did not explain how the Paris Agreement goal of net zero emissions would be incorporated into UK law' (Supreme Court, 2020a: 2).

But secondly, in attaching this narrow condition of clarity to 'government policy', the court also imposed a particular understanding of what fell under the category of 'legitimate' considerations for the Secretary of State, thus serving to exclude from consideration government commitments under the Paris Agreement. It concurred with the High Court that Paris imposed no obligation on the UK or any other state to implement its global objective in a particular way. In this way, the ratification of the Paris Agreement in November 2016 did not constitute a statement of government policy, for the Agreement did not translate into obligations in domestic law; it was therefore not 'a statement devoid of relevant qualification' (Supreme Court, 2020b: 37, paragraph 108). Indeed, the Court highlighted the fact that the ramifications of the Paris Agreement for domestic government policy, and its aviation strategy, were in the process of being reformulated at the time of the designation of the ANPS in June 2018.

The judgement also underlined how the advice of the CCC to government in September and October 2016 was not to revise at that time the agreed emissions reduction targets of the CCA (Supreme Court, 2020b: 27, paragraph 75). It did acknowledge that in January 2018 the CCC invited the Secretary of State to review long-term emissions targets, but the Court noted that the CCC suggested that this revision took place after the publication of the IPCC report on the implications of the Paris commitments – the report was published in October 2018 after the designation of the ANPS (although FoE and Plan B Earth argued that ministers had received a draft of the report and submitted final comments on the draft in June 2018) (Supreme Court, 2020b: 28–9, paragraphs 79–80; IPCC, 2018). Ultimately, therefore, by furnishing a strict and narrow definition of 'government policy', the judges of the Supreme Court reasoned that the CCA was the relevant statement of government policy to be 'legitimately' considered by the Secretary of State in formulating the ANPS (Supreme Court, 2020a: 2).

Hence, against this background, the Court concluded that there was evidence that the Secretary of State had in fact taken the Paris Agreement into account (although initially government lawyers had said that the Secretary of State had been advised that it was not legal to do so). But it also declared that the Paris obligations were already covered by the emissions targets of the CCA, and that the duties of the Planning Act were clearly taken into account by the Secretary of State in the designation of the ANPS (Supreme Court, 2020b: 42, paragraph 125). And in a belt and braces approach to the diverse challenges to the ANPS, the Court concluded that the UK's obligations under the Paris Agreement, until given effect in domestic law, fell under considerations that the Secretary of State 'may have regard if [they] think that it is right to do so' (Supreme Court, 2020b: 39–41, paragraphs 116–22).

In this interpretation, the weight given to a particular consideration, including the Paris Agreement, was at the discretion of the Secretary of State, and only to be challenged on the grounds of 'irrationality'. The Secretary of State's discretion was also invoked to reject challenges to the Appraisal of Sustainability, which was seen by the Court as a report for public consultation, with its content resting on the judgement of the Secretary of State as to what constituted a 'sound and sufficient basis for consultation' (Supreme Court, 2020a: 3). Notably in this regard, the Court warned against a 'defensive drafting' of such documents, which would 'mean that the public would be drowned in unhelpful detail ... and their ability to comment effectively ... would be undermined' (Supreme Court, 2020b: 51, paragraph 146). In short, the recognition of political discretion, and the definition of government policy as 'clear, unambiguous and devoid of relevant qualification', came together in the arguments of the Court to determine that the decision not to consider either carbon emissions after 2050, or the impact of aviation's non-CO_2 emissions on climate change, was not 'irrational'. Here the Court tapped into the uncertainties surrounding the policy debates at the time of the designation of the ANPS, in which future policies had yet to be formulated.

But, thirdly, it also bolstered its ruling through the emergent interpretation of the remit and assessment criteria of any future DCO. In fact, like the High Court, the Supreme Court deflected many of the challenges to the ANPS onto the DCO, asserting that developers would have to meet the environmental and climate change objectives at the time of the DCO assessment (not those in place at the time of the ANPS). In other words, the demands of the Paris Agreement and other objectives, including commitments to net zero emissions by 2050, or the non-CO_2 impacts of aviation would (most likely) have to be considered when granting the DCO, whatever the assertions and demands of the ANPS (Supreme Court 2020b: paragraph 157). This judgement effectively gave the Secretary of State and the ANPS a 'get out of jail free card'. But, equally, as the Planning Act emerged as a new proto-technology of government, this interpretation of the requirements of the DCO potentially framed the work of future planning inspectors, putting in place important legal precedents upon which campaigners could draw to challenge any future planning consent for the proposed third runway (Hicks, 2022: 158–60).

More broadly, the Supreme Court judgement embodied the tensions and contradictions of aviation policy. Paradoxically, its judgement used the CCA, the UK's world leading legislation on climate change, which was deemed to work hand in hand with the Planning Act, to ward off a challenge to aviation expansion and rising emissions. The Supreme Court even drew upon a series of arguments that the Secretary of State acted on the advice of the CCC. But equally, its judgement resonated with the argumentative rhetoric and tropes of the AC, as the Court referred to the 'extensive work' of the AC on capacity needs, concluding that the Secretary of State had not been irrational in thinking that the case for expansion had been sufficiently set out to designate the ANPS. It thus backgrounded the impacts of aviation on climate change by declaring that the Paris Agreement was only significant to the designation of the ANPS, if 'it is to be argued that there should not be any decision to meet economic needs by increasing airport capacity', while also concluding that sustainability included economic and social factors as well as economic dimensions (Supreme Court, 2020b: 45–6, paragraph 133). Most importantly, it displaced the assessment of the compatibility of the third runway with national commitments to net zero onto the process of gaining consent for development, a strategy which safeguarded the ANPS, though it was also a potential victory for campaigners, as it inserted questions about aviation's impact on climate change at the heart of the approval of the DCO application for a third runway.

However, the judgement did little to assuage the antagonistic coalitions contesting aviation expansion. Labelling the ruling 'the right result for the country', a spokesperson for Heathrow reiterated the economic benefits of the industry, claiming that '[o]nly by expanding the UK's hub airport can we connect all of Britain to all of the growing markets of the world, helping to create hundreds of thousands of jobs in every nation and region of our country.'[1] On the other hand, Tim Crosland of Plan B Earth leaked the judgement to the press 'to protest the deep immorality of the Court's ruling', arguing that 'the runway plan is in clear breach of climate change targets and it can't be allowed to go ahead' (Slingo, 2021a, 2021b).

Interestingly, the Johnson government had already retreated from the fray, as it distanced itself from the judgement and the infrastructure project, while declaring that 'Heathrow expansion is a private sector project which must meet strict criteria on air quality, noise and climate change, as well as being privately financed, affordable and delivered in the best interest of consumers.'[2] Yet, as we have argued, because the judgement of the Supreme Court came in the midst of the global COVID-19 pandemic and lockdown, questions remained as to if, and when, HAL would take the judgement forward. Indeed, as we shall now show, along with Brexit, the pandemic was another factor that would put more pressure on the financing and prospects of the third runway.

The post-Brexit interregnum

The political and policy complications following Britain's decision to leave the EU in 2016 posed potentially serious problems for airlines and the UK aviation industry more generally. Self-evidently, the global airline market had a strong interest in securing a seamless post-Brexit transition, especially when set against the rapid liberalisation of the European aviation market in the early 1990s, which had transformed air travel across the continent, bringing massively increased numbers of flights between the UK and Europe, and in particular an eightfold increase in passengers carried by UK based airlines to Europe between 1993 and 2014 (KPMG, 2016: 4). For airlines and airport operators working in the UK this translated into a desire to protect 'the ability of airlines to continue to access the markets into which they transport passengers and cargo' (KPMG, 2016: 9).

The eventual Brexit withdrawal agreement passed into law on 24 January 2020. It was accompanied by the trade agreement, which was signed on 24 December 2020, and came into force 7 days later, amounting to 1,449 pages, 26 of which dealt with aviation (CAPA, 2021) Although Brexit was not focused on reforming or improving the European aviation system, the industry's prime goal was to try and preserve existing conditions. And while the agreements managed to achieve this objective, although not optimally, as there remained question marks about airline ownership and control, not to mention potential divergences with respect to aviation safety and consumer protection, they still represented a major setback for the logic of liberalisation that had been underway for 30 years (CAPA, 2021). For example, in the immediate aftermath of the deal, British cargo, charter and leasing airlines claimed that they were losing contracts and business to EU rivals because the trade deal did not bring the promised level playing field. In their view, the rules and practices of the new post-Brexit regime, which Britain had unilaterally adopted, carried severe disadvantages, because they permitted more freedom and flexibility for EU-owned airlines to fly in the UK than they did for UK carriers to operate in Europe (Topham, 2021a).

Nonetheless, the overall outcome of the new legal and regulatory framework was far from revolutionary and was significantly more liberal than previous regimes built on bilateral agreements. More saliently for the aviation industry, the 'horrific' prospect of 'no deal' was avoided, though the new regime did bring some inconvenience and readjustment in its wake and promised more disputes in the years ahead. Yet the paralysis of the Brexit process did bring other costs. In particular, it heavily impacted on the plans to expand Heathrow, as the UK government and political system became preoccupied with resolving the constitutional crises and the planned infrastructure revolution stalled. Delay would prove very costly for plans that needed quick and decisive action and implementation, especially as the Brexit interregnum was suddenly filled by another dramatic global dislocation and threat: COVID-19.

The COVID-19 crisis

If Brexit produced uncertainty and worries about the regulatory future of UK aviation and its market access, then COVID-19 presented an altogether different challenge. Indeed, if anything, the wider social processes and logics that effectively 'overdetermined' the airports issue in the UK context, which we expose in our genealogical interpretations, was strongly accelerated by the COVID-19 crisis, heightening the tensions in the aviation field and its impacts on other parts of society. In the short term, the global pandemic brought about catastrophic consequences for the global aviation industry, and its attendant infrastructure such as airports and ground transportation, disclosing underlying contradictions and pathologies. And in the immediate aftermath of the pandemic in the UK, passenger air travel all but ground to a halt, as commercial flights declined by 95 per cent. Under pressure from airlines and airports, on the one hand, and environmental campaigners, on the other hand, and facing competing demands, the UK government's stated priority was to secure the income of workers, while keeping strategic routes open (Badstuber, 2020). Still, in October 2020, it was reported that nearly 200 airports in the UK and Europe were facing insolvency due to collapse in air travel (Neate, 2020a; Airports Council International, 2020).

In the UK, Heathrow announced that low passenger numbers had resulted in deep falls in revenue for 2020 and 2021. The airport lost £1.5bn up to the end of September 2020, while revenue from July to September fell 72 per cent compared with 2019 to £239m (Jolly, 2020). As the effects of the pandemic appeared to recede in the summer of 2020, travel corridors were introduced to allow people travelling from some countries with low numbers of COVID-19 cases to come to the UK without having to quarantine on arrival. But the situation worsened dramatically in the winter, as the government announced it was to close all travel corridors from 18 January, 2021 to 'protect against the risk of as yet unidentified new strains' of COVID-19 (BBC News, 2021). Anyone flying into the country from overseas was required to show proof of a negative COVID-19 test before setting off. Indeed, the owners of BA reported losses of €2 billion in the first 6 months of 2021 (Topham, 2021b). Although restrictions were removed in most cases, great uncertainty still remained about the 'normalisation' of aviation and the recovery of allied industries like tourism, hospitality and leisure.

As commentators were quick to note, the COVID-19 pandemic inflicted a devastating impact on the UK, both in terms of numbers of cases, hospitalisations and deaths, as well as severe economic dislocations for an economy disproportionately reliant on services, leisure and consumption. In early January 2021, second-wave COVID-19 cases peaked in the UK, as over 60,000 new cases were recorded in 24 hours, while on 7 January, 2021 the country recorded 1,162 COVID-19 deaths. Moreover, after a winter of discontent, which brought the imposition of further national lockdowns at the end of the October 2020 that continued into the summer of 2021, and a complex and ever mutating system of travel bans and restrictions, struggles began to surface between the more libertarian and communitarian wings of the Conservative Party and in society more generally. Such divisions reflected bitter ideological differences in the country, despite the widespread public acceptance of government measures. If anything, the much-vaunted vaccination programme exacerbated tensions in the ruling classes and within the newly emergent political elite, as libertarians and anti-vaccination groups demanded the opening up of the economy and a relaxation of travel restrictions. As the spring and summer approached, so the temperature of the political debate and the public discourses warmed up.

'Time to get flying again!' was the headline greeting readers of the *Mail on Sunday* on 20 June 2021, as Dr Liam Fox, the former Conservative International Trade Secretary, urged the 'British people' not to be 'a nation of COVID neurotics', and demanded that the UK government immediately lift the travel ban and adopt a broader perspective, which would 'balance the risks of the pandemic with the need to get our economy moving'. Couched in language that more or less replicated the discourse of the pro-aviation coalition, Freedom to Fly, which was active in the early 2000s, Fox stressed the importance of aviation to the economy, trade and tourism, but also issues of global connectedness and the need for families to meet face to face. Dismayed to observe 'a half-empty Heathrow Airport', which he described as 'one of the world's great transport hubs' and 'a centre not only of passenger travel but many of our exporting businesses', he emphasised the importance of 'our global connections' in 'a post-Brexit world'. He also stressed the importance of 'leisure travel' that he argued needed to open up before 'it goes bust and before another holiday season is lost'. Fox's intervention exemplified the growing concerns of the aviation industry and its supporters during the pandemic, while highlighting the dilemmas of the Johnson government, whose 'hard Brexit' created pressures to find new global trading partners and networks (Fox, 2021).

In the previous week it was reported that BA had resuscitated plans to curtail its operations at Gatwick airport, focusing its struggling operations at Heathrow, and creating further difficulties for Britain's second-biggest airport (Gill, 2021). Reports suggested that IAG, BA's parent company, was worried that it could lose lucrative take-off and landing slots at Heathrow, while BA had earlier intimated that it might abandon Gatwick in June 2020, predicting that demand for air travel was likely to dip for several years (Gordon, 2020). (Because of Heathrow's popularity among airlines, its take-off and landing slots are extremely desirable and can be traded by airline companies for tens of millions of pounds.) Indeed, on Thursday 17 June, 2021, the Airports Council International (ACI) – the self-named 'voice of the world's airports' – warned of a 'severe airport investment crunch' in Europe, as the industry was compelled to assume more than €20bn of additional debt in the previous year (ACI, 2021a). In terms of ownership, airports in the UK are either privately owned, or owned by local authorities and private organisations, or fully publicly owned, so that their monopoly positions are secured because they are an exclusive provider in a particular region (Tyers, 2022). And though it was the case that before the COVID-19 crisis airports were regarded as secure investments, producing income streams that were relatively stable and predictable, and which were generally linked to inflation, such assumptions were shattered by the pandemic and its effect on travel and tourism.

An important upshot of this growing crisis in UK aviation was to put into doubt the expansion plans at Heathrow, and the south-east more generally. In a revealing interview, Sir Howard Davies now claimed that he was no longer sure whether such plans were needed. 'Heathrow would be delighted to fill the two runways it has got', he told LBC, the British phone-in and talk radio station, adding: 'I suspect [that COVID-19] probably has changed the profile of demand for aviation in the future.' He also said he would have to 'redo the numbers' in order to see whether the economics of a third runway still made sense. But he remained convinced that if a new runway was needed in the south-east, then it should still be at Heathrow (Paton, 2021).

By contrast, most industry figures and the UK government believed that air travel would recover. For example, Gatwick's chief executive, Stewart Wingate, told the *Financial Times* (Plimmer and Georgiadis, 2021) that '[d]emand is expected to return to levels experienced before the pandemic by, or soon after, 2025 by which time congestion and capacity constraints will once again become an issue for the London market'. And on BBC Radio 4's flagship politics show – Any Questions – Lord Blunkett warned that Britain should not become 'a nation of puritans', who were reluctant to fly and enjoy themselves more. In his words,

> I don't think stopping people flying and the aviation industry collapsing, and any chance of this slogan about global Britain becoming a reality, is anti-climate change. What we need is sustainable aviation fuel ... which will come ... I am really quite worried about this anti-flying notion that's suddenly emerged ... Let's get the narrative right: let's make it possible to fly without affecting the climate and in a way that does not disrupt other people's lives – rather than saying we shouldn't do this, we shouldn't do that. What an awfully puritanical world we are creating for the children of the future! (BBC, Any Questions, 9 July, 2021)[3]

Certainly, demands to get the aviation industry back to 'business as usual' were strongly evident in a special Parliamentary Debate on 10 June, 2021, as the major political parties urged support for airlines and airports (Hansard, 2021a). Yet demands for a rapid return to 'business as usual' – part of the 'build back better' rhetoric – also met up with opposed demands, often intensified by the growing environmental and ecological crises.

Climate uncertainties and COP26

As if on cue, the months of July and August 2021, 5 months before the COP26 conference in Glasgow, brought a concatenation of dramatic events and news coverage, which put climate change centre-stage once again. Hundreds were killed in an unprecedented heatwave in British Columbia and the western US, followed by deadly flooding in Germany, Belgium and China, as well as wildfires in California and southern Europe, heatwaves and flooding in the UK, a devastating drought in South Africa and temperatures topping 50°C in Pakistan. In a report, the UK Met Office added the salutary warning that the age of extreme weather 'has just begun', a warning foregrounded by Ed Miliband, then Shadow Secretary for Energy and Industry in an attack on climate delay (Miliband, 2021), while Sir David King, the former UK chief scientific adviser, who along with other leading scientists established the Climate Crisis Advisory Group in June 2021, noted that 'scientists had been warning about extreme weather events for decades and now time was running out to take action' (Watts, 2021).

On top of this, the IPCC published its sixth comprehensive assessment of climate science on 9 August, 2021 (IPCC, 2021). Synthesising the work of hundreds of experts and peer-review studies for a period of 8 years, the Report provided overwhelming evidence that human activity is changing 'the Earth's climate in ways "unprecedented" in thousands or hundreds of thousands of years, with some of the changes now inevitable and "irreversible" … bringing widespread devastation and extreme weather'.[4] Combining a full and comprehensive account of 'the physical basis of climate change', the Report, which received widespread coverage across the media, 'found that human activity was "unequivocally" the cause of rapid changes to the climate, including sea level rises, melting polar ice and glaciers, heatwaves, floods and droughts'.[5]

Political and ideological turbulence

More strikingly, these events sparked bitter debate about commercial air travel and the global aviation industry as a whole. In the first wave of the pandemic, some politicians argued that support packages for airlines and travel operators 'should come at a price', and that because 'airlines, airports and travel operators are one of the biggest single contributors to global emissions', they should 'be made to do more to tackle climate change'. Support packages to airlines and travel companies thus required 'stringent

147

conditions', so that in return for financial assistance airlines were urged not to pay dividends to their owners, to refund customers for cancelled bookings and to rehire employees who had been fired during the pandemic. They were also requested to do more to tackle the climate crisis, including the implementation of 'ambitious carbon offsetting schemes' (Sarah Olney, MP, 27 April, 2020).[6]

More radical voices, like George Monbiot, argued that 'Do Not Resuscitate' tags should be attached to the oil, airline and car industries and that governments should provide financial support to company workers, while refashioning the economy to provide new jobs in different sectors. In his view, air travel is 'inherently polluting', which means that 'there are no realistic measures that could, even in the medium term, make a significant difference'. Reiterating calls for a Green New Deal, he demanded that the UK Government (and others) should abandon road-building plans, create plans to reduce the need to move and invest in walking, cycling and – when physical distancing is less necessary – public transport. Rather than expanding airports, governments should commit themselves to reducing landing slots and to an explicit policy of leaving fossil fuels in the ground (Monbiot, 2020).

Such dislocations and their accompanying demands radically reactivated and intensified the growing social unease and political contestation about the future of a more or less unregulated global aviation industry, as well as the devastating impacts on the climate and local communities affected by its many negative externalities. Along with other destructive industries and unsustainable forms of life, penetrating questions were asked about the need for and character of (global) air travel and certain forms of trade, as well as the travel and mass tourist industries more generally (see IPSOS, 2020; Cabot Institute, 2021). Alternative forms of communication and technological innovation, coupled with innovative ways of living, began to surface in different quarters, as critics sought to supplement the critique of aviation and neoliberal globalisation with the elaboration of new modes of exchange, enjoyment and pleasure.

Amidst this rapid politicisation of the future of aviation, the Johnson government reverted to a strategy of promoting technological fixes and innovation to deliver its promise of 'sustainable aviation'. Its public discourse increasingly embraced policies of ecological modernisation as the means to increase passenger numbers and mitigate the impacts of aviation on climate change. On the one hand, in April 2021, as it prepared for COP 26, the Johnson government committed itself to legislating a new target to reduce national carbon emissions by 78 per cent by 2035 compared to 1990 levels, while taking the step to include for the first time domestic and international aviation and shipping emissions in the calculations of carbon budgets by the CCC.[7] However, on the other hand, such ambitious targets were matched by a ratcheting up of the rhetoric of technological fixes in aviation. Hence, in its Jet Zero Consultation in July 2021, the Johnson government reasserted its desire to 'deliver zero emission transatlantic flight within a generation [by 2050]', as part of a means of meeting 'the requirement to decarbonise aviation … whilst allowing the sector to thrive, and hardworking families to continue to enjoy their annual holiday abroad'. Such rhetoric restated the fantasmatic narrative of sustainable aviation, announcing that 'aviation and the UK go hand in hand' before declaring decarbonisation to be 'a huge opportunity for the UK … which will see new technologies, new companies and new markets all emerge' (DfT, 2021a: 4, 5, 8). Not surprisingly, Jet Zero rehashed the government's support for technological acceleration through system efficiencies, sustainable aviation fuels, zero emission aircraft and the use of carbon markets and measures to influence consumer behaviour, all of which were to be delivered through international collaboration and partnership with industry, notably the aviation industry group, Sustainable Aviation (DfT, 2021a: 18, 21–41).

This discourse of ecological modernisation was also on display at COP26, which was held in Glasgow in November 2021 under the presidency of the UK government. The statement by the 23 states of the International Aviation Climate Ambition Coalition on 10 November, which included the UK, committed to net zero aviation by 2050 (International Aviation Climate Ambition Coalition, 2021). However, it shied away from concrete measures to curb aviation expansion, choosing instead to endorse international collaboration within ICAO, which was designated as the 'appropriate forum' to 'advance ambitious actions to reduce aviation CO_2 emissions' so as to limit any rise in global temperature to 1.5 °C. In this way, the Coalition put its faith in technological developments and market instruments. Signatories thus committed to work to deliver the 'maximum effectiveness' of CORSIA, advance sustainable aviation fuels and low-carbon aircraft, and support the adoption by ICAO of a 'long-term aspirational goal consistent' with 1.5 °C rise in global temperature and the commitment to net zero by 2050. States also agreed to formulate action plans 'detailing concrete national action' to lower aviation emissions in advance of the 2022 ICAO Assembly.[8] But the Declaration fell silent on increased taxation on aviation to blunt rising demand, moratoriums on airport expansion, a ban on short-haul flights and the substitution of rail for air travel. Rather, it validated the leadership of industry dominated institutions, relied on technological and market fixes, and displaced the meeting of any stringent emission targets to 2050 (Kennedy, 2021).

Importantly, however, falls in passenger numbers were deployed by the Johnson government to push the issue of Heathrow expansion into the future and off its political agenda. The discourse of Jet Zero and technological fixes remained silent on the issue of the third runway, which as we have argued was increasingly framed as a 'private sector project' with the government distancing itself from the appeal process of Heathrow Airport in the Supreme Court and its outcome. When Rupa Huq, the Labour MP for Ealing Central and Acton, asked Boris Johnson in Parliament for a new vote on Heathrow expansion to end any prospect of the third runway being built, the Prime Minister replied that the focus of the government was on 'net zero aviation', to which he added: 'And by the way, I think *that* has every chance of arriving a lot earlier than a third runway at Heathrow' (Hansard, 2021b).[9]

Nonetheless, his longstanding and personal commitment to oppose Heathrow expansion, which stretched back to his days as London mayor, did not automatically translate into an opposition against aviation and airport expansion per se; the latter was apparent, for example, in the embracing of Jet Zero demands and the use of green technology to sustain the growth of aviation. It was also apparent when Rishi Sunak, Johnson's Chancellor, cut APD by 50 per cent for domestic flights in economy class in his October 2021 budget (Allegretti, 2021). And only a few weeks earlier, ICCAN, which had been established in response to the Davies Commission's recommendations on noise – albeit a limited response – was quietly wound up and its functions integrated into the Civil Aviation Authority (CAA).

Conclusion

This chapter has characterised and analysed the COVID-19 conjuncture in aviation policy and politics, pulling together the multiple threads of our genealogy of the technologies and techniques designed to tackle the problems of aviation expansion and its demands for more and efficient airport capacity. Such technologies were at times castigated as costly and inefficient, but ultimately they did enable the incremental expansion of the UK's airport capacity. Yet, over time, and particularly in the aftermath of the ATWP (2003), as aviation expansion was linked to climate justice and social inequalities, the issue of airport expansion has become increasingly politicised, evolving into an intractable policy controversy.

We also suggest that this dilemma for government has been exacerbated by the multiple and interlocking crises of Brexit, climate change and the global COVID-19 pandemic, which have come to the fore in the period after the AC published its Final Report. In fact, our analysis has identified and constructed a novel problematisation facing government in the political conjuncture focused on the COVID-19 pandemic. The pandemic has exposed many citizens across the world to new modes of travel and consumption, as well as the possibilities and prospects of living in a world without aviation, or at least with a radically retrenched aviation sector. Our conclusion is that it has dramatically revealed the biggest challenge ever to the embedded fantasmatic narratives of flying as an unproblematic and valued public good, which has 'gripped' politicians and much of the public in recent times.

But is there an available and credible policy and lifestyle alternative to aviation and airport expansion? How can this policy be embedded in government and the wider society? The answer to these questions depends on the cultural battle to reshape established thinking on mobility and the demands of our future environmental geographies. Most importantly, it means a new kind of discourse and a different kind of political leadership, which does not seek to depoliticise aviation, but aims to put the conflicts surrounding its future at the heart of any dialogue. Such an intervention should give a legitimate voice to a plurality of alternative forms of expertise and competing demands, rather than trying to push them to the margins of policy formulation. In short, it requires a different regime of governing technologies and novel forms of knowledge and expertise with which to imagine new ways of living and enjoying. It is to such ethical and normative concerns that we now turn in the final part of our study.

6

'What if...?' A manifesto for the green transformation of aviation

Our genealogies have demonstrated how the UK airports issue and the problem of aviation has evolved into a deepening policy controversy involving the clash of political forces, which espouse competing ideals and values. But they also show the difficulties in challenging the myths and fantasies built into the embedded narratives of sustainable aviation and the technologies of government, which seek to depoliticise and perpetuate aviation expansion, not to mention the highly organised resources of the industry and its supporters. This means that the questioning and problematisation of continued aviation expansion is ever more necessary if we are to meet the pressing demands of the global environmental crisis and the instabilities of living in the Anthropocene. Like Thomas Princen (2005), we thus ask the 'what if?' question. What if we were to disinvest from aviation and embark on an alternative agenda of post-growth policies? What would such an imaginary look like? What would such a transformation require? And how would we achieve it?

This chapter addresses these questions by putting forward a manifesto for the green transformation of aviation. We first identify and evaluate the two leading discourses that have emerged – 'business as usual' and 'demand management' – and which have come to frame public policy dialogue around aviation in the post-pandemic world. We argue that the expansionist logic of 'business as usual', which relies on the myth of technological fixes, efficiencies and offsetting, no longer provides the effective tools or policies to tackle the environmental injustices of aviation, if it ever did. But we also conclude that demand management, which offers an alternative to the discourse of continued growth, ultimately conforms to a logic of attenuation, supporting the politics of reform rather than transition and transformation. Reformist politics in our perspective leaves intact existing economic, political and social formations, simply installing one more updated version of the same operating system. Alone, it cannot fully accommodate the radical, non-linear and continual reorganisation of the politics of transition and transformation, which are necessary to bring about changes to our social identities, political institutions and practices of economic and social reproduction, as well as our underlying relations with nature, which can in turn bring about a post-growth, just and sustainable mode of aviation (Eckersley, 2021: 247–9).

Embracing demands for a just transition and social transformation of unsustainable, inegalitarian and oppressive practices, we thus point to an emergent path that can lead to the green restructuring of aviation. Hence, we call for a radical divestment from aviation that goes beyond demand management to deliver post-growth policies that provide support for green jobs, social infrastructure and the foundational economy. Our aim is to contribute to the generation of a new 'common sense', which draws on broader social and cultural investments in alternative hedonism, while instilling new forms of political leadership and progressive alliances at the heart of a green state. We contend that it is only this hegemonic strategy of transformation, tying aviation to broader visions of post-growth societies, which will enable us to break our addiction to flying and dependency on an ever-expanding politics of airport infrastructure. We begin by analysing the limits of the discourse of 'business as usual', before turning to 'demand management'.

'Business as usual': reiterating the fantasmatic narrative of sustainable aviation

Proponents of 'business as usual' prolong what might be called a form of 'weak' ecological modernisation, as they continue to invest in the fantasmatic narrative of sustainable aviation, where the growth in passenger numbers and airport expansion is believed to be compatible with the mitigation of aviation's impact on climate change through technological innovation and market instruments (Christoff, 1996). In such quarters, continued aviation growth is framed as sustainable, for it supports social cohesion and economic well-being, and most effectively enables airlines and airports to invest in new technologies. On the whole, then, this is an argument which re-casts government sponsorship of the industry in the wake of the COVID-19 pandemic as enhancing the sustainable transformation of aviation as a whole (Pickard and Pasqualino, 2022).

Putting their faith in the mechanisms of the market to deliver innovation, thereby maintaining the potential for growth and environmental protection, its adherents invest in the promise of new propulsion systems, low carbon biofuels and operational efficiencies to address the negative externalities of flying. The Jet Zero Council, for example, which was put in place by the Johnson government in 2021, brought together government departments and industry partners to coordinate approaches towards the delivery of 'zero-emission transatlantic flights' within a generation (DfT, 2021a). Similarly, Airbus has pledged to deliver hydrogen-powered planes by 2035, while the Electric EEL project is developing electric hybrid planes for short journeys between regional airports (Boyle, 2020; Morris, 2021). Typically, in its road-map to decarbonise aviation, the UK-based Sustainable Aviation industry group proposed a host of efficiencies, ranging from improved operations, fleet upgrades, sustainable fuels and carbon removal to market-based measures such as the EU ETS and CORSIA schemes. It forecast that such initiatives will permit a 70 per cent growth in passengers through to 2050, alongside a reduction in net emissions levels to zero (Sustainable Aviation, 2020: 5).

To legitimise this unlikely combination of continued growth and environmental protection, market mechanisms like global carbon offsetting schemes are accorded an important strategic role, even if the accountability and effectiveness of such schemes are doubted by some industry insiders (Pickard and Pasqualino, 2022). The aviation industry and governments thus place much faith in the market to calculate where and how cuts to emissions are best made. It is claimed, for example, that CORSIA – the global carbon offsetting scheme heralded by the ICAO – which comes fully into operation in 2027, will offset any growth in carbon emissions from international flights above 2019 levels. Airlines taking part in the scheme will be obliged to either buy emission reduction offsets from other sectors to compensate for increases in their own emissions or use lower carbon eligible fuels (Carbon Brief, 2019). In line with such aspirations, ICAO set the target for global greenhouse gas life-cycle emissions from international aviation not exceeding 2020 levels in 2035 (revised to 2019 following the COVID-19 pandemic), reducing to at least 50 per cent of 2005 levels by 2050. And the industry has been quick to publicly embrace such targets and also realign their operations with the net zero commitments of the Paris Agreement. By May 2021, 235 airports across Europe had committed to deliver net zero emissions by 2050, with 91 airports on course to deliver on their commitment by 2030 (ACI, 2021b). In the UK, the launch of 'Heathrow 2.0' in 2017 established the airport's own path towards zero-carbon emissions, in which it aimed to create a 'culture of sustainability' that would go beyond the narrow preoccupation with carbon emissions and structure its engagement with local communities, its supply chains, the career development of its employees and its policies towards air quality and respite (Heathrow Airport, 2018b).

However, the implementation of these targets and technological innovations is beset with obstacles. At best, the presumed trajectories articulated within the discourse of 'business as usual' require intensive and sustained funding, as well as collaboration across the industry and its partners, alongside government investment and international coordination. At worst, they are flawed in that they do little more than repeat the 'greenwashing' peddled by the fantasmatic narrative, which suggests that we can continue to fly *and* mitigate the impacts of our flying on the environment. They also downplay the relative weight of aviation to global carbon emissions, while overplaying its economic and social contributions to sustainability, and drawing equivalences between demands to tackle carbon emissions and those to address noise and air quality (Pickard and Pasqualino, 2022).

And although laudable, commitments from airports to achieve net zero emissions do little to account for the emissions from flights, which is part of their 'core' business. For example, United Airlines' ambition to become '100 per cent green' by 2050 masks an expansion of daily flights to London, new routes to Amman and Tenerife, as well as an investment in supersonic jets, which use five to seven times more fuel than conventional aircraft (Paddison, 2021). Mobilising these tried and trusted fantasmatic appeals, the narrative of 'business as usual' hampers rather than supports the implementation of our commitments under the Paris Agreement. Instead, it functions as a legitimising discourse for inaction and the bolstering of the status quo.

Why 'business as usual' is no longer an option

Technological fixes will not come quickly enough

Meeting the Paris target of limiting global warming to 1.5 °C requires global CO_2 emissions to decline by 45 per cent from 2010 levels by 2030 and to reach net zero in 2050 (IPCC, 2018). The timescales of these international commitments do not tally with the speed of supposed technological improvements in aviation, which will remain heavily reliant on kerosene fuels for the foreseeable future (Royal Society, 2023). For example, the Air Transport Action Group (ATAG) argues that at a global level, with the continued use of offsets, net zero aviation is likely to be possible only by 2060–2065. But even this pathway depends on a set of questionable assumptions, including the continued dependency on reductions in other sectors; the substantial contribution to the reduction of emissions of hybridisation and electrification by 2050–2060; sustainable aviation fuels reaching 100 per cent emissions reduction or emitting no emissions by 2060; the use of hydrogen to be attainable; and an acceptance of the continued reliance on offsetting and on direct air carbon capture technologies that have yet to come into being (ATAG, 2020b: 27–8).

In practice, fuel efficiencies are not being delivered quickly enough to offset the continued growth in flights (ICCT, 2020: 3). Between 2013 and 2019, air passenger transport-related carbon emissions rose by 33 per cent, with passenger air traffic increasing almost four times faster than improvements in fuel efficiency (ICCT, 2020: 3). At the same time, alternatives to kerosene are in short supply. The CCC has argued that full electric flights, particularly for long-haul trips, are 'unlikely to be feasible by 2050' and it forecasts only a 10 per cent take-up of sustainable fuels in aviation by the middle of the century, pointing out that there will be pressure on biomass production from its alternative uses in the economy and from its land use (CCC, 2019b: 9). And this use of biofuels would require a rapid scaling up of production: at the end of 2021, sustainable aviation fuels accounted for less than 0.1 per cent of aviation fuel, while costing three to four times more than conventional kerosene (Paddison, 2021). In fact, it is predicted that the use of alternative aviation fuels would require the doubling of current global palm oil production and the clearance of 3.2 million hectares of forest, producing an additional 5 gigatonnes of carbon emissions through land use change, not to mention the social justice concerns of removing land from agricultural use for food crops (Rainforest Foundation Norway and Cerulogy, 2019). Even optimistic forecasts predict that new long-range hydrogen planes could not come into service until 2040 (Clean Sky 2 JU and CH 2 JU, 2020; see also IATA, 2019).

Technological transformation also depends on the fleet replacement strategies of carriers. With most commercial planes staying in service for up to 30 years, there will be a time lag between the arrival of new technologies onto the market and their introduction into fleets, adding to the initial time lags between the development of alternative technologies and their gaining of regulatory approval to go to market (ATAG, 2020b: 46; Pickard and Pasqualino, 2022). But, in any case, it is far from certain that new propulsion systems or alternative fuels will deliver 'net zero' pathways for flying. Water emissions from hydrogen planes would continue to create contrails at high altitude as the combustion of hydrogen releases 2.6 per cent more water vapour than kerosene, although the larger ice crystals of the contrails created may reduce their radiative forcing effects (IATA, 2019). Even more importantly, the production of liquid hydrogen currently uses fossil fuel methane and doubts remain over whether it is possible to competitively scale-up its production without adding to carbon emissions. Its use as an aviation fuel will require sustained investment in storage, production and distribution, as well as changes to aircraft design and airport infrastructure to accommodate its new technologies. Moreover, liquid hydrogen is likely to be at least twice as expensive as kerosene in the near future, with larger fuel tanks on hydrogen planes requiring airlines to choose between flying with fewer passengers or introducing larger planes (Henderson, 2021). The same investments in storage, production and distribution also apply to the development of electric or hybrid planes.

Offsetting will continue to fuel expansion and perpetuate climate injustice

Simply put, CORSIA will not impose any effective constraints on the growth of carbon emissions from international aviation (Transport and Environment, 2021a). The scheme is designed to offset any growth above 2019 levels in carbon emissions from international flights, whereby participating airlines are obliged to buy offset credits from listed programmes or substitute lower carbon eligible fuels to compensate for increases in their own emissions. But it does not include the impacts of other non-CO_2 greenhouse gases emitted at high altitude, which can double the climate change impacts of flights, and nor does it impose a requirement to reduce emissions from aviation. Rather, it merely ensures no net growth in carbon emissions from aviation above 2019 levels, thus allowing emissions to continue to grow as long as they are offset. And, significantly, in waiting for CORSIA to come into place, it is our contention that the EU lost time in reducing aviation carbon emissions by 'stopping the clock' and withdrawing international aviation from outside Europe from its more robust cap and trade ETS (Transport & Environment, 2021a).

In fact, the effectiveness of the CORSIA regime is flawed in terms of delivering the reductions in emissions required across the aviation sector before 2030 and 2050. First, participation in CORSIA remains voluntary until 2027, with China, Russia, Brazil, India, and Vietnam deciding not to join the scheme in its initial stages. The US has joined but its continued participation rests on widespread engagement in the scheme by other leading nations, while the participation of American airlines remains voluntary and not a legal obligation (Transport & Environment, 2021a: 9). Non-participation by some states means that any flights to or from these countries will not be counted in emissions targets, even if the flight departed from a participating state. Taking these omissions into account, it is predicted that CORSIA will account for as little as 35 per cent of global CO_2 emissions from aviation (Transport & Environment, 2021a: 2).

But, secondly, the operation of the regime rests heavily on the market determining a sufficiently high price for carbon offsets to incentivise airlines to make carbon efficiencies. However, as airlines recover from the pandemic, it is projected that there will be an oversupply of inexpensive carbon offset credits for airlines, in part because of the decision of ICAO to take 2019 as its sole baseline year, removing the collapse of passenger traffic in 2020 due to the COVID-19 pandemic from any calculations, and also because, at least in the short-term, the pandemic has led to a fall in passenger numbers and demand. In this particular conjuncture, there is little incentive for airlines to experiment with alternative sustainable fuels, as it remains less costly to 'continue polluting' and buy cheap offsets (Transport & Environment, 2021a: 7).

Thirdly, uncertainty surrounds the quality and transparency of carbon offset programmes, with fears expressed that carbon offsets will be double counted, simultaneously matched against emissions from aviation and emissions from other sectors. In fact, offsets do not guarantee carbon neutrality, allowing emissions to grow on the promise of delivering carbon reductions in the near future through schemes which are not necessarily carbon neutral in the first instance (Transport & Environment, 2021a, 2021b). At the same time, carbon offsetting poses important questions of environmental justice. For one thing, the availability of, and access to, land and resources for nature-based offsetting is not unlimited, requiring choices over which activities to prioritise, or which demands to privilege. At the same time, because schemes are often located in developing countries, offsetting is derided as a form of green imperialism, which transfers the environmental costs of aviation onto those communities, who have historically made little contribution to climate change, but who are increasingly impacted by it. Here Klein (2014: 223) questions the unjust practices that accompany the act of devoting land to offset schemes, arguing that 'it's easier to cordon off a forest inhabited by politically weak people in a poor country than to stop politically powerful corporate emitters in rich countries'.

Flying is an environmentally unjust activity

The environmental injustice of aviation carries over into the stark social inequalities of who flies and who does not. Dominant policy narratives repeatedly popularise air travel, emphasising how cheap fares and increasing competition have opened up flying to the masses. Yet, once again, this is only part of the story. Air travel remains highly socially stratified. It bears repeating that most people across the world do not fly, with close to 90 per cent of the global population not flying in any given year. Only 2 to 4 per cent of the global population flew internationally in 2018, while North America accounted for some 25.6 per cent of global air travel, Asia-Pacific for 32.5 per cent and Europe for 22.7 per cent (Gössling and Humpe, 2020: 4, 7). The three largest markets – the US, the EU and China – were responsible for over 50 per cent of all passenger CO_2 emitted in 2019 (ICCT, 2020: 1).

There are also stark inequalities among those who do fly. 'Super-emitters', the top 10 per cent of the most frequent fliers, account for more than half of carbon emissions from travel on commercial aviation, to which can be added the emissions of private jets (Gössling and Humpe, 2020: 9). Similarly, in the UK, 20 per cent of the most frequent non-business travellers produce 60 per cent of related emissions, while the contribution of highest income groups (above £40,000 per person per annum) is 3.5 times greater than lower income groups (£10,000 per annum) (Gössling and Humpe, 2020: 9). These inequalities are amplified by the larger carbon footprint of premium class passengers, which is approximately three times larger than that of economy class. Some 20 per cent of carbon emissions from commercial aviation emanates from passengers in premium seating classes, which is more than all of the carbon emissions from dedicated freight and freight carried in the hold on passenger flights (ICCT, 2020: ii). And this is not to mention the growth of private air travel, demand for which remained resilient, if not buoyant, during the global pandemic (Neate, 2020b), after an increase of nearly one third in carbon emissions from private jets within the EU between 2005 and 2019 (Transport & Environment, 2021c: 3). Principles like 'polluter pays' are again not being applied, as patterns of over-consumption by the minority have in part been fuelled by the fact that average ticket prices in 2020 were 61 per cent cheaper in real terms than in 1998 (Tyers, 2020). In short, commercial aviation is a global site of environmental injustice.

The economic numbers do not stack up

The discourses of 'business as usual' tend to overstate the economic benefits of commercial aviation. Commercial aviation is heavily subsidised, as airlines benefit over time from government bailouts, grant support on routes to remote places, reduced charges for transfer passengers and government investment in local transport infrastructure, not to mention the absence of fuel tax on kerosene and VAT on tickets for international flights (Gössling et al, 2017). When considering VAT exemptions, government support for infrastructure to and from the airport and artificially low airport charges, it was conservatively estimated that a round trip flight from Schiphol Amsterdam to Toulouse drew upon subsidies totalling almost 100 per cent of the cost of the ticket (Bannon, 2019). In the UK, exemptions from fuel tax and VAT on tickets amount to a £7 billion per year subsidy to the industry (NEF, 2020: 5). Indeed, APD, which for the majority of air travellers has fallen in real terms since 1997, would need to be more than three times its current level to match the value of the industry's blanket exemption from fuel duty and VAT (AEF, 2020: 2). Finally, aviation pays the lowest effective carbon price of all sectors in the UK (Sturge and Day, 2021). It is the most carbon intensive but least taxed sector of the economy, effectively undermining once again the principle of polluter pays in environmental policy (Transport & Environment, 2021b).

More broadly, business air travel is generally overestimated in terms of volume and economic benefits, while the benefits of aviation tourism and overseas travel exacerbate the UK's trade deficits. In 2019, British residents undertook 93.1 million visits abroad, nearly two thirds of which were for holidays, while approximately a quarter were to visit family and friends. The number of business trips fell slightly to 9 million, but it has remained relatively stable for over 20 years, even if the 'higher yield' of business passengers remains central to the economic model of many airlines (Chapman, 2020; Boin et al, 2022). Moreover, because an estimated four-fifths of flights are recorded as leisure travel and/or visits to friends and family, aviation cannot be divorced from a trade imbalance in tourism of approximately £33.9 billion in 2019: UK residents spent £62.3 billion on visits overseas, while the 40.9 million visits made to the UK generated £28.4 billion spend by overseas residents.[1] Importantly, most of the UK residents who flew abroad for their holidays visited countries within the EU, where alternative modes of transportation were available. At the same time, business trips are less and less necessary given the expansion of information technologies and online meetings. Unlike tourism and leisure, where the experience of visiting places or relaxation is difficult to substitute, business is not dependent on travel.

In fact, the economics behind the construction of new terminals and runways as large infrastructure projects are extractivist. Take, for example, the case of Heathrow expansion, where there are growing concerns that the costs of building the third runway could surge to £31 billion, over double the initial estimates of £14 billion, throwing doubt on the viability of the private-funded project and threatening the investment grade credit rating of Heathrow Airport Holdings (AirportWatch, 2019). Concerned with spiralling costs, the CAA introduced a new clause into Heathrow's licence in early December 2019, which could be used to penalise the airport if it did not build the third runway 'economically and efficiently' (Collingridge, 2019). But funding rules mean that the airport has little interest in containing the capital costs of the construction project, because the costs of expansion are added to the calculation of the airport's Regulated Asset Base (RAB) on which it gets a permitted return. In short, increasing the costs of the proposed third runway inflates the airport's revenues, passing on costs to airlines and customers. Since taking over Heathrow in 2006, for example, Ferrovial has tripled the airport's RAB to some £15 billion, enabling it to finance expansion with relatively low levels of equity capital (AirportWatch, 2018; NEF, 2018). As Mitchell (2020) points out, such financial and investment strategies follow a broader trend: large infrastructure projects enable capital to extract wealth from the future as the construction of runways and terminals delivers investors the opportunity to reap the benefits of the discounted purchase of future revenues. Moreover, the delay and postponement of projects after construction begins can work to maximise further discounted opportunities. Also, despite private funding, taxpayers do not escape 'the bill' for expansion, because the funding of improvements to public transport infrastructure and road access to airports often comes from the public purse (Plimmer and Ford, 2018).

Finally, much is also made of the direct and indirect employment supported by the aviation industry. In government consultations and white papers aviation is invariably framed as a significant source of employment, in which it is estimated that the UK aviation sector directly provides over 230,000 jobs across the country, and 'many more' are 'supported indirectly' (DfT, 2018b: 97). However, such assertions must be increasingly questioned. In recent years, the number of jobs per passenger has been falling by 2.6 per cent a year, triggering disputes and strikes over pay and conditions across the industry, notably the highly publicised strike of pilots in British Airways (BBC News, 2019). In reality, therefore, any airport expansion will produce fewer jobs per passenger over time, while some jobs will inevitably be displaced from other airports as one airport expands and another does not (NEF, 2020: 7). Indeed, the pandemic has led to cutback management and widespread redundancies throughout the aviation industry, coming on top of the rapid moves towards automation across the industry. In the UK, by March 2021, over 35,600 workers directly employed in the aviation industry had lost their jobs following the outbreak of the pandemic in February 2020, including 12,000 jobs at British Airways. When indirect employment, and employment in aerospace and companies with a significant presence in UK airports was taken into account, this loss of employment in the aviation sector rose to an estimated 62,000 jobs (Acuity Analysis, 2021: 11–13).

Yet, ultimately, the economic value of any jobs created by aviation expansion will be outweighed by the growing costs of addressing carbon emissions. In September 2021, the government, allowing for the rising costs of technologies to cut emissions to net zero by 2050, more than tripled its calculation of 'carbon value' – the abatement cost of a tonne of CO_2 or equivalent. This has doubled the carbon costs of emissions of current proposals for expansion, adding £500m to the climate costs at Leeds Bradford and Southampton and £1 billion to those at Stansted, while increasing climate costs at Heathrow to over £100 billion from 2025 to 2050.[2] But, due to the 'holes' in the UK ETS, its awarding of free carbon allowances for up to 82 per cent of emissions, as well as its low carbon pricing and failure to include either flights departing to non-EU countries or non-CO_2 emissions, such additional costs will be carried by taxpayers, to the benefit once again of the industry and frequent flyers (Chapman, 2022). In 2021, the UK government awarded 4.4 million free carbon allowances to airlines, which was approximately 1 million more than they needed, a direct subsidy to airlines that resulted in them not having to pay for their carbon emissions (Transport & Environment, 2022).

There is no capacity overload, and airport expansion is simply a strategy to beat off the competition

Claims of capacity overload in the UK have been undermined by the impact of the global pandemic on passenger numbers. Optimistic forecasts predict that passenger numbers will return to pre-pandemic numbers by 2024, while more pessimistic forecasts argue that it might take until the second half of the 2030s for passenger numbers to bounce back to pre-pandemic levels. For its part, industry experts predict a 20–30 per cent drop in business travel following the COVID-19 pandemic, although it is contended by some analysts that the number of business travellers on flights peaked in 2006 (Chapman, 2021: 24). Of course, even before the pandemic, predictions that suggested the need for further airport capacity in the next 10 to

20 years were highly contested. The case set out by the AC relied on the exclusion of Stansted airport from its calculations and the narrowing of its focus on the need for a global hub and perceptions about the unwillingness of passengers to travel to alternative airports in and outside London. The threat of capacity overload at London airports was also projected to 2030, which was the deadline set by the IPCC for governments to act to ensure that global temperature rises remain at 1.5 °C or below and when it might be expected (or hoped) that demand management policies in aviation had begun to lower the demand for flights. Finally, the trend to larger aircraft, assuming it continues in the aftermath of the COVID-19 pandemic (Grimme et al, 2021), will always lessen demand for more runway capacity as it will enable more passengers to be accommodated on individual planes.

But, if capacity overload is not a significant constraint, why are airports continuing to propose plans to build more runways and terminals? In February 2020, it was reported that all UK airports have plans for expansion in place (*Air Quality News*, 2020). In September 2021, Gatwick Airport, which was the ostensible 'loser' in the battle with Heathrow to win approval from the AC, started public consultation on its plans to bring its existing Northern Runway into routine use. One month earlier, it was reported that the airport was in talks with lenders after losses of £245 million in the first half of the year (Georgiadis and Ralph, 2021). Such financial losses shed a new light on the drivers behind growth and plans for expansion: they are generally not the consequence of an overall gap in airport capacity across the UK, but the result of the market competition installed between airports in the privatisation and liberalisation of the 1980s and 1990s. Airports have become multi-national companies, often owned by foreign investors eager for increasing dividends. Operating in the context of a competitive market, the expansion of an airport's infrastructure becomes intertwined with the promise of increasing returns and market share, the opening up more of more take-off and landing slots for airlines, more commercial and shopping venues within terminals, and increasing opportunities to reap car parking revenues, and so on. Continual growth becomes the condition of an airport's very existence within the market – such is the drive behind the discourse of 'business as usual'. But it is possible to challenge such logics and demand management seeks to do so.

The logic of attenuation: demand management

The discourse of demand management, whose propagators have elaborated alternative policy trajectories for the regulation and governance of commercial aviation, recognises that climate change mitigation and adaptation pose particularly stringent challenges in the field of aviation. Because of this threat, the proponents of this discourse argue that flying represents 'the quickest and cheapest way for a consumer to increase their carbon footprint' in high-income European countries (Carmichael, 2019: 7). But, despite the increasing public recognition of the environmental impacts of aviation, apart from the COVID-19 hiatus, consumer demand for aviation has grown steadily largely due to the deregulation of the airline industry, the growth of low-cost carriers and the continued array of financial subsidies awarded to the industry. In the absence of any short-term fixes to aviation's dependency on kerosene, advocates of demand management thus argue that there is little option but to constrain passenger demand in aviation. In other words, unrestricted growth in aviation is simply not compatible with the delivery of the government's net zero commitments (Carmichael, 2019; AEF, 2021).

Supporters of demand management thus call for a 'stronger' version of ecological modernisation, in which the state regulates, rather than enables, the market for aviation, moving beyond the reliance on technological innovation and economic instruments to advance deliberative and institutional change strategies (Christoff, 1996). They call for an end to airport expansion, including the construction of additional runways and terminals across the UK, while emphasising the advice of the CCC in its Sixth Carbon Budget, published in December 2020, that there should be no net increase in the UK's airport capacity (CCC, 2020: 176). Advocates of this discourse also call for the imposition of stringent caps on growing passenger demand. In line with this thinking, the Climate Assembly UK, the first UK-wide citizens' assembly on climate change, rejected any future in which air passenger numbers would rise by up to 65 per cent between 2018 and 2050, 'labelling it "counterproductive"' (Climate Change Assembly UK, 2020: 121). Yet the AC had endorsed such 'counterproductive' forecasts in making its case for expansion. In contrast, members of the Assembly supported a cap on the increase air passenger numbers of between 25 and 50 per cent from 2018 until 2050, depending on technological improvements. Such limits would translate in practice to an annual growth rate in passenger numbers of between 0.7–1.3 per cent, compared to 2.8 per cent between 2000 and 2018 (Climate Change Assembly UK, 2020: 121).

Alongside such caps on passenger numbers and airport capacity, advocates of demand management propose the application of 'polluter pays' principles in aviation, with the aim of shifting consumer behaviour, substituting low carbon rail for short-haul air travel and further facilitating the switch to information communication technologies in order to replace face-to-face meetings and business conferences. In the first instance, this logic of demand management projected into the future would result in the government: imposing duties on aviation fuel and VAT on air tickets and increasing APD, so as to remove state subsidies to aviation; 'levelling the playing field' with other forms of less carbon intensive modes of transport; and ensuring that air passengers pay the full carbon costs of their flights. However, fearing the regressive impacts of non-discriminatory aviation fuel taxes, for example, some advocates of demand management call for the adoption of a frequent flyer tax and/or an air miles levy whereby flying becomes more expensive the more miles flown (Carmichael, 2019; Chapman et al, 2021). Hence, the Free Ride Campaign proposes that passengers each receive one tax fee return flight each year, with each additional flight being subject to increasing rates of taxation, ensuring environmental and tax justice in the consumption of aviation.[3] Such measures would go hand in hand with the transparent carbon pricing of flights, reflecting the increased carbon costs of flying in business or premium class seats, as well as the carbon intensity of specific planes and distances travelled (ICCT, 2020). Over time, personal quotas for carbon emissions accounting for international flights could also be introduced.

Finally, CORSIA, the global offsetting regime designed by the ICAO, would be replaced by a more heavily regulated cap and trade carbon emissions scheme, building on the EU ETS into which aviation was incorporated in 2012. The Scheme covers all airlines operating in Europe, although it is limited to flights solely within the European Economic Area, because the EU took the decision to support the ICAO 2016 resolution to develop CORSIA (ICAO, 2016). The EU will review its support for CORSIA in 2024 after an assessment of the operationalisation of the implementation of the global offsetting regime in aviation. Following the end of the Brexit transition agreement in January 2021, the UK ETS came into being, covering all domestic flights and flights from the UK to the European Economic Area. The UK scheme will operate in parallel to that of the EU, although the British government has suggested that it will impose a 5 per cent tougher cap than those set by the EU and ensure the alignment of the scheme with its 2050 net zero targets by 2024 (HoCL, 2021). In this regard, scenarios envisaged by the discourse of demand management envisage the immediate UK and EU withdrawal from CORSIA, ensuring that the emissions of all flights in and out of Europe return to a heavily policed emissions trading system with decreasing caps every year designed to meet net zero 2050 carbon targets. In the aftermath of Brexit, this would entail the potential integration of EU and UK schemes in order to avoid overlap and the possibility of 'carbon leakage' between schemes.

Why demand management will not go far enough and not quickly enough

Measures and proposals articulated in the discourse of demand management are best characterised as a logic of attenuation, which seek to constrain the impacts of aviation by flying less and substituting alternative forms of travel and communication for aviation where and if possible. It offers a 'strong' version of environmental modernisation in which the state regulates the market and seeks to embody the public good in its efforts to shape patterns of consumer behaviour. But ultimately, flying less or taxing aviation more does not challenge the embedded discourses of accelerated mobility and the consumption of positional goods, and our personal attachments to them. In other words, strategies of demand management still invest partially in the fantasmatic narrative of 'sustainable aviation', as they adhere to the promise of a 'balanced' resolution in which people continue to fly but can mitigate the environmental impacts of doing so. Hence, the logic of attenuation constrains demand by reducing the growth of air passenger numbers, promising to reduce the impacts of aviation on noise and air quality pollution, as well as rising carbon emissions. Yet managing demand does not put into question the acceptance of aviation as a valuable public good. On the contrary, if anything, it might further legitimise flying as an essential practice of everyday living, which is incompatible with the creation of a more sustainable world. In short, it remains attached to the politics of reform and continuity, and the limits of such strategies.

Consider, for example, the proposal of a frequent flyer tax, one of the central planks in the platform of demand management. Much has been made of the potential for political opposition to such a rise in taxation, particularly in the aftermath of the collapse of aviation during the pandemic, as well as the administrative costs of delivering a levy on frequent flyers. However, more importantly, the imposition of such a measure runs the risk of legitimising the practices of frequent flying, because in paying for the right to take additional flights frequent flyers are contributing to the public purse, while the practices of mobility and consumption are not problematised and left unchanged. At the same time, as it is often formulated, the frequent flyer tax offers consumers one return flight per year before the frequent flyer tax kicks in, so as to 'spare the large majority of travellers any extra cost' (Carmichael, 2019: 7). While such measures may well address the concerns of social justice, they also endorse flying as a positional good and run the risk of taking no account of the distance and class of such a flight, further embedding the possibility of unsustainable lifestyles dependent on international mobility (Stay Grounded, 2019a, 2021b).

In fact, we believe that such demand management measures would only change the behaviour of price-sensitive or cost-conscious consumers, while potentially shifting demand away from long-haul flights (Carmichael, 2019: 7). They would not necessarily work on 'quality conscious' consumers who might be prepared to carry the additional costs of the frequent flyer tax. So, to counter such consumer calculations, any measures of demand management would require politicians to act as exemplars, that is, by shifting their practices of flying, establishing guidelines for how revenues from frequent flyers' levy will be used and showing how scaling back on flying produces benefits in terms of health, well-being, biodiversity and employment (Carmichael, 2019).

But, most importantly, demand management strategies come up against the pressing constraints of time that we face as a society if we are to address the environmental impacts of flying in order to meet the 2015 Paris commitment to keep any rise in global temperatures to 1.5 °C. Such temporal pressures require a quick and brutal disinvestment from harmful climate change behaviours and collective choices over which practices or sectors to privilege in order to address the immediacy of climate change. Calls for demand management that lessen the growth in air passengers continue to sidestep such choices. In practice, any expansion in aviation, even if constrained, requires other sectors of the economy to take up the slack and impose deeper cuts to carbon emissions than aviation. This means that the discourse of demand management simply implies that less slack must be taken up by other sectors, so that we can continue with our addiction to flying under 'business as usual' scenarios. In other words, changes to aviation cannot be divorced from the projections of alternative futures, in which we move away from the privileging of mobility and accelerated lifestyles and the consumption of positional goods. With this in mind, we thus call for a more radical disinvestment from aviation that questions the utility of flying in a post-pandemic and sustainable world. After all, flying is a minority activity and one of the fastest growing sources of emissions, and it exhibits little prospect of reducing its dependency on kerosene in the short-term.

Post-growth aviation in the UK: a manifesto for a just green transformation

Given the limitations and uncertainties of demand management, we propose a third trajectory, which has already been prefigured by environmentalists and campaigners: post-growth aviation. We argue that with little or no prospect of a technological fix to rising carbon emissions in commercial aviation, as well as severe limits in the logic of attenuation evident in the strategies of demand management, there is little option but to plan for a *rapid contraction* of air travel if we are to meet the commitments and requirements to transition towards net zero societies. Continuing to privilege aviation over other economic and social activities is neither politically acceptable nor environmentally just. On the contrary, permitting the continued expansion of aviation simply perpetuates the embedded myths of aviation as a 'great British success story'. It also accentuates the associated environmental injustices in a world that has to break its habit of growth and hypermobility, bolstered by a 'belief that more is always better' (Stay Grounded, 2019b: 6).

We thus call for a radical transformation of commercial aviation by invoking a logic of sufficiency, which moves away from economic growth and consumption towards the stewardship of the environment (Princen, 2005). As a principle of social organisation, sufficiency recognises that in the pursuit of any activity, there reaches a point where 'there can be enough and there can be too much' (Princen, 2003: 43). It thus embeds core ideals in our decision-making, asking critical questions about: whether or not our current patterns of resource use threaten ecological integrity and social cohesion, or prevent and jeopardise future material gains; when the gratification of consumption and investment returns put into doubt economic security; and when social activities bring about an unacceptable disjuncture between internalised benefits and externalised costs (Princen, 2003: 44). In responding to such questions, the logic of sufficiency incorporates the values of frugality, moderation and prudence, embodying them in the principles of restraint, precaution, polluter-pays and reverse onus, which oblige us to show that social and environmental harms are unlikely before going ahead with any experimentation. In particular, for our analysis and normative orientation, it endorses the pre-emptive zero principle, which 'recognises that if a little of a dangerous activity is allowed, more is likely, and catastrophe is possible, even likely' (Princen, 2003: 48).

Levering such principles of sufficiency into the field of aviation compels us to consider policies and practices that reduce flying so as to lower its environmental impacts, while challenging the ideology of growth that flying and hypermobility lifestyles promote and reflect. At the very least, given the difficulties of developing alternatives to the use of kerosene for commercial aviation, it leads us to conclude that a new post-growth regime requires political leaders to accept that 'for some period, we'll all stop using aeroplanes' (UK FIRES, 2019: 1). We thus call for a divestment from commercial aviation, seeking to install a discourse of post-growth, which actively transforms existing practices of aviation, disclosing a scenario in which the use of commercial aviation is scaled back, used only for events such as humanitarian emergencies or where it is socially accepted that there is no alternative to air travel (Stay Grounded, 2021a: 3). Our five core sets of demands for the transformation of UK aviation policy and its associated attitudes towards flying are elaborated here. (We articulate a broader set of demands and measures in the concluding chapter).

Suppressing demand and ending expansionist 'go for growth' aviation policies

In the first instance, our principles and values lead us to support the introduction of demand management measures, including increased passenger taxes for frequent flyers and ending all subsidies to the aviation industry. Such proposals are starting to gain traction in various contexts. For example, the French Citizens' Convention for Climate Change proposed the introduction of an eco-tax on flights by kilometre, adding that governments should cooperate to coordinate aviation taxation policies at the European and eventually the global level (Convention Citoyenne pour le Climat, 2021: 252–62). As part of the suppression of demand, advertising of air travel would be banned, like tobacco and alcohol in some states, while industry lobbying of government and representatives would be stringently policed and frequent flyer programmes banned (Stay Grounded, 2021a).

But such measures would be delivered in tandem with a series of interventions designed to transform practices of flying. To begin with, in the UK, the national government should commit itself to a complete moratorium on airport expansion and an immediate withdrawal of the ANPS, with its expansionist endorsement of proposals for a third runway at Heathrow airport. Government should begin a new process of consultation, putting in place a citizens' convention or assembly for aviation, which builds on the work of the UK Climate Assembly, and supports the UK government and parliament in devising deliverable plans to tackle decarbonisation within aviation, plans which challenge the fantasmatic investment in rapid technological change and the promise of Jet Zero. At the end of this public deliberation, government should endeavour to gain cross-party parliamentary approval for plans for the disinvestment from commercial aviation and the planned closure of airports. Any current local planning applications for airport expansion should be refused.

Divestment

Secondly, local authorities should withdraw all investment from regional airports and work towards ending any controlling ownership of airports. Such practices run counter to the principles of sufficiency and it remains troubling that certain local authorities, which are dedicated to tackling the climate emergency, continue to invest and own shares in airport infrastructure. Equally, members of pension funds should lobby for pension fund managers to divest from investment in airports as part of their corporate responsibility. For example, the Universities Superannuation Scheme (USS), a pension scheme for university lecturers, owns 10 per cent of Heathrow Holdings Ltd, while there is local authority investment in Birmingham, East Midlands, Manchester and Stansted airports (Budd and Ison, 2021).

Ending short-haul flights and promoting alternatives

Thirdly, passenger demand should be suppressed through direct bans on short-haul flights. This would entail in the first instance a ban on all domestic flights in the UK, as well as travel by private jets and pleasure flying. Short-haul international flights would be banned where low carbon rail alternatives of below 5 hours are readily available (Stay Grounded, 2019b: 16). Such measures would compel travellers to use low carbon rail, night trains and buses, and telephone or video conferences can be used to replace face-to-face meetings, a practice that has become part of our everyday experiences as a result of the global COVID-19 pandemic. In its exemplary intervention, the French Citizens' Convention for Climate Change proposed the ending of short-haul domestic flights where a low carbon alternative was available for a journey of less than 4 hours (Convention Citoyenne pour le Climat, 2021: 255). Of course, additional state funding to enhance existing rail connections and reliability would be essential to deliver such bans, shifting existing subsidies away from aviation towards local rail services and ensuring that increased taxation on flights was transparently and publicly diverted into programmes to support the green transformation of aviation, including the phasing out of some forms of mass aviation. In the short-term, any government bailouts and financial support for aviation businesses should be attached to conditions, including the suspension of shareholder dividends, curbs on excessive executive pay and tax avoidance, and the development and implementation of green technologies and decarbonisation (NEF, 2020: 14–16).

A just transition

Fourthly, policies and measures should be developed to ensure that plans for divestment from aviation do not jeopardise the economic security of workers and communities who currently depend on the commercial aviation industry for employment (New Economics Foundation, 2020; PCS et al, 2020; Safe Landing, 2020). Post-growth needs to be accompanied by a government-funded transition support programme for workers in aviation. In the short term, UK airports should be brought back into public control, for the democratic state is better positioned than the market and dividend-driven shareholders to deliver a programme of support for workers across the industry. The transition programme should be led by a collaborative board or taskforce with representatives from unions, businesses, affected residents and airport communities, as well as national and local government, and it should cultivate practices of decision-making that enable airport workers to voice their demands for training and job creation programmes. The collaborative transition board must also oversee a 'union-negotiated limit on redundancy rates' and the 'delivery of a skills and employment strategy', which keeps workers in employment while they transition towards other jobs (with costs covered by all employers) (NEF, 2020: 3; PCS et al, 2020).

Divesting from aviation presents new economic opportunities for increasing employment in low carbon activities, such as retrofitting housing, expanding reuse and recycling in a circular economy, developing renewable energy and restoring nature and ensuring biodiversity (PCS et al, 2020: 18–25). But it also offers the opportunity to strengthen the social infrastructure, investing in the 'socially useful production' that supports the foundational economy and the work of teachers, carers and nurses upon which communities depend (PCS et al, 2020: 5, 20). More broadly, closed airport sites may well provide land for new affordable housing, particularly where airports are close to urban centres. At the same time, terminals can be converted into art centres and museums or transformed into parks, nature reserves and biodiverse habitats (Glancey, 2014).

In fact, the authors of the Green New Deal for Gatwick argue that transitioning the airport workforce towards 'green deal' employment opportunities has the potential to create directly some 16,100 jobs in the Gatwick area (compared to the existing 18,125 aviation-linked jobs prior to the pandemic) (PCS et al, 2020: 27). Of course, a green transformation of this kind requires a programme of sustained financial investment from the state, which it is estimated equates to between £287–523 million per year for 10 years. Nonetheless, in relative terms, this investment represents 'less than half', and potentially only a quarter, of 'Gatwick Airport's share of the annual tax break' awarded to the UK aviation industry in, for example, fuel duty and VAT exemptions (estimated at £1.25 billion in 2019). Equally, while the cost of such a programme is more expensive than the 12-month suspension of APD demanded by the industry to support jobs during the pandemic, transitioning the workforce would create thirteen times more jobs in and around Gatwick than those created by the suspension of APD (PCS et al, 2020: 30–1).

Of course, flying is also intrinsically linked to, and supportive of, a chain of other technological and services industries, not least the aerospace sector and the tourist industry. Hence, proposals and planning for the degrowth of aviation will need to coordinate with national governments and international organisations to fashion just transition schemes for workers in affected industries and the communities dependent upon them (de la Plaza, 2021). The rapid spread of low cost aviation has, for example, enabled the growth of a mass tourism industry, whose extractivist dynamics are often driven by narrow and exclusionary interpretations of heritage, which are usually tied to colonial narratives, neoliberal forms of infrastructure provision, the privatisation of public space, logics of gentrification and economic precarity, all of which lead to negative impacts on the local environment and climate change (Córdoba Azcárate, 2020; Hall et al, 2020). In short, the degrowth of aviation must be linked to slow tourism, where communities re-take control of local facilities and schemes in ways that promote small-scale and sustainable alternatives to the destructive travel and practices of mass tourism (Everingham and Chassagne, 2020; Manthiou et al, 2022).

Envisioning an alternative hedonism

Finally, however, flying and infrastructure are so pivotal to our current growth-oriented economies that any green transformation requires us to imagine alternative forms of hedonism, which can form part of a new eco-egalitarian and radically democratic 'common sense' (Soper, 2020). This paradigm shift should enable us to envisage and exercise different lifestyle choices, so that we can engage and invest in more enjoyable and sustainable ways of living, consuming and enjoying, which do not require the existing patterns and structures of mobility and social reproduction. In aviation, this requires the challenging of 'business as usual' trajectories, coupled with the construction and institutionalisation of alternative narratives that challenge our current addiction to accelerated mobility.

The narratives that constitute this putative hegemonic project would showcase the benefits of slow living and slow travel. They would foreground, for example, the values and benefits of localised vacations, as well as the potential enjoyments of taking the time to travel, where time spent on the journey is included in the experience of the holiday or leisure itself (UK FIRES, 2019; Stay Grounded, 2019b). In this way, the deceleration of tourism and leisure is pivotal to the development and installation of an 'alternative hedonism', which does not involve the destructiveness and one-dimensionality of industrialised and mass air travel (for the relatively small minority), nor the excesses and pathologies of global tourism. Finally, such appeals would have to go hand in hand with the production of more regionalised, 'circular economies', which aimed to reduce air freight and food miles, rebalancing uneven and exploitative spatial dynamics and inequalities.

Hence, the transformation of aviation cannot be considered within narrowly defined sectoral boundaries. Challenges to aviation must incorporate demands to transform our practices of flying within revisioned collective social imaginaries, which tackle the ideology of the free market and the privileging of growth and consumption, as well as the ways in which the latter create strong equivalences between consumption and citizenship. In the words of Soper (2020: 177), the exercise of choice as a moment of individual freedom has to be reframed as a moment of 'republican pressure for sustainable living' or 'an expression of duty and concern for the wider community and future generations'. Moreover, in creating the momentum for a new Green Republic, progressive social movements and campaigns should not only tie the critique of aviation to climate change, but also to the negative impacts of noise and air pollution on health and well-being so as to establish deep and long-term cultural, social and political change in attitudes and practices. In other words, the task is how to make aviation the 'new tobacco industry', even though this will require much ideological work and will prove difficult to achieve. The threats of carbon emissions, climate impacts and the impending destruction of natural and everyday life, provide an important impetus for change, but it is still necessary to develop strategies and tactics through which ingrained practices and habits can be overturned.

Delivering the green transformation in aviation

The pressures of time are widely recognised as a key constraint in bringing forward the eco-egalitarian and democratic transformations that we are calling for, as societies and governments battle to keep rises in global temperature to 1.5 °C or below and to reach net zero emissions by 2050 at the latest. Nonetheless, in keeping with our genealogical approach, it is important to build upon those demands against aviation expansion, which are already being voiced and mobilised. In this way, the image of a post-growth future and aviation divestment is not a utopian vision or policy. On the contrary, campaigns against airport expansion in different countries across the globe have brought together novel alliances of local residents, environmental pressure groups and direct action campaigners, as well as anti-corporate activists, trade unions, think tanks, local authorities and political parties. Such initiatives have engineered equivalences between 'traditional' demands for conservation and the regulation of noise and air pollution, alongside demands for climate change, democratic decision-making, international social justice, corporate regulation, 'slow' living and investment in social infrastructure. These interventions have also prefigured new ways of living that break with our dependency on the market and mobility, be it through the 'no fly movement', the 'flight free pledge' or the construction of alternative communities on land designated for development (as in Go Heathrow or the ZAD ('Zone to be Defended') on the proposed site for the now cancelled international airport at Notre-Dame-des-Landes to the northwest of Nantes). Anti-aviation groups and movements like these envisage a life in which flying is deemed socially unacceptable, as they prefigure and bring into being the joys and possibilities of different counter-imaginaries, which are opposed to our continued investment in 'business as usual' expansion.

Support for such anti-expansionist movements and solidarity with their international networking is and remains a vital ingredient in the articulation of a new 'common sense' in aviation. Highly visible protests, challenges in court, as well as the media communications and interventions of anti-expansionist groups and activists, are a necessary element in rebutting the continued protectionist campaigns of the aviation industry. The industry's 'greenwashing' campaigns, which peddle a vision of 'sustainable aviation' that enables us to continue to fly and protect the environment, as well as campaigns for state support and subsidies, which quickly emerged in the crisis of the pandemic, can be expected to continue as the aviation sector challenges the political will of governments to deliver post-growth policies and transformation (see, for example, the calls by the Airport Operators Association in 2021 for the relaxation of APD to ensure the 'competitiveness' of the UK aviation industry (Airport Operators Association, 2021: 10)). Indeed, in his 2021 Autumn Budget and Spending Review, Rishi Sunak unveiled plans to slash taxes on domestic flights, which was forecast to lead to a 3.5 per cent increase in passenger numbers in the UK, equivalent to an extra 400,000 extra air journeys per year.[4] Only a couple of weeks later, the UK Government announced an additional £4.3 million funding for domestic flight routes, supporting flights between London and Newquay and London and Dundee.[5]

It is thus imperative to expose the ideological and policy contradictions of these campaigns and their outcomes, as anti-expansionist movements endeavour to generate more accurate and telling sets of 'numbers' to counter the rehashing of embedded myths trumpeting the economic contribution of aviation, capacity overload and technological fixes on the horizon. As our genealogical narratives show, such myths resonate with many politicians, trade unions, voters and communities. Political leaders will need therefore to remain resolute in their stances, seeking to forge cross-party alliances and commitments to divest state subsidies from aviation. But equally, campaigners and environmentalists will need to provide ideological cover for political leaders who want to deliver change, and where necessary hold governments to account for their actions in the field, while advancing alternative measurements of societal well-being.

The current conditions and realities thus draw attention to the critical role of political leadership and representative government in bringing about transformation. Movements and activists should continue to manufacture networks within and between like-minded political parties: locally, nationally and globally. In the UK, the success of the movement against the proposed third runway at Heathrow during the New Labour government rested in part on its efforts to connect their opposition to expansion to the efforts by David Cameron to 'detoxify' the Conservative party and foreground the role of the environment and citizen well-being. However, the specific configuration of political conditions that enabled the Conservatives – the traditional party of business – to go against the interests of the aviation industry, partly made possible, paradoxically, by the dislocatory effects of the GFC and its short-term impacts, are no longer as clear-cut. As Prime Minister, Boris Johnson opposed expansion at Heathrow, but his government still retained the highly contested ANPS, which supports the expansion of Heathrow. Indeed, the Secretary of State for Transport rejected all demands to review the ANPS in a letter that was published in early September 2021, pushing back any review of the ANPS in relation to climate change and carbon policy to after the finalisation of the Government's Jet Zero strategy (DfT, 2021b: 1–2).

In the short term, the UK government and state's endorsement of the aviation industry's discourse of 'business as usual' means that a radical transformation in aviation policy and governance requires the construction of a broad progressive alliance, bringing together supportive politicians and parties, notably Labour, the Greens, Liberal Democrats and the SNP. Of course, this progressive alliance will not be easy to assemble particularly given the institutional pressures of the 'first past the post' electoral system in the UK, which favours two-party systems of the left and right, squeezing out third and minority parties. Ideologically, it is noteworthy that the growth-oriented productivism of the Labour party (Latour, 2022) has often militated against any such alliance, particularly in the field of aviation, where New Labour's 2003 ATWP envisaged the biggest expansion of airports since the Second World War.

As public intellectuals like Bruno Latour (2018: 56–8, 2022) argue, along with theorists like Jane Bennett (2009), Romand Coles (2016), William Connolly (2019), Kate Soper (2020) and others, progressive politics has too often been dogged by a binary opposition between, on the one hand, the focus on social and cultural issues, and on the other hand ecological and natural questions, hampering the development of political practices that can address the challenges of climate change in the Anthropocene. In the place of such an opposition, Latour proposes the concept of the Terrestrial as a new political actor in the Anthropocene, because 'we are no longer dealing with small fluctuations in the climate, but rather with an upheaval that is mobilising the earth system itself' (Latour, 2018: 43). The recognition of the Terrestrial as a mobilising 'attractor' for political struggles and change requires a new unprecedented politics, which goes beyond the oppositions of left and right, and the social and the ecological, so as to re-politicise the meaning of attachment or belonging to land, as prefigured, for example, in the politics of the ZAD (Latour, 2018: 53–4). In Latour's view, such politics spark new conversations, which 'get out of the impasse [of the separation of the social and the ecological] by imagining a new set of alliances: "you have never been a leftist? That doesn't matter, neither have I, but like you, I am radically Terrestrial!"' (2018: 56).

At the same time, this new politics calls for the development of what has been called an 'ecological', 'green' or 'environmental' state (Duit et al, 2016), though this demand carries risks. On the one hand, if we are to manage the dislocations of a green and just transformation in the field of aviation, it is not possible to 'go around' or 'do without' the coordinative and regulatory administrative resources of the state (Eckersley, 2021: 248). Collective action and the mechanisms of environmental governance are entangled with practices of state legitimation and regulation at multiple scales, whether local, national or global, so that to bypass the apparatus of the state is to fail to understand that in tackling the challenges of sustainability, 'it is not just that states actually wield power, but also that they are understood to embody legitimate authority' (Duit et al, 2016: 3). On the other hand, however, as our genealogical narratives have demonstrated, the existing apparatus of the state and its sponsorship of the logics of production and growth are incompatible with meaningful green transformation: the key ministries and departments of state are generally locked into the sedimented logics of production and growth. As our genealogical narratives of the aviation sector have demonstrated in the UK since the end of the Second World War, the DfT has developed and repeated numerous technologies and techniques of government to enable the growth of aviation, while trying to depoliticise its unsustainable impacts and practices.

A radically democratic project of green transformation thus requires the design and construction of a 'green state', which acts as an 'ecological steward and facilitator of transboundary democracy rather than a selfish actor jealously protecting its territory and ignoring or discounting the needs of foreign lands' (Eckersley, 2004: 3). Decisions about investment, production and consumption cannot continue to be consigned to the private realm or to the vagaries of the market, where the logics of privatisation tend (at least initially) to depoliticise decision-making and disregard the embedded logics of productivism, which constrain choices and transfer costs onto marginal groups (Eckersley, 2004). On the contrary, they should be brought back into the public domain, that is, they must be subject to the outcome of a broad and meaningful process of political representation and dialogue, which allows contestation and challenge.

But, more concretely, and most importantly, the direction of public policy and decision-making must be grounded in the principles and logic of sufficiency, which are articulated within wider struggles for radical democracy. The project of radical democracy, for its part, involves the articulation and extension of the values of freedom, equality and solidarity to ever-increasing spaces and sets of social relations, and is predicated on the linking together of a plurality of democratic and popular demands governed by the principle of democratic equivalence. Finally, following Connolly (1995), Norval (2007) and Mouffe (2013), it also involves the fostering of an ethos of agonistic respect and critical responsiveness among diverse and sometimes opposed communities and identities (Howarth and Roussos, 2022) – an ethos that is crucial to the politics of transformation and the reproduction of everyday alliances.

Conclusion

This chapter has sketched out a manifesto for the green transformation of aviation, setting out our demands and the radical strategies of eco-egalitarian and radical democratic transformation, which we believe must be supported by the actions of individuals across different institutional and organisational arenas throughout society. The global pandemic has brought home to many the benefits of 'slow' living and the possibilities of innovative practices of work and leisure, from empty and quiet skies to cycling, walking and staycations. As the skies are regrettably filled again with aircraft, noise and polluting contrails, such practices must not be discarded or forgotten, but translated into a new 'common sense'. Individuals must act as exemplars to others, committing themselves to 'no flying' pledges, while challenging practices of intensive mobility too.

Alongside a host of citizen actions and democratic interventions in the public sphere, they must also engage as activist consumers, using their spending power to lobby and push for change in companies and corporations, and by moving away from everyday practices of intensive consumption. Hence, individuals can exercise their voice in the workplace to transform organisational commitments to sustainability. In universities, for example, individuals can lead the development of sustainable research policies by restricting travel to international conferences and changing modes of travel for fieldwork; encouraging online and virtual interactions; and changing the nature of teaching, examining and conversing. And finally, as Soper (2020) urges, individuals can vote strategically for those political parties that offer the opportunity to bring about the green transformation we require in aviation and other sectors. As citizens, we can put pressure on local and national political leaders and parties at the ballot box, and by using other combinations of voice and exit, demand that they deliver the required radical green change in aviation and society as a whole.

Conclusion: Staying grounded

'Staying grounded' captures one of the central concerns of this book: our critique and evaluation of the dominant discourses of airport expansion in the UK and across the globe, where the growth of the aviation industry, despite its accelerating contribution to rising carbon emissions, is universally supported and promoted by most governments and states. Our book has investigated the efforts by the UK state, the aviation industry and public authorities to sponsor the industry over many decades, often in the face of hostile protests and political campaigning, and lodged in this genealogical investigation is a quest to articulate and refine our normative alternatives to 'binge flying'. But 'staying grounded' also alludes to our preferred approach in exploring these issues, as we have sought to analyse our objects of study by assembling detailed genealogies of the ways governments, parties and politicians, public authorities (including local councils), departments of state, the aviation industry, environmental groups, campaigners and citizens have problematised, argued about and fiercely contested *where*, *when* and *if* airport expansion should occur in any conjuncture.

For more than 25 years, we have adopted and developed a 'slow' approach in this research, benefitting from a longitudinal study that has gathered and interpreted the 'common sense' of actors expressed in this complex policy field (Almond and Connolly, 2020: 69). At times, we have also hovered above the fray at varying altitudes, seeking to show the various connections and differences between the multiple strands of the seven main problematisations of the UK airports issue since 1945, as well as the continuities and discontinuities in its evolution. This perspective has enabled us to deconstruct the dominant myths, narratives and fantasies underpinning the vicissitudes of UK aviation policy, and to propose alternative pathways and futures.

Our book has shown that the case of UK airport politics and policy, especially the future of Heathrow, is what John McDonnell calls an 'iconic, totemic battleground of climate change' (Johnson, 2018). It also illuminates a number of pressing issues in the present, including the role of government and their different technologies and techniques in addressing the dilemmas of large infrastructure projects, the paradoxes of depoliticisation, the role of courts and judicial review, the dialectics of protest, campaigning and policymaking, and the future trajectories and possibilities of new ways of travelling, working and enjoying. Put succinctly, we argue that the creation and implementation of plans and intended policies of airport development and aviation expansion have run up against the fundamental problem of politics.

Our core argument is that the political costs of expansion, the inability of government and/or the industry to forge an efficient and stable political will, the uncertain dynamics of electoral and party politics and a changing and unpredictable external environment marked by the logics of privatisation and deregulation, coupled with the persistent opposition of campaigners, has generally resulted in policy delay, failure and reversal. Such costs have been substantially increased as the issue of carbon emissions and climate change has been added to the traditional suite of environmental disbenefits associated with airport expansion, namely noise, air quality, the impact of surface transport facilities, the destruction of houses and property, and the disruption of everyday life. And the issue has been exacerbated by the peculiar path dependency of Heathrow airport, and the desire of key stakeholders, especially airlines, governments and airport operators, to expand an airport that, with the gift of hindsight, was located precisely to magnify its 'public bads' to use Aldrich's terms.[1]

Put more fully, in their endeavours to resolve the issues and engineer workable solutions, governments of various hues have devised and used a series of different technologies and techniques. Yet, while their recourse to governmental technologies like public inquiries, expert Commissions and national public consultations have invariably delivered the pro-expansion proposals and recommendations they wanted to hear, governments have still been unable to implement their policies and plans. Indeed, their failures have often required supplementary devices and mechanisms, such as rhetorical redescriptions, the production of fantasmatic images and narratives, and a range of ideological concealments to try and bring about airport construction and expansion.

Our concluding chapter reiterates some of our core arguments and explores the implications of this exemplary case for a wider set of social and political issues. We begin by reflecting upon the power of numbers and the logic of quantification before exploring the relationships between different technologies of government and depoliticisation. We then set out the implications of our cases for the role of legal institutions and spaces in the structuring of policy and campaigning, before focusing more closely on the dilemmas and opportunities of political campaigning against expansions. Our focus then turns to the crucial dimension of politics in our story, where we examine the role of party politics, government and the state, as well as campaigners and social movements, in shaping airports policy, and the implications of our arguments and conclusions for democratic decision-making. In particular, we analyse the linkages between political costs and the creation and exercise of political will, showing that this factor played a crucial part in the explanation of airports policy and the development of the aviation policy regime. We conclude by restating our demands for the transformation of aviation policy, which stem from the normative orientation that we outline.

The grip of numbers and the logic of quantification

In vital respects, our genealogy of aviation is a story of numbers and the increasing role of quantification in policy-making. We show how the technique of forecasting – embodying the social logic of 'predict and provide' – inscribed into the decision-making process a wealth of categories, economic models, statistical techniques and variables, which were used to create, normalise and sediment expectations of ever-increasing passenger numbers and expanding transport infrastructure. In turn, it determined the boundaries of the formal terrain upon which the competing arguments about aviation policy were conducted, as the rhetoric of government was suffused with a battery of graphs, tables and diagrams of future estimates of passenger numbers, noise contours, load factors and route assessments, or the economic benefits of expansion and more recently predictions of carbon emissions from UK flights. Somewhat paradoxically, the present was submerged under the weight of the future, as projections of the 'inevitable' rising numbers of passengers contributed to the displacement of demands for the regulation of the noise and environmental costs of flying.

Our research demonstrates that the work of numbers promised to bring about the depoliticisation of airport expansion in the UK, and still does so, as forecasting has naturalised the continued growth of aviation and the need to meet that demand. Rhetorically, it negated contestation, confining the politics of airport expansion to the realm of expertise and value-free scientific calculation and data. Particular techniques of quantification, such as CBA, conveyed the promise of comparison between multidimensional and complex site locations, seeking to remove the shadow of politics by simplifying such decisions into a 'straightforward' judgement based on numbers. In practice, these techniques of data generation also installed the DfT as a nodal actor, excluding all but the most knowledgeable and powerful 'numerate and calculating' citizens (Rose, 1991: 691), who possessed the resources to generate novel forms of counter-expertise. Local knowledge and the experiences of residents were sidelined as 'soft data', which were deemed unable to grasp the 'reality' of technological improvements to aircraft noise and flight movements. Politically, this dismissal of local knowledge served to transform opposition to expansion from a challenge to the dominant logics of quantification into a broader lack of trust in government, as well as grievances and demands over the absence of impartial information. Even when opponents to expansion possessed the counter-expertise to challenge the forecasts of government, which they often did, direct challenge was often constrained by the failure of the DfT or short-term Commissions to 'show their workings' and engage with citizen experts. In short, the production of forecasts was often cloaked in complex assemblages of seemingly fixed, yet ultimately contingent assumptions.

Indeed, as our genealogy of airport expansion demonstrates, numbers do not speak for themselves. Quantification and its political work implies a plurality of other social practices, including categorisation, measurement, aggregation and reification (see Rose, 1991; Porter 1995; Espeland and Stevens, 2008; Stone, 2021). So, in keeping with our approach to discourse, we thus underline how the political work of numbers owes much to the *articulatory practices* of categorisation, for such actions and decisions partly determine *what* counts (and what does not), precisely *how* they count and indeed *whether or not* certain things should be counted in numbers at all. The logic of equivalence is also important here: numbers allow things to be compared and rendered commensurate, even if they are qualitatively different. At the same time, categories reflect (even if unconsciously) the underlying assumptions of decision-makers and their interpretive schemas, coordinating actions across various policy arenas.

In the field of aviation, complex and contestable categories were devised, such as passenger demand, which itself was broken down into leisure and business travel, short-haul and long-haul flights, and different market segments and groupings, all of which depended upon and partly constituted sets of assumptions about economic growth, ticket prices, fuel costs and changes within the industry itself. Such categories were also an integral part of the constitution and reconstitution of the hegemonic discourses of mobility, market competition, the national interest and social progress. Finally, it is important to stress that categorisation cannot be separated from values and the attribution of values, or what the state claims it values and what it does not. In the field of aviation, practices of categorisation were tied to the values embedded in the post-war policies of the state sponsorship of aviation, so that the logics of categorisation, measurement, aggregation and the reification of numbers served to materialise these perceived goods and their commitments.

In the seven problematisations we have analysed in this book, 'headline' predictions of rising passenger numbers and the economic benefits of aviation were generally highlighted and weaponised as elements of the fantasmatic narratives of 'capacity overload', longer delays at airports, threats to – and rising costs of – annual holidays, not to mention the loss of jobs and economic growth. In different combinations, they were employed to try and depoliticise airport expansion, and to legitimise policy narratives in which expansion was portrayed as a necessary response to inevitable pressures on demand and the means of protecting economic benefit. Forecasts were thus reiterated by differently positioned actors in multiple policy arenas, where each repetition mobilised their particular reputational resources in the endorsement of the underlying scientific models. Predictions of expansion thereby assumed a life of their own as they migrated from their originators, acquiring greater weight and solidity.

Yet the limits of the logics of quantification and the rhetorical appeal of numbers were also tangible. The dissemination of forecasts opened up possibilities for politicisation or repoliticisation, even translating into moments of hyper-politicisation, as local residents and campaigners collected and presented alternative 'numbers' that exposed the failed logic of government policy. Engaging in myriad forms of 'statactivism' (Bruno et al, 2014), campaigners exploited public inquiries to present rival readings of rising demand, capacity limits, or the economic benefits of aviation. Indeed, as the logic of quantification spread into environmental and climate change policy through, for example, the carbon budgets of the CCC, campaigners were able to harness these alternative modes of counter-expertise to challenge the legitimacy and justification of aviation forecasts; one institution of the state was thereby brought into conflict with another, re-politicising airport expansion and exposing the internal struggles within the state. Of course, such strategies of politicisation were hampered by the exclusionary dynamics of the logics of quantification, not least the availability of the necessary resources to measure and aggregate data.

In fact, confirming and developing what Feldman and Milch (1982) discovered more than 40 years ago, forecasts remained consistently inaccurate, largely because they were based on questionable assumptions that over-inflated the rate of growth in passenger demand, while fears of capacity overload did not materialise when anticipated, as economic recessions weakened aviation markets in different periods. In addition, when the numbers did not add up, it was noticeable that government disregarded them, elevating instead the role of judgement and the duty of government to decide the public interest. Again, the appeal of objective numbers and their potential to depoliticise aviation cannot be divorced from the hegemonic discourses lodged in the core institutions of the British state and civil society which constructed aviation as a necessary public good. Nonetheless, such hegemonic discourses were increasingly challenged as demands to counter the environmental impacts of aviation were progressively voiced from the 1960s onwards. In the face of such challenges, the British state resorted to various technologies of government as it sought to ward off political contestation and opposition to expansion.

The arguments and empirical evidence for the complex politics of quantification presented in this book enable us to extend and develop Marx's theoretical insights about the role of commodities and money into our understanding of numbers, measurement and quantification, as well as the logic of reification (Marx, 1973). Using Marx's conceptual infrastructure, numbers are 'real abstractions', which despite their apparently formal and universal qualities do not preclude their role in shaping political decisions and public policy-making (Sohn-Rethel, 1978). Like money, numbers are ideal elements that facilitate various social practices of measurement, forecasting, comparison and commensuration. Indeed, just as Marx spoke about the fetishisation of commodities, which inverts the agency of human beings vis-à-vis the things they buy and sell in capitalist social relations – subject and object – so we can talk about the fetishisation of numbers in our increasingly digital and corporate universes (Gudeman, 1998; Wood, 2021). Numbers are not just instruments that social actors employ to analyse, assess and decide. On the contrary, they often actively shape the very actors and systems within which they function and are deployed, often imbued with a power, potency and agency of their own (Marx, 1976). Hence, as our research shows, in certain conditions numbers are fetishised and reified: they are turned into or acquire the status of things endowed with mysterious powers to shape perceptions and thinking, influencing and determining decisions. In short, numbers alter behaviour and practice, though they also at times require the supplemental role of judgement and will (Horkheimer and Adorno, 2002).

Politicisation, depoliticisation and the technologies of government

In our problematisations of UK aviation, we have defined technologies of government as those particular bundles of concrete techniques or policy instruments, which are deployed by governments to engineer policy agreements among affected parties and communities. From our perspective, governments employ such technologies in order to try and secure political consensus by tackling potential opposition to decisions, thus rendering a controversial issue more 'governable' or tractable. The genealogies of these problematisations disclose that technologies like public inquiries, expert Commissions and national consultations are intrinsic components of the practices of hegemonic politics and statecraft, where their purpose is often to conceal or displace conflict to the margins of a policy arena, constructing a contingent settlement as a necessary 'common sense'.

More fully, our genealogies have described how successive governments have installed and utilised such technologies mainly to manage or defuse opposition to airport expansion. Our evidence suggests that they were designed and rolled out to transfer the issue of airport expansion into quasi-judicial or deliberative spaces, so as to constrain and orchestrate the voice of local residents and campaigners. In such spaces, much was made of the personal reputational power of individual chairs or inspectors, while rules of engagement and deliberations were tightly framed, notably through the constraints of government-determined terms of reference or planning legislation. In turn, such spaces privileged rational methods of inquiry, marginalising local knowledge, while reproducing dominant modes of discourse, which privileged calculative reasoning and quantification.

Ultimately, our studies affirm that governments consistently endeavoured to monopolise the definition of the public interest, as it pursued a logic of difference that sought to incorporate and depoliticise protesters and their demands, often via the rhetoric of 'balance' and 'reasonableness', within the confines of expansionist policies. This is clearly illustrated with respect to the core issue of noise and the work of the AC. Its chair, Howard Davies, identified aircraft noise as the major obstacle in securing the consent of local residents and adjacent airport communities, presenting campaigners with an acute dilemma: should they engage with the Commission to advance their demands on aircraft noise pollution, but risk the possibility of legitimising a process, which they believed would ultimately lead to the recommendation of a third runway? In this way, the dangers presented by the logic of difference created tensions and fragmentations within the coalition against the proposed runway infrastructure. In HACAN's self-interpretations – one of the main local resident groups opposed to expansion at Heathrow – their engagement with the AC delivered 'ground-breaking noise recommendations'. But HACAN's strategy of separating the fight against noise from the fight against a proposed new runway was to taint its legitimacy within the broader coalition and lead to a rupture with fellow campaign organisations (Stewart, 2021: 18–28).

In many respects, technologies of government count as some of the key mechanisms and conditions through which governments and states seek to depoliticise, engineer differences and strike compromises in order to resolve policy dilemmas. Yet the eventual outcomes are often mixed. For one thing, our analysis underlines how such strategies of depoliticisation rest on the selection of particular venues within which issues are to be debated and settlements thrashed out. The recourse to an expert Commission or public inquiry brings a specific set of spatial and temporal logics into the field of aviation policy. In other words, as Riker (1986, 1996) argues in his discussion of the art of strategic manipulation, venue selection – the determination of the arena or setting in which policy controversies are debated – shapes access to decision-making and formulates specific rules of engagement and deliberation (Fouilleux and Jobert, 2017): different venues privilege particular rhetorical strategies, repertoires and performances. Technologies of government thus facilitate a series of rhetorical and argumentative strategies of depoliticisation, whether this involves the invention of fantasmatic narratives of capacity overload, the rhetorical redescription of noise as an issue of trust and information, the appeal to expertise and scientific method, or the decoupling of demands to address climate change from demands to halt airport expansion.

Viewed through this prism, our analysis of these technologies proffers novel insights into depoliticisation and post-politics. Indeed, it is tempting to read the story of airport expansion as yet further evidence that the logic of depoliticisation is a form of political statecraft, which is synonymous with the post-political market and technocratic-managerial orientations of neoliberal consumerism (Swyngedouw, 2014). In keeping with such arguments, the marketisation and deregulation of aviation is intimately associated with the reproduction of the ideological tenets of neoliberalisation, while flying is itself central to the mobility of people and goods inherent to late or advanced capitalism. More precisely, seen through such a depoliticising and post-political lens, our genealogy of airport expansion underlines how political power has been relocated to arenas where corporate interests dominate and decision-making is increasingly delegated to markets, consumer decisions and expert agencies or regulatory institutions. The Planning and Climate Change Acts (2008), as well as the AC, bear witness to such developments.

However, while it is tempting to endorse such interpretations, we shy away from attaching practices of depoliticisation to any particular mode of capitalism or periodisation. Alongside Blühdorn (2014: 149; see also Beveridge and Koch, 2017), we challenge the tendency to impose subsumptive narratives, which presume over-simplified accounts of the movement of policymaking from political and politicising domains towards depoliticised and post-political spaces. First, we view depoliticisation as a core dimension of any form of politics and hegemonic struggle. Since the late 1940s, as the struggles over the location of London's mythical third airport, or the battles surrounding the expansions at Heathrow, Manchester and Stansted attest, the British state has persistently sought to depoliticise the issue of aviation expansion, rolling out different technologies of government and rhetorical strategies of depoliticisation. Secondly, our analysis foregrounds the complex *interplay* between politicisation and depoliticisation in the struggle for policy hegemony in the aviation policy sector. On the one hand, our genealogies reveal that policymaking in aviation has been marked by successive bouts or episodes of politicisation, depoliticisation and repoliticisation. Expert Commissions in particular have, as Offe notes (1984: 113), provided temporary moments of unstable depoliticisation or 'phoney wars', which quickly break down on the publication of final reports or recommendations. But, on the other hand, even this cyclical understanding of depoliticisation and politicisation fails to grasp the continual and complex intertwining of practices of politicisation and depoliticisation in aviation. Both ministers and campaigners roved between or combined together multiple strategies of politicisation and depoliticisation, moving from issue to issue and from demand to demand, as they constructed a mobile set of storylines to advance their causes, particularly during moments of hyper-politicisation and crisis (Kettell and Kerr, 2022).

This dialectic is amply demonstrated in the AC's endeavours to deal with the thorny issue of noise. The depoliticisation of noise arose first because of its intense politicisation by citizens and campaigners. Paradoxically, of course, for Davies to try and depoliticise noise through the appeal to expertise, information and proposals to construct mediating institutions (like ICCAN), it first had to be re-politicised and thus rendered more visible. So the very endeavour to depoliticise required *more* politicisation on behalf of government and its agents, which then opened up further possibilities for contestation and challenge by local residents and campaigners opposed to expansion. More generally, the spaces constituted by different technologies of government, as well as their attendant rhetorical strategies, were rapidly politicised, as campaigners and local residents manoeuvred and intervened to create arenas of resistance. In so doing, they provoked a dialogue with alternative forms of knowledge, and engaged in practices of statactivism, which enabled them to change existing rules of engagement. But, most notably, employing their own heresthetical manoeuvres, campaigners endeavoured to politicise airport expansion by exploiting alternative arenas and different audiences, especially targeting politicians and the party political arena, the media and the courts through legal challenges to airport expansion. It is to the latter that we now turn.

The politics of law and judicial review

Aviation policy and the contestations of airport expansion in the UK, and other countries in varying degrees, have been encroached upon by a growing judicialisation of politics and policymaking (Hirschl, 2011). However, the increasing use of the courts to resolve moral issues, define the common good, or settle policy disputes is controversial and remains disputed (see for example Bellamy, 2007). On the one hand, it can be read as yet further evidence of the depoliticisation of decision-making and the capacity of the law, or rather judges, to act as a shield for politicians, taking issues out of the political domain and wrapping them in the legitimacy of independent and neutral legal expertise. But, on the other hand, as our genealogies testify, law and judicial review are increasingly seen by climate change activists and campaigners as a means of holding governments to account for their national and international climate change commitments (Walls, 2018; Balounová, 2021; Setzer and Higham, 2021). What is certain, as Marshall (2021) has argued, is that the last decade and a half has brought new planning duties and climate change commitments, which were in certain respects put in place to decontest climate change and constrain participation (though they were also the result of successful campaigning and lobbying). Yet, they have been skilfully repurposed through judicial review to deliver the opposite: the repoliticisation of aviation and a halt to government plans for airport expansion.

Legal interventions and the use of the courts thus punctuate our genealogy of UK airport policy and politics, notably in the campaign against Heathrow expansion. In October 2001, eight local residents won a landmark case against night flights when the European Court of Human Rights ruled that a good night's sleep was a human right (Brown, 2001). Some 10 years later, in March 2010, in a case brought by a coalition of six local authorities, Greenpeace and the Campaign to Protect Rural England, the High Court ruled that the decision to give the go-ahead for a third runway at Heathrow in January 2009 took insufficient account of the government's changing climate change policy commitments since the ATWP (2003), particularly the demands of the Planning and Climate Change Acts (2008).[2] Moreover, some 10 years later, in February 2020, the Court of Appeal ruled that plans for expansion were unlawful because the government had given insufficient consideration in the 2018 ANPS to its climate change commitments, which they had agreed to in the 2015 Paris Agreement. In the run-up to this judgement, the impact of Heathrow expansion on air quality had also become ensnared in the highly publicised court cases by ClientEarth against the failings of the government's plans to tackle air pollution. By 2018, these cases had delivered three successful rulings against the government's air pollution strategy, exposing the contradictions between government plans for airport expansion and its commitment to improve air quality (ClientEarth, 2018).

The recourse to judicial review thus opens up opportunities for resistance by expanding audiences and switching political debates into new venues, where the contradictions and inconsistencies of policy can be articulated. The grounds for review often rest on procedural arguments, rather than the substance of policy. For example, the judicial review of the ANPS in 2020 came to focus on the Secretary of State's compliance with Sections 5 and 10 of the Planning Act (2008), rather than the contradictions of airport expansion and the third runway at Heathrow with the carbon budgets of the CCC. Nonetheless, once underway, legal debates in courts often move beyond procedural arguments, so that complex debates about the legality or irrationality of the actions and decisions of government can ultimately spill over into the policy domain, bringing into play broader questions about the direction of policy (though the grounds on which permission to appeal are granted are notoriously difficult to secure). At the same time, the staged practices of judicial review – its legal rhetoric, performance and theatrical rituals – cannot escape the logic of adversarial argument and contestation, pitching teams of lawyers against one another under the glare of the media – a dramaturgy that contrasts with the therapeutic deliberations of consultation. And, ultimately, in their delivering of a judgement, judges are once again obliged to set out their interpretation of the law, exposing the argumentation of government to challenge.

Yet, in many ways, it makes little sense to talk of *the* 'space' of judicial review, as its logics cannot be confined to the narrow domain of the law court. Judgements and debates are rapidly harnessed and taken into other venues, as daily press releases, briefings and media reports rapidly circulate between various groups across different policy domains. Publications of rulings and the statements of judges are thus moments of hyper-politicisation, channelling political attention, while offering up opportunities to articulate alternative framings and policy narratives. When the High Court announced its ruling in March 2010, both campaigners and the DfT claimed 'victory', while Lord Justice Carnwath in his judgement declared that he was 'unable wholly to support the position taken by either party', though he went on to argue that the ruling of the court did not 'amount to a "show stopper"' for the proposed third runway – over time he was to be proved right (Bowcott et al, 2010).

The truth of the matter is that rulings in one court can be overturned in another. The ruling of the European Court of Human Rights on night flights in October 2001 was thus reversed in July 2003 on the appeal of the British government (Brown, 2003). Equally, after the Johnson government declined to contest the Court of Appeal ruling in February 2020, HAL pursued the case, having been granted the right to appeal and challenge the ruling in the Supreme Court. The Supreme Court subsequently overturned the decision of the Court of Appeal in December 2020, reinstating the 2018 ANPS on the grounds that it judged that the Secretary of State had adequately taken into account the government's climate change commitments under the CCA and that the decision not to give further weight to the 2015 Paris Agreement was not 'irrational'. Seen in these terms, it is tempting to reduce judicial review to little more than a strategy of obstruction and delay, a last-ditch effort by campaigners to snarl government policy up in further rounds of scrutiny when other avenues of opposition have ultimately failed to prevent expansion.

Moreover, as a strategy for campaigners, judicial review is not without its costs. For one thing, it requires a specific form of legal and planning expertise, which is often beyond local campaigning groups and has to be bought in, potentially at significant cost. The first hurdle is the right to go to appeal, which may not be granted. In 2011, after the successful ruling against Heathrow expansion in March 2010, campaigners at Bristol were refused permission in the High Court to challenge the decision of North Somerset District Council to approve the expansion of Bristol Airport. The court ruled on this occasion that officers were right to advise councillors that climate change 'was not a material consideration' to be taken into account in any planning decision on expansion and that they were 'bound' by the policies of the expansionist ATWP (2003) (BBC, 2011). Secondly, the grounds for judicial review do not directly challenge the 'merits' of any government decision. They are often limited to accusations of procedural failings, be it unfair processes of decision-making, or the failure of government to comply with duties or parliamentary statutes. Even successful reviews that deliver judgments that result in 'quashing orders', which demand that the government retake decisions, do not prevent the government from reaching the same conclusions again. Finally, there is the risk that the campaigning organisations, local authorities, or individuals that called for review end up paying the financial costs of large global companies or developers. In October 2021, Uttlesford District Council's application for a statutory planning review of proposals to expand Stansted Airport was rejected as 'unarguable' by a High Court judge, leaving the council to add further costs of £60,000 to a legal bill totalling close to £2 million – costs that would have to be paid in part to the ten metropolitan borough authorities, which in the alleged interests of their local residents have heavily invested in the MAG, and thus own and operate Manchester, Stansted and East Midlands airports (Corr, 2021).

But delay is not necessarily a negative outcome for campaigners. In delaying a decision, the rationales for the existing policy settlement, as well as the constellation of forces behind them, can become vulnerable to changing political fortunes and public moods, as well as events and economic and social crises. New governments can be elected with different policy platforms. If nothing else, then, political will and timetables can be dented or weakened by legal requirements to rerun consultations or rework evidence, while political costs can be recouped as judicial review minimises the reputational damage of withdrawal or the kicking of a decision into the long grass. For instance, after winning a majority to govern in the general election of December 2019, and with Brexit dominating the political agenda, Boris Johnson, who had opposed Heathrow expansion as Mayor of London, was quick to let it be known that his government would not challenge the Court of Appeal's decision in February 2020. He later refused to back the third runway after the ruling of the Supreme Court in December 2020 had reinstated the ANPS (Paton, 2020). Judicial review thus produces political uncertainty, or at least moments of delay and unpredictability.

For campaigners, such undecidability has itself to be channelled and acted upon, so that the politics of judicial review can be incorporated into a hegemonic strategy that proposes or generates an alternative pathway, or perhaps offers ideological cover to a government. It may also enable the inducement of a shift in the public mood that will not be ignored by judges and the public alike. But without their incorporation into wider hegemonic strategies, the practices and processes of judicial review do risk becoming simply a delaying tactic, and thus vulnerable to being overturned by another round of judges in a higher court. Indeed, over time, the weight of political pressures can sometimes come to bear on judges, with evidence suggesting that increasingly vocal and public criticisms of the courts by government ministers and party leaders is connected to the diminishing success of legal challenges to government (Siddique, 2022).

Overall, then, legal spaces such as the courts and the practices of judicial review, constitute sites of political contestation, even though they are still constrained by dominant structures and relations, and the broader balance of forces in society. Indeed, despite having to endure severe psychological, financial and personal costs, campaigners can even use criminal trials, which arise from the coercive use of the law by the state to punish and constrain protest, as strategic arenas to publicise and advance their cause (Doherty and Hayes, 2015). Seen from the perspective of political practices and public policy, the more pragmatic tasks of advancing political struggles and demands requires action in the here and now, and so actors and groups must decide whether or not to engage with the existing institutions and arrangements as best they can. Of course, it is our task as analysts to evaluate such decisions and to assess the ways in which legal spaces and practices affect struggles, as well as their role in resolving pressing policy controversies.

More generally, our conclusion is that the turn to the courts and legal proceedings should be seen as part and parcel of ongoing and wider hegemonic struggles, and best viewed as heterogeneous and relational *sites of struggle*, though always constrained and shaped, as we have acknowledged, by the dominant structures and the overall balances of forces in society. It might be the case that their use is mainly defensive, but it is also possible that the turn to the legal sphere may also be offensive, if and when connected to other struggles and demands. Our evidence shows that the practice of judicial review serves in many cases to re-politicise issues through the repetition and publicising of adversarial rhetoric, modes of argumentation and performances of counter-expertise, down to the demand on judges to make a public statement of their conclusions. Such evaluations also have to take account of the increasing juridification of social and political life, and the critical role of courts and human rights at different levels of the political system (Blichner and Molander, 2005). With these reflections in mind, we turn to a more detailed consideration of the dilemmas and strategies of campaigning that arose in our specific case.

Campaigning, dilemmas and hegemony

Our analysis of the interplay between politicisation and depoliticisation highlights questions of political agency and challenge, as campaigners have skilfully exploited the systematic attempts by government to depoliticise aviation and push it beyond the realms of politics. With each new technology of government they have rendered the rules of decision-making open to anti-expansion forces, politicising airports policy and aviation. In other words, attempts by government to depoliticise aviation have consistently met with rival strategies to *re*-politicise issues and events. Hence, opposition groups have been able to exploit and re-politicise the technologies, arenas and policy instruments, which governments have engineered in their efforts to take aviation expansion out of the political domain. Indeed, we have charted an array of strategies of politicisation, stretching from different modes of statactivism, to the creation of equivalences between struggles against airport expansion and climate change, as well as shifting political attention and strategies to different arenas, and thus expanding their potential audiences, especially with respect to the media and legal systems.

This repertoire of strategies and tactics continues to be enriched and deployed at struggles against planned expansion, whether it be at Gatwick, Heathrow, Stansted, Bristol, Leeds Bradford, Luton, Manston or Southampton. At Southampton, for example, AXO (Airport eXpansion Opposition), the local anti-expansion campaign group, has explicitly drawn equivalences between the struggles against noise and air pollution, as well as climate change, in its fight to stop the proposed runway extension, as part of a 'myth busting' strategy that exposes the holes in the case for expansion. At Bristol, despite the decision of the Planning Inspectorate in February 2022 to rule in support of expansion, the campaign of SBAEx (Stop Bristol Airport Expansion) pursued legal challenges to expansion, arguing that the decision was based on legislation that is no longer in line with national climate change commitments, goes against local democracy, and undercuts local and regional policies to improve public health and address climate change. Its demands against expansion include a ban on night flights, a Citizen's Charter for Bristol Airport, and full transparency over the 'permitted development' rights that free the airport from a number of planning regulations. Moreover, as our research shows, such campaigns and actions are not without success. In early 2022, the campaign of GALBA (Group for Action on Leeds Bradford Airport) effectively pressurised the airport to revise its commitment to expansion, with the Chief Executive of Leeds Bradford Airport announcing on 10 March 2022 that it had removed its planning application (although as GALBA acknowledged, the airport believed that it could expand flights without planning).[3]

But what are the limits of this style of politics? To begin with, different technologies of government brought campaigners face to face with novel sets of dilemmas, including how to strike a balance between the interests of residents concerned about noise pollution and the participation of their campaigns in wider coalitions against climate change and for environmental justice. Furthermore, such tensions spill over into debates about the merits of pursuing what some have problematically termed NIMBY-led particularistic campaigns to prevent 'local' airport expansions vis-à-vis the more universal and collective strategy of working to block airport expansion at all airports across the UK. Indeed, such problems were clearly heightened by the AC and the decision as to whether to engage or not with the work of Howard Davies and his fellow Commissioners. As we have noted, the Commission's approach to the amelioration of noise and the mitigation of other issues, including night flights and compensation, as well as its consideration of the advantages of London airports, provoked splits and ruptures between campaigners at Heathrow and Gatwick, and between local campaign groups in and around Heathrow. But it must also be said that at other times the technologies of government provided new opportunities for campaigners. For example, the decision of the Labour government to convene a national consultation on airport policy in the early 2000s enabled campaigners to bring together a national coalition against proposed expansions, although this alliance still had to be constituted and maintained by activists, and required the generation of new strategies and tactics in order to hold together the multiple demands, actions and interests of different groups and organisations.

In fact, as our genealogical inquiry brings to light, the campaigns against airport expansion are best conceptualised as a politics of persistence and obstruction that challenged plans for growth, not least by delaying the decision to expand Heathrow. But, for all their innovation and doggedness, the fantasmatic narrative of aviation as a 'public good' remains hegemonic in government circles and indeed across much of society, thus disclosing the limits of a pure politics of obstructionism. For one thing, hegemonic battles take place in and across multiple spheres – not only within the policy and institutional domains, but also in the broader cultural and societal sphere. At the same time, the struggle for hegemony ought not to rely solely on a strategy of resistance and political negation, but should also seek to articulate and disseminate a credible policy alternative, which is rooted ideally in different lifestyles, which can counter the demands for more aviation and runways.

Against this background, political opposition and social action, no matter how concerted and sustained, which lacks a credible and viable vision of the future, has its limitations. At key moments in the genealogy of airport expansion, when aviation expansion was challenged by political parties, most notably in 2010 when the Conservative-Liberal Democrat government imposed a moratorium on airport expansion in South East England, the fact that the anti-expansion movement could *not* construct a feasible alternative to the hegemonic discourse of a neo-liberalised aviation and tourist industry meant that the Cameron government, and particularly ministers in charge of the DfT, were left with little or no ideological cover to embed its newfound commitment to the environment.

The result was that the growing demands, and even expectation, for high-speed rail to replace short-haul flights, or for a more efficient and spatially fair use of existing airport capacity, not to mention a serious consideration of appropriate aviation fuel taxes, were soon dissipated. In part, this was due to the considerable and unequal resources that the aviation industry devoted to propagate its case. But it was also tied to ideological splits in the Conservative Party and the Coalition. Indeed, there is a strong argument that the moratorium was little more than a delaying tactic, and that Cameron and especially Osborne were never really signed up to it in the first place. Whatever the case, the reversal of Cameron's public commitment to oppose Heathrow expansion was also due to the absence of a transformational alternative to expansion, coupled with its dissemination in different policy and institutional arenas, and, most importantly, to the vital societal and cultural spheres of hegemony. Put differently, the politics of obstructionism lends itself to strategies of politicisation, but the creation and institutionalisation of a different regime of aviation has itself to be accompanied by a strategy of depoliticisation, which installs novel discourses and strategies like aviation divestment as the new 'common sense'.

The tasks of imagining, making available and embedding a new social order for aviation are no doubt challenging. The politics of persistence and obstruction does bring coalitions together to delay airport expansion and, in many respects, often succeeds in politicising broader commitments to the current logics of mobility and consumerism. But, if environmental campaigners want to see their ideas implemented in the longer term, they must continue to amplify the cultural battle to reshape established thinking on mobility and the escalating demand for aviation in the future. It is striking that the crises of the current conjuncture, including the global pandemic and the climate emergency, as well as crises in the supply and security of energy, coupled with growing concerns about austerity, social exclusion and the cost of living, present an opportunity to reignite this struggle, much like the late 2000s, when aviation began to act as a universal symbol of the threat of climate change. Indeed, we are witnessing a nascent and deepening dislocation of the hegemonic 'grip' of air travel among numerous actors across society, as emergent alternatives to flying and aviation expansion are being voiced and gain support, while concerns are raised about the economic feasibility of airlines and mass global tourism.

The potential attraction of these new ideas and practices depends on the hegemonic battles to reshape conventional discourses on mobility and the demands of our future environmental geographies. Most importantly, the politics of obstruction must go hand-in-hand with the voicing of more eco-egalitarian visions, which can lay the grounds for a new regime and social order. In part, this requires campaigners to politicise more aggressively the hegemonic discourses of airport expansion, putting aviation struggles at the heart of any future dialogue, while providing a legitimate voice to multiple forms of excluded expertise, as well as competing demands that are often pushed to the margins of policy formulation. But, as we have stressed, it also requires campaigners to fabricate an alternative vision and image of society, based on progressive principles, in which we divest from aviation and fossil fuels more generally. Campaigners and social movements are thus faced with the challenge of developing a 'new normal', as they simultaneously engage in radical strategies of politicisation *and* depoliticisation, in which the latter can decontest and sediment an emergent set of new practices. In short, it is not only the forces of capital or the state that engage in the logic of depoliticisation. Rather, opposition assemblages must also seek to 'become' a new 'integral state' (Gramsci, 1971: 56), though, of course, in our radically democratic perspective, they should do so in ways that are ultimately contingent and contestable, and which encourage agonistic forms of debate and discussion. But this brings us again to the primacy of politics and its implications for our understanding of government and the state.

The British State, party politics and political will

If our genealogy of the contested politics of airport expansion exposes the strategic and tactical dilemmas faced by campaigners, then it also raises critical questions about the willingness and capacity of politicians, governments and ultimately the British state to deliver planning consent and support for large infrastructure projects. The UK government is not the only government to have retreated from its plans for new runways or airports. Delays and challenges to planning applications and programmes, not to mention policy reversals, are in many ways part and parcel of the architecture of megaprojects. For example, the retreat of the 'strong' French state from its long-mooted plans for the construction of an international airport at Notre-Dame-des-Landes near Nantes in January 2018 indicates the complex politics of infrastructure planning, as do the travails surrounding the building of Berlin Brandenburg Airport in Germany. Nonetheless, it remains striking how in the UK context, such delays and reversals have often been interpreted in terms of doubts about the allegedly endemic inability of the political system to balance the competing demands that are mobilised in large infrastructure projects (see King and Crewe, 2013). Public accusations of British 'amateurism', 'pub talk' and 'dithering' over the provision of infrastructure still continue to be levelled at Whitehall and Westminster (Institute for Government, 2021; Public Accounts Committee, 2021).

What are we to make of such allegations? To begin with, our genealogies of the ebbs and flows of the emergent and fragile regime of aviation expansion show a number of political discontinuities and delays, highlighting the uneven temporalities and rhythms of policymaking. They also demonstrate that these discontinuities frequently arise from the ambiguous complexities of the centralising and pluralising logics nested in the British political system. Only too often the politics of large infrastructural projects is punctuated by the traditions of Whitehall dirigisme, first-past-the-post electoral majorities and adversarial party politics, which then come up against administrative fragmentation and departmental competition, the mechanisms of planning consent and participation and inhibitions about the use of public power in the private sector and civil society (see Jordan and Richardson, 1982; Feldman, 1985; Dearlove and Saunders, 1991; O'Riordan and Jordan, 1996; Wurzel, 2002; Ward, 2021). In other words, what we might see as the opportunity structures of the British political system produce a heady dialectic of centrifugal and centripetal pressures, and this dialectic lends itself to patterns of decision-making, which are mired in different rhythms and spatial configurations. More concretely, policymaking often lurches from episodes of 'go for growth' to moments of 'steady as she goes', if not policy stagnation.

Within such moments of policy acceleration or stagnation, our account also foregrounds the importance of electoral and party politics. Arguments of this sort have become somewhat unfashionable in recent policy studies, as attention has shifted towards governance and the 'hands off' management of collaborative networks. But our case demonstrates that partisan politics, most notably evident in the actions and representations of backbench MPs, who are opposed to expansion plans, which can threaten parliamentary majorities, as well as divisions in Cabinets, often generates significant political risks and costs for any government seeking to give the go-ahead for expansion at one location over another. Such political costs are not easily quantified in terms of the 'numbers' and preferences, which are fed into the cost-benefit analyses of airport expansion. However, it is still the case that when political leaders (or parliaments) make decisions, either to endorse or reject proposals for infrastructure projects like airports, they are making judgements about the impacts of their actions or inactions on key electoral constituencies, the coherence and cohesion of their parties, existing and future ideological and programme commitments, as well as the capacity of issues to swallow up agenda time and detract politically from other platforms (McConnell, 2018). In fact, residents and anti-expansion campaigners, and supporters of expansion for that matter, often strive to amplify or reduce such political costs for politicians, which may involve, for example, the exploitation of intra-party networks to shape political agendas, or the highlighting of policy contradictions to broader audiences through media-friendly actions, public letters and demonstrations.

In short, political costs and strategic calculations are intertwined with the construction and exercise of political will. Political will is articulated and manifests itself in different currencies, both individually and collectively. While it can be forged and used by powerful politicians pursuing a pet project, cause, or policy programme, it often requires or depends upon the active production of a collective will by the political representatives of a group, class or class fraction. The construction and reproduction of a collective political will is thus a vital ingredient in the battle for hegemony and policy change. Of course, the fabrication of a (collective) political will is always fraught with difficulty and uncertainty, and its expression is often equally precarious and reversible (Gramsci, 1971).

Moreover, from our theoretical perspective, the creation and character of a political will cannot be reduced to underlying social structures, and thus simply read-off the objective or 'real interests' to which they give rise. Instead, it is contingently manufactured out of disparate beliefs, desires and intentions, which are internally connected to ideologies and fantasies, as well as the perceived costs and benefits of actions. Over the life cycle of large infrastructure projects, therefore, political will can wax and wane. Contingent combinations of policy fatigue, shifting attention, uncertainty, changing institutional leadership and ideological values and commitments, can alter or transform perceptions of political costs, tempering the will of ministers and political leaders in driving forward large infrastructure projects (McConnell and 't Hart, 2019).

Yet there is often an unstable relationship between political costs and political will. As political costs rise, political will may dissipate, but not necessarily so; indeed, it may be the case that the actual or perceived political costs of a proposal or project function to galvanise a flagging will, while provoking the development of new strategies. For example, the volatile debates and changes that emerged in the UK's Brexit saga showed how the actual and potential political (and other) costs of certain decisions and commitments, such as exiting from the EU, for the Conservative Party (and others) did not necessarily undermine the Leave position, but strengthened the will of its core believers, leading to the development of new strategies and rhetoric. Also, in certain contexts, skilful campaigners and politicians can often use rhetoric and heresthetic to redescribe political costs as opportunities and indeed benefits for themselves, parties and their constituencies.

Seen in this light, our seven problematisations of UK airports policy show that at crucial moments in our story, when airport expansions looked imminent, if not inevitable, political will was found lacking, gelatinous and dissipated, resulting in 'delay and dither' (Civil Service World, 2016). Such exigencies come strongly into play, for instance, when we reflect upon the political judgement and calculations of the Cameron government in the wake of the AC and its support of a third runway at Heathrow. Our empirical evidence shows that following the AC's recommendations to expand Heathrow there was no consistent desire and persistent drive to act on the proposals (comparable, for example, to that provided by Lord Adonis in driving forward the high-speed rail link from London to the North West, or HS2). Cameron and Osborne had a short window of opportunity to do so in the middle of 2015, when they secured an overall majority in Parliament after the general election, but they were then overtaken by the decision (which was not favoured by Osborne) to call a referendum on the UK's membership of the EU. The loss of the Brexit referendum, and the resignation of Cameron, followed by years of political instability and policy paralysis, and eventually the election of Johnson as PM in July 2019, followed by his resignation in July 2022, further weakened the project of airport expansion. Such events were overdetermined by the devastating impact of the COVID-19 pandemic on the industry, so that eventually the unpersuasive economic arguments in favour of expansion and its environmental consequences proved too strong. In this sense, timing is crucial.

The political costs of endorsing the third runway for David Cameron as Prime Minister were no doubt significant, given his 'no ifs, no buts' pledge not to expand. More broadly, there was also opposition in the ranks of Conservative backbenchers, not to mention splits in the Cabinet. Moreover, with the election of Jeremy Corbyn in September 2015 as Leader of the Labour Party, the Conservatives faced an opposition leadership which was publicly opposed to Heathrow expansion, and a Shadow Chancellor, John McDonnell, who had long campaigned against the third runway as the MP for Hayes and Harlington. But political will and opportunity was also significant, particularly in the short window of possibility that opened in the summer of 2015. Such elements are evident in Cameron's own miserable interpretation of the events and decisions surrounding the breaking of his 'no ifs, no buts' promise not to expand Heathrow when he was the leader of the opposition in October 2009. In his autobiography, he reduces the episode to a few cursory and rather pathetic sentences designed to conceal, rationalise and ultimately displace his apparently feeble will in both making his promise and then in not acting more courageously when he changed his mind:

> For this reason, one battle I regret not confronting was our long-term airport needs. The debate over Britain's airport capacity had been going on for decades. Heathrow was now the busiest two-runway airport in the world, and a third runway was the favourite option for fixing this problem. And yet ... we decided to push it into the next Parliament. (Cameron, 2019: 473)

Indeed, it is interesting to observe that Cameron's excuse implies that he had no real intention of adhering to his much publicised commitment to alter the trajectory of UK airport's policy at all, and that he then decided to defer the issue to a later date, even though he had already promised not to expand Heathrow.

Similar arguments pertaining to political costs and political will surfaced in the New Labour governments of the 1990s and 2000s, and their national plans to expand UK airports at the start of the century. As Chancellor of the Exchequer and Deputy Prime Minister respectively, Gordon Brown and

John Prescott pushed for airport expansion in the lead up to, and during the aftermath of, the ATWP (2003). In his account, Brown recalls that he took a 'principled stand' in favour of expansion, which he thought in the 'national interest' (Brown, 2017: 371). But this desire was confounded and ultimately undermined by Labour's broader policy focus and internal disputes between ministries and key personalities, as well as its fluctuating political fortunes in the aftermath of the Iraq war, the growing salience of climate change politics, and then the GFC of 2007–2008, which made the eventual decision to give the go-ahead for expansion in 2009 little more than a pyrrhic victory for the proponents of airport expansion (Brown, 2017: 371). While Brown readily affirmed his desire to develop the UK's infrastructure, it is notable that Heathrow expansion and the aviation issue is not even mentioned in Tony Blair's memoirs (Blair, 2010). Moreover, within the Labour Party, the feuds about airport expansion continued under the Miliband leadership, in which Ed Balls as Shadow Chancellor, firmly in the Brown camp of the Labour Party, was keen on Heathrow expansion and sceptical about high speed rail, while Miliband expressed opposite views on both counts (McBride, 2013). Finally, it is important to stress that such political costs and fractures were amplified by opposing political forces, particularly in the aftermath of the ATWP (2003). In this conjuncture, anti-expansionist campaigners forged new equivalences and coalitions, which foregrounded the 'greenwashing' of the fantasmatic narrative of 'sustainable aviation', thus removing any ideological cover for expansion from the Labour government, while heavily framing the internal policy review undertaken by the Conservative opposition.

The upshot of these conclusions is that the production and sustenance of an effective collective political will often requires a 'sponsor' to forge equivalences and resonances between competing demands and to bring networks together, and in some instances to act as the symbolic embodiment of the project itself. In the UK aviation context, the tasks of sponsorship have become increasingly difficult as privatisation and deregulation have brought new actors into the policy arena, often articulating competing interests. At the same time, the audiences for airport expansion have expanded and become polarised, as aviation has been connected to issues of environmental and social justice. Paradoxically, perhaps, the Blair government's efforts in the early 2000s to bring together a governance network in aviation expansion served only to heighten antagonisms, leaving a policy arena crisscrossed by competing alliances and multiple alignments, which ultimately led to an abandonment of New Labour's ambitious programme for expansion.

If only through its forecasts of rising passenger demand, and its vested interest in supporting the aviation industry, the work of the DfT and its core administrative rationality of 'predict and divide' has stridently, if intermittently, brought the attention of government back onto aviation and pushed the issue of expansion onto and up the political agenda. But, in the institutional environment of the British state, the DfT and the Secretaries of State for Transport often lacked sufficient political weight and influence when competing against the other offices of state. One effect of this institutional unevenness is that the sponsorship of airport expansion has increasingly been taken up by the Treasury and successive Chancellors, or relied on the Prime Minister, whose support was by no means guaranteed. And, of course, while the Treasury can act as a sponsor for aviation expansion and infrastructure investment, it can also mobilise its resources to obstruct and delay plans; either way, the relative weakness of the DfT in the hierarchy of Whitehall and the fragmentation of the British state can undermine the political will for expansion.

Taken together, our interpretation of the case of airport politics underlines how partisan politics and political agency matters a great deal. Policy is made by individuals and networks of actors making judgements in specific historical contexts; and in making such judgements they are actors with distinctive personal histories and identities (Hirschman, 1982). Political judgement and craft are always part of the game of politics, whether it involves the leaders of protest movements and citizen campaigns or political parties. In short, the work of policymaking is not delivered on auto-pilot. Nonetheless, as our genealogical inquiry also underlines, political judgements cannot simply be reduced to short-term tactical manoeuvres, for they are ultimately clashes between different values and ways of being, and it is to this aspect that we now turn.

Critique, normative evaluation and demands

An important focus of our book has been the critique of the hegemonic myths, narratives and fantasies, which structure UK aviation and airports policy, showing how such ideological concealments and fixations have been used to cover over the failure to legitimise plans for airport expansion and secure the active consent, or at least the compliance, of affected groups and parties. Our genealogies highlight the contingent emergence of the dominant regime of aviation expansion through various problematisations, and stress the primacy of politics in the resolution of the ongoing disputes and contestations, while exposing its multiple contradictions and negative environmental and social impacts. But in response to those who rightly ask for our solutions to such obsessions and pathologies we have also sought to set out our demands and preferred normative alternatives, and it is on this note that we conclude our book.

The slogan 'Build Back Better', which has been enunciated and circulated during the global pandemic, admits competing interpretations.

In Chapter 6 we set out three different scenarios – demands for a speedy return to business as usual, a reform of aviation based on the idea of demand management, and a more thoroughgoing radical critique and restructuring of the aviation industry and neoliberal capitalism – each relying upon different underlying imaginaries and hegemonic projects. Contributing to the third scenario, our projected normative ideals arise from our commitment to the logic of sufficiency (and its reworked relationship with the logic of efficiency), the call for an alternative hedonism and an ethos of slow living, which we articulate together in a project of plural and radical democracy.

In brief, this putative hegemonic project advocates an eco-egalitarian and inclusive vision of a future of social order, in which public ownership and the democratic control of key infrastructure are core ingredients. More concretely, this new social imaginary can be productively supplemented and fleshed out with a specific set of demands pertaining to aviation and airports policy, which arise from our genealogical investigations and our elaborated normative commitments and assumptions. Our preferred political infrastructure to represent and reach decisions about the ongoing dilemmas and directions of aviation, transport policy and social relations, involves the promotion of agonistic forms of democratic politics, and its institutional requirements, which are placed within a reworked and transformed mode of production, exchange and consumption. But we shall first set out our demands.

Our demands for the green transformation of UK aviation

1. An immediate moratorium on all plans for airport expansion across the UK. The government should embed this commitment in a new Air Transport White Paper and legislation, which divests and transitions away from all the unsustainable elements of the aviation industry, putting in place a programme of airport closure. The White Paper should also introduce bottom-up Citizen's Charters at every airport to govern local development towards transition and provide a means for holding airport management teams to account.

2. An end to all domestic and short-haul flights. Long-haul flights should be rationed and regional airports closed or restricted to the bare minimum with no state financial support. As part of this transition, government, particularly in England, must reinvigorate approaches to spatial planning, moving away from unequal competitive regionalism towards collaborative and balanced regional integration and coordination. A re-invigorated logic of spatial planning is fundamental to the pursuit of a National Green Plan for aviation and the delivery of local Citizen's Charters.

3. A complete suspension of all *de facto* subsidies for the aviation industry. Government must impose VAT on aviation fuel and airplane tickets and end other forms of public subsidies that lower the costs of aviation travel. Government should increase APD on domestic flights and scrap financial subsidies for regional airlines and domestic routes.

4. Legislation to ensure that passengers pay the costs of the pollution caused by air travel. Government should introduce a frequent flyer tax, as well as considering a carbon air miles tax. Airlines must fully reflect the carbon costs of flying in pricing for different seats and planes, with mandatory emissions labels on tickets.

5. The immediate abandonment of CORSIA and the inclusion of all flights to and from the UK in a stringent cap and trade regime which aims to reduce aviation emissions. This emissions regime should take account of the non-carbon impacts of flying on climate change. At the same time, government should call on the CCC to revise its carbon budgets for aviation so that aviation can move towards a net zero, which does not rely on reductions in other sectors or offsetting.

6. All advertising for commercial flights, and frequent flyer programmes, should be proscribed, alongside strict regulation of casual support for flying in news programmes (images and reports), TV documentaries and forms of product placement and endorsement in films.

7. Government should support alternative forms of travel, with a programme of investment in low carbon rail and coach travel.

8. Public authorities, companies and places of work should facilitate the use of video-conferencing and online meetings, with public organisations such as universities acting as exemplars to discourage, rather than promote, practices of taken-for-granted hyper-mobility. Conferencing and business travel should be deemed unacceptable and phased out.

9. Engaging with trade unions, civic associations and local communities, government ought to put in place a National Green Plan for aviation, which converts jobs at airports and airlines into green jobs for local communities.

10. In keeping with such principles, planned measures should incorporate the impact of degrowth in aviation on other sectors, notably tourism, seeking to support radical transformation and innovation across the economy and promote international collaboration to meet the demands of transition and net zero. Governments, think tanks and social movements should also advance new forms of enjoyment and slow living, providing ideological and material support for staycations and new forms of tourism, while restricting UK hosting of international sporting events.

11. Public inquiries, judicial review and other mechanisms of public accountability must be developed and strengthened, so that local

communities and campaigners can hold government to account for their climate change commitments.

12. The UK Government should lobby internationally for the reform of ICAO and the governance of international aviation. The global institutions governing air transport were designed to facilitate the expansion of aviation, and they are no longer fit for purpose and thus cannot meet the demands of transition and transformation. Moving forward, aviation must be brought into the 'mainstream' of international climate change politics with international agreements about aviation agreed and binding at COP meetings. Echoing the demands of those who have evoked nuclear non-proliferation treaties as an 'analogy' for multilateral coordinated action to end the use of fossil fuels (Newell and Simms, 2020; see also Buck, 2021), we thus call for an international air transport non-proliferation treaty (AT-NPT) informed by the principles of 'burden sharing' and 'polluter pays'. The AT-NPT would thus provide a mechanism to disrupt the embedded policies and practices of ICAO, while planning for non-proliferation of airports and routes and the transformation of existing infrastructure, as well as international financial support for the development of alternative economies, low carbon forms of transport and 'slow tourism'. The implementation of the treaty, or the monitoring and regulation of the supply of aviation, should fall firmly under the auspices of the UNFCCC, charged with regulating the phasing out of fossil fuels (Piggot et al, 2018). But, importantly, applying principles of environmental justice to aviation, the treaty should deliver differential targets for mature aviation markets, recognising their historical contributions to rising aviation emissions and responsibility to lead the phasing out of aviation.

The politics of transformation

There is little doubt that the satisfaction of these demands will require a radical restructuring of our entire society, including the basic logics and accumulation regimes of our current economic structure, and a transformation of our current modes of producing, consuming and living. Such demands will also have to be articulated and pursued in conjunction with other struggles and demands, including programmes to transform the production and use of energy in cities, homes and the countryside; more sustainable forms of agricultural production, distribution, eating and consuming; more affordable and greener forms of transport, including the provision of electric buses, cycle lanes and footpaths, and their attendant infrastructures; and the construction of new forms of enjoyment such as staycations and new attachments to possessions and places (Pretty, 2013).

Bringing about such transitions in aviation, not to mention the wider societal transformations within which they have to be nested, will be immensely challenging, for given the absence of a technological fix in aviation, stopping or cutting back on flying will involve sacrifice (Barasi, 2017: 171–6). And, somewhat pessimistically, we must accept that previous efforts to encourage people to incur such sacrifices have had little, or at best a limited impact, on patterns of consumption in aviation. People keep on flying despite growing awareness of its contribution to rising carbon emissions. For some, cutting back on flying is often dogged by a classic challenge of collective action, leading individuals to question why they should stop flying when others continue to do so. (It also leads some governments and states to question the virtue of curbing aviation when other countries continue to build airports and expand their aviation industries.) Moreover, for others, in aviation, as in other fields of environmental politics, demands to tackle climate change are little more than a kind of 'simulative politics', expressing demands that are 'not supposed to be taken seriously and implemented, but which are nevertheless constantly rearticulated' (Blühdorn, 2007: 267).

Against this background, we recognise the need for a new campaign of public persuasion and political communication in climate change politics and policy. As Barasi (2017) argues, such a campaign should focus on the equivalent of the 'swing voters' of climate change politics. It should articulate a set of messages that conveys how climate change impacts directly on them, their families and their communities. Such appeals have to reframe climate change as a cross-partisan issue to maximise support in these constituencies, while climate change 'talk' has to accentuate the benefits of cutting emissions for the well-being of communities and as a means of softening the demobilising horrific narratives of climate change (Barasi, 2017: 178–82). Of course, the impact of flying on climate change must be woven into each of these messages, clarifying, for example, the intensity of flying's emissions in relation to other activities, as well as highlighting the injustices of frequent flying and government subsidies for the industry. An ecologically informed project of radical democracy and democratisation should also demonstrate how the transition away from aviation opens up new opportunities for upskilled green employment, while improving public health through the alleviation of air and noise pollution, and supporting investment in new forms of public transport and connectivity. In fact, support for alternative forms of hedonism should counter perceptions of individual sacrifice, reshaping individual and collective interests in flying less.

However, the politics of transition has also to create a moral imperative for action that generates a common purpose rooted in solidarity between individuals in communities, different nations and future generations. It is in part a task for political leaders to cultivate and forge ties of solidarity, and we must demand that politicians lead from the front in cutting back on flying and stand firm in legitimising and arguing for transition. Ironically, it is vital for politicians *not* to play politics with aviation divestment, and to ensure a fair transition, for people's willingness to suffer costs and 'lost' opportunities collapses if such costs are deemed to fall unequally on them and not on others (Barasi, 2017: 173–4). A just and democratic transition in aviation must also harness the role and resources of the administrative state, with politicians and campaigners working in, for and at times against the state to deconstruct and reverse institutionally embedded discourses of aviation expansion. Indeed, given the centrality of the state apparatus in facilitating the production of air transport through the legalisation of production via Air Service Agreements (ASAs), the granting of monopoly protection for airlines, the control of land for airports and the regulation of the entire air transport system, the state is a logical place to start in transitioning aviation. For example, state power could theoretically be activated to insist on carbon pricing, rationing or other market-based mechanisms, such as multi-lateral carbon cap and trade regimes (Young, 2020).

But politicians and political leaders must also be supported by actions in civil society. Campaigning organisations should continue to hold politicians to account for their actions and climate change commitments, raising the political costs of inaction and delay, while providing ideological cover for those political leaders who advance the cause of climate justice. In this regard, we should not forget that protests against airport expansion have been successful in the past and that transnational movements have emerged to lobby for change in international arenas. Therefore, it is imperative that such transnational alliances continue to be fostered so that they can create linkages and equivalences at multiple levels and scales, while continuing to mature politically. But individuals can and should also act on this issue. We can pledge not to fly, or voice demands for transition within our families, associations, civil society organisations and our workplaces, challenging unnecessary forms of travel and unsustainable logics of mobility. As academics, we should publicise the contradictions between, on the one hand, the public commitments of our institutions to sustainability, and on the other hand, the continued pressure applied to students and researchers to engage in unsustainable forms of international travel by attending conferences and conducting short and fast research fieldwork, as well as competing for global exchanges and the recruitment of international students, not to mention the ideological grip of such travel for many across the profession. Ultimately, the continued expansion of aviation and the attendant narratives of technological fixes and efficiencies are no longer tenable. Projections of hydrogen or electric planes coming into service construct alternative futures, which have flimsy roots in the present reality, and mask the challenges facing us as a global society. They are in fact little more than flights of fantasy – and it is now time for us to dismiss them.

Notes

Introduction

[1] For a further discussion, see: https://www.republicworld.com/world-news/australia/qan tas-launches-flight-to-nowhere-for-frequent-flyers.html [Accessed 8 January 2023].

[2] See Quantas Group, 'Managing climate risk', Available from: https://www.qantas.com/gb/ en/qantas-group/acting-responsibly/our-planet/managing-climate-risk.html [Accessed 4 November, 2021].

[3] See Stay Grounded (2020) *Airports conflicts – Struggles for Environmental Justice*, Available from: https://stay-grounded.org/airport-conflicts-struggles-for-environmental-justice-webinar-summary/ [Accessed 12 December, 2021].

[4] A return flight from London Stansted to Edinburgh generates approximately 0.298t CO_2. The estimated maximum annual allowance per person of CO_2 if we are to stop climate change is 0.600t CO_2. Based on MyClimate calculations, Available from: https://co2. myclimate.org/en/flight_calculators/new [Accessed 18 October, 2021].

[5] See Greenskies, Available from: http://www.aef.org.uk/downloads/Factsheetairquality. pdf [Accessed 21 October, 2021].

[6] In the summer of 2022, Heathrow Airport announced that the HCEB was to be succeeded by a new body, the Council for the Independent Scrutiny of Heathrow Airport (CISHA). Echoing the rhetorical appeals of the Airports Commission for Heathrow to be a 'better neighbour', the mission of CISHA was to 'hold the airport to account and work to help ensure it is the best neighbour it can be.' The first chair of the new body was announced as Baroness Liz Sugg, Minister for Aviation, 2017-2019. To view the commitments and work of the CISHA, see https://www.cisha.org/about [Accessed 5 March, 2023].

[7] Our methodological approach builds upon and extends ideas and research, which have been developed in: Howarth, 2000; Glynos and Howarth, 2007; Griggs and Howarth, 2013, 2019; Barnett et al, 2019.

Chapter 1

[1] We share Hay's concerns about Schmitt's strong definition of the political as the opposition between friend and enemy. But, along with Chantal Mouffe (1993, 2005), we accept the importance of conflict and contestation as a defining feature of the political, so long as this fundamental opposition is rendered compatible with the requirements of a liberal and plural democracy. Ideally, for us, the opposition between friend and enemy should take the form of an agonistic struggle between adversaries, who share a commitment to an underlying set of democratic norms and values, rather than a singular and purely antagonistic relation between friends and enemies that seek to destroy one another.

[2] We are indebted to Daniel Little's blog 'Hirschman on the passions', which we draw upon in the development of our argument here, see: https://understandingsociety.blogs pot.com/2013/05/hirschman-on-passions.html [Accessed 20 October, 2021].

Chapter 2

[1] Airport developments and projects can be classified as public goods, where the 'operating costs cannot be fully recovered from all beneficiaries and must be wholly sponsored or partially subsidised by the state' (see Brion, 1991: 37, cited in Aldrich, 2008: 3), though they differ from standard public goods in that they 'involve "entrepreneurial politics" that confer general (though perhaps small) benefits as a cost to be borne chiefly by a small segment of society' (Wilson, 1980: 370, cited in Aldrich, 2008: 3). Indeed, for this reason,

infrastructure projects like airports, roads, nuclear power stations and so on, are more accurately categorised as 'public bads', which increase overall welfare but impose net costs on the individuals living in the host community (Frey et al, 1996: 1298, note 1).

2   The World Bank, 'GDP growth (annual %) – United Kingdom 1961–2020', Available from: https://data.worldbank.org/indicator/NY.GDP.MKTP.KD.ZG?locations=GB [Accessed 17 September, 2021].

3   House of Commons Procedure Committee, Evidence Sessions, 19 June, 2002, Available from: https://publications.parliament.uk/pa/cm200102/cmselect/cmproced/823/2061 901.htm [Accessed 24 May, 2021].

4   House of Commons Procedure Committee, Evidence Sessions, 19 June, 2002, Available from: https://publications.parliament.uk/pa/cm200102/cmselect/cmproced/823/2061 901.htm [Accessed 24 May, 2021].

5   For further details, see SSE (2007) 'Inuit leader to give evidence at Stansted public inquiry', Press release, 21 July, Available from: https://stopstanstedexpansion.com/press-releases/ inuit-leader-to-give-evidence-at-stansted-public-inquiry/ [Accessed 23 May, 2021].

6   Reprint of speech by Harold Wilson at the Labour Party Annual Conference, 1 October, 1963, Available from: http://nottspolitics.org/wp-content/uploads/2013/06/Labours-Plan-for-science.pdf [Accessed 5 December, 2022].

Chapter 3

1   This term was used by to the chair of the Transport Committee to question Howard Davies on the outcomes of the Airports Commission when he gave evidence in January 2014 (Transport Committee, 2014).

2   For an overview of the career of Sir Howard Davies as reported for the Airports Commission, see 'Chair-Airports Commission', Available from https://www.gov.uk/ government/people/howard-davies [Accessed 31 December, 2022].

3   Based on the list of Airport Commission meetings with stakeholders from September 2012 to July 2015. The list full of meetings can be found at: https://www.gov.uk/gov ernment/publications/airports-commission-meetings-with-stakeholders [Accessed 21 October, 2021].

Chapter 4

1   For an overview of the criticisms of the Final Report made by the Local Authorities Aircraft Noise Council, see https://www.airportwatch.org.uk/2015/07/laanc-local-auth orities-aircraft-noise-council-to-consider-legal-action-against-biased-and-flawed-airpo rts-commission-report/ [Accessed 20 October, 2021].

2   Wandsworth Council Press release, 20 August, 2015, Available from: www.wandsworth. gov.uk/news/article/12978/airports_commission_buried_doubts_over_heathrow_grow th_forecast [Accessed 20 October, 2015].

3   For a full version of the letter, see www.wandsworth.gov.uk/news/article/12948/ campaigners_take_heathrow_concerns_to_prime_minister [Accessed 20 October, 2015].

4   BBC News, 10 October 2015, Available from: www.bbc.co.uk/news/uk-england-lon don-34495393 [Accessed 9 March, 2017].

5   Howard Davies made a public statement on 19 August, 2015 to counter criticisms from Gatwick, see https://www.gov.uk/government/news/sir-howard-davies-statement. He also wrote a letter to the Secretary of State dismissing the criticisms made by Gatwick Airport of the work of the AC, see https://assets.publishing.service.gov.uk/government/ uploads/system/uploads/attachment_data/file/463769/howard-davies-to-patrick-mcl oughlin-070915.pdf [Accessed 21 December, 2021].

6   Interview on Today programme with George Osborne can be found at: www.bbc.co.uk/ programmes/p034d84j [Accessed 6 October, 2015].

7   In October 2015, the Cameron government established the National Infrastructure Commission (NIC) charged with providing analysis and advice to government, notably through the delivery of a national infrastructure assessment each Parliament. Its first chair was Lord Adonis, a former Secretary of State for Transport in the Brown government. He was replaced in December 2017 by John Armitt, previously a member of the AC. Significantly, the NIC became an Executive Agency of the Treasury at the beginning of 2017.

8   For a discussion of the roles of these institutions, see HCEB, 'About us', Available from: https://www.hceb.org.uk/who-we-are; ICCAN, 'Our remit', Available from: https://iccan.gov.uk/about-iccan/ [Accessed 21 December, 2021].

9   See Gatwick Airport Press release, 25 October, 2016, Available from: https://www.mediacentre.gatwickairport.com/press-releases/2016/16-10-25-gatwick-airport-responds-to-government-decision-on-airport-capacity.aspx [Accessed 14 November, 2021]; Davies, P. (2016) 'Heathrow charges rule out more domestic links, says BA', *Travel Weekly*, [online] 23 November, Available from: https://www.travelweekly.co.uk/articles/64075/heathrow-charges-rule-out-more-domestic-links-says-ba, [Accessed 14 November, 2016].

10 See AirportWatch (2016) 'CAA writes to heathrow setting out its expectations, including preventing airline cost rises', [online] 27 October, Available from: https://www.airportwatch.org.uk/2016/10/caa-writes-to-heathrow-setting-out-its-expectations-including-preventing-airline-cost-rises/ [Accessed 14 November, 2021].

11 To review the letter from Andrew Tyrie to the Chancellor, see 'Chair urges Chancellor to publish details on airport expansion', 9 December 2016, Available from: https://committees.parliament.uk/committee/158/treasury-committee/news/98600/chair-urges-chancellor-to-publish-details-on-airport-expansion/ [Accessed 20 October, 2021].

12 For an overview of the claims made by Teddington Action Group, see https://www.airportwatch.org.uk/2016/10/teddington-action-group-commence-judicial-review-proceedings-against-government-re-heathrow-runway-decision/ [Accessed 4 August, 2022].

13 For the Reclaim the Power press release, see https://reclaimthepower.org.uk/news/press-release-protesters-blockade-mock-runway-outside-parliament-to-oppose-airport-expansion/ [Accessed 2 January, 2023].

14 Andrew Pendleton, FoE's head of campaigns, see https://www.edie.net/news/11/Heathrow-airport-expansion-approved-by-UK-Government-/ [Accessed 19 November, 2021].

15 BBC News, 21 June, 2018, Available from: https://www.bbc.co.uk/news/uk-politics-44561170 [Accessed 21 December, 2021].

16 To review the case of claimants and the final judgement, see [2017] EWHC 121 (Admin) Case No: CO/6287/2016, Available from: https://vlex.co.uk/vid/london-borough-of-hillingdon-793131273 [Accessed 2 January, 2023]; for press reports of the case, see *The Daily Telegraph*, 28 January, 2017, Available from: https://www.telegraph.co.uk/news/2017/01/28/heathrow-third-runway-unlawful-locals-made-life-choices-tory/ [Accessed 2 January, 2023].

17 For a discussion of the judgement and the intervention by Ravi Govindia, see https://news.sky.com/story/high-court-grounds-heathrow-third-runway-challenge-10748838 [Accessed 2 January, 2023].

18 Details of the case for judicial review can be found at: https://www.airportwatch.org.uk/2018/08/lawyers-acting-for-a-consortium-of-local-authorities-and-others-have-issued-jr-proceedings-in-the-high-court-re-heathrow-runway/ [Accessed 2 January, 2023].

19 See Plan B's 6 August 2018 Press release announcing its legal challenge at: https://planb.earth/plan-b-begins-legal-action-against-heathrow-expansion/ [Accessed 2 January, 2023].

20 See Friends of the Earth's 7 August 2018 Press release announcing its legal challenge at: https://friendsoftheearth.uk/climate/friends-earth-launches-high-court-legal-challenge-heathrow-expansion [Accessed 2 January, 2023].

21 To view the statement of the CCC, see https://www.theccc.org.uk/2016/10/25/uk-aviation-emissions-must-be-consistent-with-uk-climate-change-commitments-ccc-says/ [Accessed 11 January, 2022].

22 The letter from Lord Deben to Greg Clarke, the Secretary of State for Business, Energy and Industrial Strategy is available from: https://www.theccc.org.uk/wp-content/uploads/2016/11/CCC-letter-to-Rt-Hon-Greg-Clark-on-UK-airport-expansion-November-2016.pdf [Accessed 5 July, 2022].

23 The Planning Act (2008) can be found at: https://www.legislation.gov.uk/ukpga/2008/29/contents [Accessed 2 January, 2023].

24 The full text of the letter can be found at: https://www.theccc.org.uk/wp-content/uploads/2018/06/CCC-letter-to-DfT-on-Airports-National-Policy-Statement.pdf [Accessed 4 July, 2022].

25 Chris Grayling MP (2019) 'Heathrow expansion: judgements from the High Court in the Judicial Review', Written statement to Parliament, 1 May, Available from: https://www.gov.uk/government/speeches/heathrow-expansion, [Accessed 5 December, 2021].

26 Press release, FoE, Available from: https://friendsoftheearth.uk/climate-change/heathrow-third-runway-uk-government-actions-ruled-illegal [Accessed 5 December, 2022].

27 Tim Shipman appeared on the BBC's *Politics Live* on 27 February 2020. The details of the episode can be viewed at https://www.bbc.co.uk/programmes/m000frqk [Accessed 6 April 2020].

Chapter 5

1 BBC News (2020) 'Heathrow wins court battle to build third runway', 16 December, Available from: https://www.bbc.co.uk/news/business-55322340 [Accessed 21 November, 2021].

2 BBC News (2020) 'Heathrow wins court battle to build third runway', 16 December, Available from: https://www.bbc.co.uk/news/business-55322340 [Accessed 21 November, 2021].

3 For a recording of the *Any Questions* programme, see https://www.bbc.co.uk/sounds/play/m000xn09, [Accessed 20 August, 2021].

4 For a press summary of the report, see https://www.theguardian.com/environment/2021/aug/08/worlds-climate-scientists-to-issue-stark-warning-over-global-heating-threat [Accessed 17 December, 2021].

5 For further discussion of the IPCC report, see https://www.theguardian.com/science/2021/aug/09/humans-have-caused-unprecedented-and-irreversible-change-to-climate-scientists-warn [Accessed 12 December, 2021].

6 To read Sarah Olney's letter to the Chancellor, see Liberal Democrat Voice (2020) 'Lib Dems leads cross-party call for urgent support for airlines in return for climate action', 27 April, Available from: https://www.libdemvoice.org/lib-dems-lead-crossparty-call-for-urgent-support-for-airlines-in-return-for-climate-action-64283.html [Accessed 2 May, 2021].

7 To review the policy statement of the Johnson government see GOV.UK (2021) 'UK enshrines new target in law to slash emissions by 78 per cent by 2035', Press release, 20 April, Available from: https://www.gov.uk/government/news/uk-enshrines-new-target-in-law-to-slash-emissions-by-78-by-2035 [Accessed 26 November, 2021].

8 To review the full declaration, see International Aviation Climate Ambition Coalition (2021), *COP-26 Declaration*, 10 November, Available from: https://ukcop26.org/cop-26-declaration-international-aviation-climate-ambition-coalition/ [Accessed 21 November, 2021].

9   For the official Hansard record of the exchange, see https://hansard.parliament.uk/comm ons/2021-11-03/debates/DA26E685-87E2-430D-AD81-919688AE9400/Engagements [Accessed 3 January, 2023].

Chapter 6

1   Figures based on Office for National Statistics (2020) 'Travel trends: 2019', 22 May, Available from: https://www.ons.gov.uk/peoplepopulationandcommunity/leisureand tourism/articles/traveltrends/2019#uk-residents-visits-and-spend-abroad [Accessed 19 November, 2021].

2   These figures are based on departing flights for schemes at Leeds Bradford, Stansted and Southampton airports, while figures for Heathrow are based on both arriving and departing flights. See Chapman (2022).

3   For further information on the aims and policy proposals of A Free Ride, see https:// afreeride.org/ [Accessed 20 December, 2021].

4   See BBC News, 28 October, 2021, Available from: https://www.bbc.co.uk/news/uk-politics-59062696 [Accessed 12 November, 2021].

5   For further discussion of these subsidies to the aviation industry, see https://www.edie. net/news/11/UK-Government-unveils--4-3m-funding-for-domestic-flights--despite-green-backlash/; https://www.business-live.co.uk/economic-development/governm ent-pays-18m-ensure-round-22238956 [Accessed 21 November, 2021].

Conclusion

1   In exploring the different calculations and strategies through which politicians, states and public agencies decide to locate controversial infrastructure, Aldrich (2008: 54) concludes that it is the relative strength of civil society in a potential host community which is the key determining factor in their location. Naming such facilities 'public bads', because they appear to furnish some good for the community as a whole, but bring unfair burdens and strong negative externalities on the communities that host them, Aldrich argues that the state targets those sites which display weaker community and civil society networks, which also enable the use of 'coercive methods such as land expropriation and police action' (Cooley, 2009: 386).

In part, seen against this perspective, the UK case is something of an outlier, mainly because Heathrow was 'chosen' to be London's main airport in 1944, just at the start of what might be termed a 'golden age' of infrastructure development in many capitalist democracies, when the extent of their social and environmental impacts was relatively unknown, and the political opposition emanating from civil society was negligible. Yet our research does confirm Aldrich's argument that the strength of civil society is a crucial factor in the siting and expansion of large-scale facilities like airports and nuclear power stations, which is evident in the widespread opposition to the expansion of Heathrow and other airports in South East England, and indeed in Manchester. In this respect, the UK government was confronted with the problem of path dependency, and the reluctance of airlines, business and passengers to shift away from Heathrow, or even spread the load between different airports in the South East. The failure of the Boris Island option supports this proposition. Moreover, Aldrich's claims are borne out further in the failed endeavour to develop a third London Airport in the 1960s and 1970s, which we discussed in relation to the Roskill Commission, when the latter decided upon Cublington and then after political resistance chose Maplin Sands instead, mainly because it was perceived to be more politically compliant.

2   To review the final judgement of Lord Justice Carnwath, see http://www.bailii.org/ew/ cases/EWHC/Admin/2010/626.html [Accessed 21 November, 2021].

3   For an overview of these local campaigns and their strategies, see https://axosouthamp ton.wordpress.com/ [Accessed 25 June, 2022]; https://www.stopbristolairportexpansion. org/ [Accessed 24 June, 2022]; https://www.galba.uk/ [Accessed 23 June, 2022].

References

Acuity Analysis (2021) *Final Call for UK Civil Aviation?*, London: Unite.

Adams, J. (1970) 'Westminster: the fourth London airport?', *Area*, 2(2): 1–9.

Adams, J. (1981) *Transport Planning: Vision and Practice*, London: Routledge & Kegan Paul.

Adelman, J. (2014) *Worldly Philosopher: The Odyssey of Albert O. Hirschman*, Princeton: Princeton University Press.

Air Quality News (2020) 'Revealed: Every UK airport has plans to expand', *Air Quality News*, [online] 18 February, Available from: https://airqualityn ews.com/2020/02/18/revealed-every-uk-airport-has-plans-to-expand/ [Accessed 23 October, 2021].

Air Transport Action Group (ATAG) (2020a) *Aviation: Benefits Beyond Borders*, Aviation Benefits, Available from: https://aviationbenefits.org/media/ 167517/aw-oct-final-atag_abbb-2020-publication-digital.pdf [Accessed 9 October, 2021].

ATAG (2020b) 'Waypoint 2050. Balancing growth in connectivity with a comprehensive global air transport response to the climate emergency', Aviation Benefits, Available from: https://aviationbenefits.org/media/167 187/w2050_full.pdf [Accessed 4 September, 2021].

Airlines UK (2021) 'UK-based airline CEOs unite to call for government aviation recovery roadmap announcement', Press release, 18 February, Available from: https://airlinesuk.org/uk-based-airline-ceos-unite-to-call-for-government-aviation-recovery-roadmap-announcement/ [Accessed 21 November, 2021].

Airport Operators Association (2021) *A UK Airport Recovery Plan*, London: AOA.

Airports Commission (AC) (2013a) *Airports Commission: Interim Report*, December, London: AC.

AC (2013b) *Guidance Document 01: Submitting Evidence and Proposals to the Airports Commission*, February, London: AC.

AC (2013c) *Discussion Paper 01: Aviation Demand Forecasting*, February, London: AC.

AC (2013d) *Discussion Paper 02: Aviation Connectivity and the Economy*, March, London: AC.

AC (2013e) *Discussion Paper 05: Aviation Noise*, July, London: AC.

AC (2014a) *Consultation Document: Gatwick Airport Second Runway, Heathrow Airport Extended Northern Runway, Heathrow Airport North West Runway*, November, London: AC.

AC (2014b) *Heathrow Public Discussion Session*, Official transcripts, 3 December, Available from: https://assets.publishing.service.gov.uk/gov ernment/uploads/system/uploads/attachment_data/file/386011/heath row-area-transcript.pdf [Accessed 21 November, 2021].

AC (2015a) *Airports Commission: Final Report*, July, London: AC.

AC (2015b) *Strategic Fit: Forecasts*, July, London: AC.

Airports Council International (ACI) (2020) 'Almost 200 European airports facing insolvency in coming months', Press release, 27 October, Available from: https://www.aci-europe.org/downloads/mediaroom/20-10-27%20 Almost%20200%20European%20airports%20facing%20insolvency%20 in%20coming%20months%20PRESS%20RELEASE.pdf [Accessed 16 December, 2021].

ACI (2021a) 'Airport financial stress & investment crunch call for regulatory revamp', Press release, 17 June, Available from: https://www. aci-europe.org/downloads/mediaroom/21-06-17%20Airport%20Fi nancial%20Stress%20%20Investment%20Crunch%20Call%20for%20 Regulatory%20Revamp%20%20PRESS%20RELEASE.pdf [Accessed 16 December, 2021].

ACI (2021b) 'Airport industry reconfirms and accelerates net zero CO2 targets', Press release, 20 May, Available from: https://www.aci-europe. org/downloads/mediaroom/21-05-20%20Airport%20Industry%20Rec onfirms%20and%20Accelerates%20Net%20Zero%20CO2%20Targets.pdf [Accessed 20 October, 2021].

AirportWatch (2015a) *The Truth about the Airports Commission and Airport Expansion*, N. Ferriday (ed) April, Available from: https://www.airportwa tch.org.uk/wp-content/uploads/AC_and_airport_expansion_28.4.2015. pdf [Accessed 11 December, 2021].

AirportWatch (2015b) 'Great majority of election candidates around Gatwick oppose a 2nd runway', *News*, 26 April, Available from: https://www.airportwatch.org.uk/2015/04/great-majority-of-election- candidates-around-Gatwick-oppose-a-2nd-runway [Accessed 29 January, 2023].

AirportWatch (2015c) 'London Assembly votes decisively that "there is no circumstance under which Heathrow expansion would be acceptable"', *Latest News*, 8 September, Available from: https://www.airportwatch. org.uk/2015/09/london-assembly-votes-decisively-that-there-is-no- circumstance-under-which-heathrow-expansion-would-be-acceptable/ [Accessed 9 February, 2023].

AirportWatch (2018) 'How Heathrow is happy to pay way over the odds, to increase its RAB, allowing more revenue', 28 March, Available from: https://www.airportwatch.org.uk/2018/03/how-heathrow-is- happy-to-pay-way-over-the-odds-to-increase-its-rab-allowing-more-reve nue/ [Accessed 21 November, 2021].

AirportWatch (2019) 'Who will pay for Heathrow's 3rd runway?', 12 December, Available from: https://www.airportwatch.org.uk/2019/12/ who-will-pay-for-heathrows-3rd-runway-there-is-no-simple-answer-can- heathrow-afford-it/ [Accessed 21 November, 2021].

Aldrich, D.P. (2008) *Site Fights: Divisive Facilities and Civil Society in Japan and the West*, Ithaca: Cornell University Press.

Allegretti, A. (2021) 'Rishi Sunak defends halving domestic flight taxes in Cop 26 run-up', *The Guardian*, 28 October, Available from: https://www.theguardian.com/uk-news/2021/oct/28/rishi-sunak-defends-halving-domestic-flight-taxes-in-cop26-run-up [Accessed 23 July, 2022].

Almond, P. and Connolly, H. (2020) 'A manifesto for "slow" comparative research on work and employment', *European Journal of Industrial Relations*, 26(1): 59–74.

Anderson, P. (1976) 'The antinomies of Antonio Gramsci', *New Left Review*, 1(100): 5–78.

Andersson, J. (2018) *The Future of the World*, Oxford: Oxford University Press.

Appleyard D. (1983) 'Case studies of citizen action and citizen participation in Brussels, Covent Garden, Delft, and Camden' in L. Susskind and M. Elliott (eds) *Paternalism, Conflict, and Coproduction*, Boston: Springer, pp 67–117.

Apter, D.E. (1987) *Rethinking Development: Modernisation, Dependency and Postmodern Politics*, London: Sage.

Apter, D.E. and Sawa, N. (1984) *Against the State*, Cambridge, MA: Harvard University Press.

Arnstein, S. (1969) 'A ladder of citizen participation', *Journal of the Institute of American Planners*, 35(4): 216–24.

Aviation Environment Federation (AEF) (2007) *Fallible Forecasts. A Critique of the 2007 Air Passenger Forecasts*, London: AEF.

AEF (2015a) *The Airports Commission's Economic Fudge*, August, London: AEF.

AEF (2015b) *All Set for Take Off? Aviation Emissions to Soar Under Airports Commission Proposals*, June, London: AEF.

AEF (2015c) *The Airports Commission's Final Report – Has it Closed the Carbon Gap?*, August, London: AEF.

AEF (2016a) *Aircraft Noise and Public Health: The Evidence is Loud and Clear*, January, London: AEF.

AEF (2016b) 'What answers has the government found to the environmental hurdles facing a third runway?', Available from: https://www.aef.org.uk/2016/10/25/what-answers-has-the-government-found-to-the-enviro nmental-hurdles-facing-a-third-runway/[Accessed 10 November, 2021].

AEF (2020) *Briefing on the Importance of Maintaining Air Passenger Duty as Part of a Green Recovery for the Aviation Sector*, 2 July, Available from: https://www.aef.org.uk/uploads/2020/07/AEF-APD-briefing-July-2020.pdf [Accessed 24 October, 2021].

AEF (2021) 'Challenging airport expansion', Available from: https://www.aef.org.uk/campaigns/challenging-airport-expansion/ [Accessed 11 September, 2021].

AEF (undated) *How do I Present at a Public Inquiry?*, Available from: www.aef.org.uk/uploads/PlanningGuide8.pdf [Accessed 20 May, 2021].

Badstuber, N. (2020) 'Flights are grounded – is this the moment we give up our addiction to flying?' *The Guardian*, 9 April.

Balounová, E. (2021) 'Climate change and the expansion of airports in court', Global Network for Human Rights and the Environment [Blog] 29 April, Available from: https://gnhre.org/climate-change-2/blog-climate-change-and-the-expansion-of-airports-in-court-are-there-any-arguments-at-all/ [Accessed 17 November, 2021].

Banatvala, J., Peachet, M. and Münzel, T. (2019) 'The harms to health caused by aviation noise require urgent action', *British Medical Journal*, 366: 15329.

Bang, H. (2005) 'Among everyday makers and expert citizens' in J. Newman (ed) *Remaking Governance*, Bristol: Policy Press, pp 159–79.

Bannon, E. (2019) 'A cheap airline ticket does not fall from the sky', *Transport & Environment*, Available from: https://www.transportenvironment.org/news/cheap-airline-ticket-doesn%E2%80%99t-fall-sky [Accessed 7 September, 2021].

Barasi, L. *The Climate Majority*, Oxford: New Internationalist.

Barnett, C. (1995) *The Lost Victory: British Dreams, British Realities, 1945–1950*, London: Macmillan.

Barnett, N., Griggs, S. and Howarth D. (2019) 'Whatever happened to local councillors?', *Political Studies*, 67(3): 775–94.

Bates, S., Jenkins, L. and Amery, F. (2014) '(De)politicisation and the Father's Clause parliamentary debates', *Policy & Politics*, 42(2): 243–58.

BBC (2011) 'Bristol airport expansion approval "was legal"', [online] 26 October, Available from: https://www.bbc.co.uk/news/uk-england-bristol-15469445 [Accessed 21 November, 2021].

BBC (2019) 'BA strike threat removed after pilot pay deal', [online] 16 December, Available from: https://www.bbc.co.uk/news/uk-50807348 [Accessed 15 September, 2021].

BBC News (2019) 'Greta Thunberg: teen activist says UK is "irresponsible" on climate change', 23 April, Available from: https://www.bbc.co.uk/news/uk-48017083 [Accessed 2 February 2023].

BBC News (2021) 'Covid: UK to close all travel corridors from Monday', 15 January, Available from: https://www.bbc.co.uk/news/uk-55681861 [Accessed 6 August 2022].

Bednarek, J. (2016) *Airports, Cities and the Jet Age: US Airports Since 1945*, London: Palgrave MacMillan.

Bell, J. (2020) 'Did the Court of Appeal "kill off" the Heathrow third runway?', 19 May, Available from: https://www.seh.ox.ac.uk/blog/did-the-court-of-appeal-kill-off-the-heathrow-third-runway [Accessed 6 February, 2023].

Bellamy, R. (2007) *Political Constitutionalism: A Republican Defence of the Constitutionality of Democracy*, Cambridge: Cambridge University Press.

Bennett, J. (2009) *Vibrant Matter*, Durham, DC: Duke University Press.

Beveridge, R. and Koch, P. (2017) 'The post-political trap?', *Urban Studies*, 54(1): 31–43.

Bevir, M. (2010) *Democratic Governance*, Princeton, NJ: Princeton University Press.

Blackman, T. (1991) 'Planning inquiries: A socio-legal study', *Sociology*, 25(2): 311–27.

Blair, T. (2010) *A Journey*, London: Hutchinson.

Blichner, L.C. and Molander, A. (2005) 'What is juridification?', Working paper No. 14, March, Oslo: Centre for European Studies, University of Oslo.

Blühdorn, I. (2007) 'Sustaining the unsustainable: symbolic politics and the politics of simulation', *Environmental Politics*, 16(2): 251–75.

Blühdorn, I. (2014) 'Post-ecologist governmentality', in J. Wilson and E. Swyngedouw (eds) *The Post-Political and its Discontents*, Edinburgh: Edinburgh University Press, pp 146–68.

Boin, R., Bouwer, J., Bozarth, D., Krishnan, V., Kuchibholta, P., Loubeau, A. and Tufft, C. (2022) 'Trying to boost corporate travel sales? Five questions for airline executives', Available from: https://www.mckinsey.com/ind ustries/travel-logistics-and-infrastructure/our-insights/trying-to-boost-corporate-travel-sales-five-questions-for-airline-executives [Accessed 23 June, 2022].

Boström, M. (2021) 'Take the opportunity afforded by the Covid-19 experiences', *Frontiers in Sustainability*, 10 September, DOI: 10.3389/frsus.2021.726320.

Bowcott, O. and agencies (2010) 'Heathrow protesters win third runway court victory', *The Guardian*, 26 March, Available from: https://www.theguardian.com/environment/2010/mar/26/heathrow-third-runway-travel-and-transport [Accessed 29 December, 2022].

Bowen, J. (2010) *The Economic Geography of Air Transportation*, Abingdon: Routledge.

Bowen, J. (2013) 'Continents shifting, clouds gathering: the trajectory of global aviation expansion' in L. Budd, S. Griggs and D. Howarth (eds) *Sustainable Aviation Futures*, Bingley, UK: Emerald, pp 37–63.

Bowen, J. (2019) *Low Cost Carriers in Emerging Countries*, Amsterdam: Elsevier.

Boyland, A. (2008) *Report to the Secretary of State for Communities and Local Government and the Secretary of State for Transport. Town and Country Planning Act 1990. Appeal by BAA plc and Stansted Airport Ltd*, Stansted Airport, Stansted, Essex, Bristol: Planning Inspectorate.

Boyle, L. (2020) 'Airbus reveals plan for first ever "zero emission commercial planes", potentially by 2035', *The Independent*, 21 September, Available from: https://www.independent.co.uk/climate-change/news/airbus-emissions-planes-2035-hydrogen-climate-b517838.html [Accessed 5 February, 2023].

Bradshaw, J., Wright, B. and Martin, B. (2015) 'Heathrow expansion: government to report back in the autumn as Tory MPs vow to fight recommendations', *The Daily Telegraph*, 1 July, Available from: https://www.telegraph.co.uk/finance/newsbysector/transport/11709288/Heathrow-third-runway-wins-over-Gatwick-live.html [Accessed 15 February, 2023].

Brion, D. (1991) *Essential Industry and the NIMBY Phenomenon*, New York: Quorum Books.

Brown, P. (2001) 'Ruling puts airport night flights in doubt', *The Guardian*, 3 October, Available from: https://www.theguardian.com/travel/2001/oct/03/travelnews [Accessed 7 February, 2023].

Brown, P. (2003) 'Night flight blow to million residents', *The Guardian*, 9 July, Available from: https://www.theguardian.com/business/2003/jul/09/theairlineindustry.transportintheuk1 [Accessed 7 February, 2023].

Brooker, P. (2008) 'ANASE: measuring aircraft annoyance very unreliably', *Significance*, 5(1): 18–24.

Brooker, P, Critchley, J. Monkman, D. and Richmond, C. (1985) *United Kingdom Aircraft Noise Index Study. DR Report 8402*, London: CAA/DfT.

Brown, G. (2017) *My Life, Our Times*, London: Bodley Head.

Bruno, I., Didier, E. and Vitale, T. (2014) 'Statactivism: forms of action between disclosure and affirmation', *Partecipazione e Conflitto. The Open Journal of Sociopolitical Studies*, 7(2): 198–220.

Buchan, L. (2018) 'Boris Johnson faces calls to resign after jetting off to Afghanistan to dodge crucial Heathrow vote', *The Independent*, 25 June, Available from: https://www.independent.co.uk/news/uk/politics/heathrow-boris-johnson-third-runway-vote-aiport-parliament-afghanistan-kabul-foreign-secretary-a8416471.html [Accessed 6 February, 2023].

Buchanan, C. (1981) *No Way to the Airport*, Harlow: Longman.

Büchs, M. and Mattioli, G. (2021) 'Trends in air travel inequality in the UK: from the few to the many?', *Travel Behaviour and Society*, 25: 92–101.

Buck, H.J. (2021) *Ending Fossil Fuels: Why Net Zero is Not Enough*, London: Verso.

Budd, L. and Ison, S. (eds) (2020) *Air Transport Management*, 2nd edn, London: Routledge.

Budd, L. and Ison, S. (2021) 'Public utility or private asset? The evolution of UK airport ownership', *Case Studies on Transport Policy*, 9(1): 212–18.

Burnham P. (2001) 'New Labour and the politics of depoliticization', *The British Journal of Politics & International Relations*, 3(2): 127–49.

Burnham. P. (2006) 'Depoliticisation: a comment on Buller and Flinders', *British Journal of Politics and International Relations*, 8(2): 303–6.

Butcher, L. (2010) *Aviation: Manchester's Second Runway, 1993–2001*, Standard Note: SN/BJ/101, London: HoC Library.

Butcher, L. (2018) *Heathrow Airport*, Briefing paper: CBP 1136, London: HoC Library.

Cabot Institute (2021) 'Survey reveals many people have reservations about flying in the future', Press release, 23 April, University of Bristol, Available from: https://www.bristol.ac.uk/neuroscience/news/2021/flying.html [Accessed 18 September, 2021].

Cairns, S. and Newson, C. with Boardman, B. and Anable, J. (2006) *Predict and Decide*, Oxford: Environmental Change Institute.

Cameron, D. (2019) *For the Record*, London: William Collins.

CAPA-Centre for Aviation (2021) 'Brexit and aviation: all's well that ends. Well, almost ...', 7 January, Available from: https://centreforaviation.com/analysis/reports/brexit-and-aviation-alls-well-that-ends-well-almost-548205 [Accessed 29 November, 2021].

Carbon Brief (2019) *Corsia: The UN's Plan to 'Offset' Growth in Aviation Emissions*, 4 February, Available from: https://www.carbonbrief.org/corsia-un-plan-to-offset-growth-in-aviation-emissions-after-2020 [Accessed 24 October, 2021].

Carmichael, R. (2019) *Behaviour Change, Public Engagement and Net Zero*, London: Committee on Climate Change, Available from: https://www.theccc.org.uk/publications/ and http://www.imperial.ac.uk/icept/publications/ [Accessed 24 October, 2021].

Carrington, D. (2020) 'Heathrow third runway ruled illegal over climate change', *The Guardian*, 27 February, Available from: https://www.theguardian.com/environment/2020/feb/27/heathrow-third-runway-ruled-illegal-over-climate-change [Accessed 1 January, 2023].

Chapman, A. (2020) 'The dodgy economics behind expanding our airports', New Economics Foundation, 15 September, Available from: https://neweconomics.org/2020/09/the-dodgy-economics-behind-expanding-our-airports [Accessed 23 June, 2022].

Chapman, A. (2021) *Proof of Evidence of Dr Alex Chapman. Economic Impacts, Expansion of Bristol Airport to 12 mppa*, Planning application ref: 18/P/5118/OUT, PCCA/W5/1-Proof of evidence, Available from: https://gat04-live-1517c8a4486c41609369c68f30c8-aa81074.divio-media.org/filer_public/69/b9/69b94941-bf15-4459-a4f7-bc0152971d13/5_alex_chapman-_finalised.pdf [Accessed 7 January, 2022].

Chapman, A. (2022) 'The £62Bn carbon giveaway', New Economics Foundation, 27 January, Available from: https://neweconomics.org/2022/01/the-62bn-carbon-giveaway [Accessed 23 June, 2022].

Chapman, A., Murray, L., Carpenter, G., Heisse, C. and Prieg, L. (2021) *A Frequent Flyer Levy: Sharing Aviation's Carbon Budget in a Net-Zero World*, New Economics Foundation, Available from: https://neweconomics.org/2021/07/a-frequent-flyer-levy [Accessed 23 October, 2021].

Choat, I. (2020) 'Climate campaigners condemn "joy flights" for travellers who miss flying', *The Guardian*, 18 September, Available from: https://www.theguardian.com/travel/2020/sep/18/climate-campaigners-condemn-joy-flights-for-travellers-who-miss-flying [Accessed 8 October, 2020].

Chorley, M. (2015) 'Cabinet "stitch-up" on Heathrow', *The Daily Mail*, 22 July, Available from: https://www.dailymail.co.uk/news/article-3170781/Cameron-takes-charge-Heathrow-airport-decision-locks-Cabinet-ministers-oppose-expansion.html [Accessed 21 August, 2021].

Christoff, P. (1996) 'Ecological modernisation, ecological modernities', *Environmental Politics*, 5(3): 476–500.

Civil Aviation Authority (CAA) (2014) *Managing Aviation Noise, CAP 1165*, London: CAA.

Civil Service World (2016) 'National Infrastructure Commission chief Phil Graham on 2017 and why Britain must "banish the culture of dither and delay"', 19 December, Available from: https://www.civilserviceworld.com/in-depth/article/national-infrastructure-commission-chief-phil-graham-on-2017-why-britain-must-banish-the-culture-of-dither-and-delay [Accessed 12 December, 2022].

Clean Sky 2 JU and CH 2 JU (2020) *Hydrogen-Powered Aviation*, Luxembourg: Publications Office of the European Union.

Clementine, K. (2015) 'Heathrow Airport van protest', *SurreyLive*, 3 July, Available from: https://www.getsurrey.co.uk/news/heathrow-airport-van-protest-third-9573809 [Accessed 31 December, 2022].

ClientEarth (2018) 'UK government loses third air pollution case as judge rules air pollution plans "unlawful"', Press release, 21 February, Available from: https://www.clientearth.org/latest/latest-updates/news/uk-government-loses-third-air-pollution-case-as-judge-rules-air-pollution-plans-unlawful/ [Accessed 20 November, 2021].

Climate Assembly UK (2020) *The Path To Net Zero*, Available from: https://www.climateassembly.uk/report/read/final-report.pdf [Accessed 9 September, 2021].

Climate Change Committee (CCC) (formerly the Committee on Climate Change) (2016) 'UK Aviation Emissions Must be Consistent with UK Climate Change Commitments, CCC says', Public statement, 25 October, Available from: https://www.theccc.org.uk/2016/10/25/uk-aviation-emissions-must-be-consistent-with-uk-climate-change-commitments-ccc-says/ [Accessed 14 June, 2022].

CCC (2018) *Reducing UK Emissions. 2018 Progress Report to Parliament*, London: CCC.

CCC (2019a) *Net Zero: The UK's Contribution to Stopping Global Warming*, London: CCC.

CCC (2019b) 'Net-zero and the approach to international aviation and shipping emissions', Letter from Lord Deben to Rt Hon Grant Shapps MP, Secretary of State for Transport, 24 September, Available from: https://www.theccc.org.uk/wp-content/uploads/2019/09/Letter-from-Lord-Deben-to-Grant-Shapps-IAS.pdf [Accessed 20 December, 2021].

CCC (2020) *The Sixth Carbon Budget*, London: CCC.

Colebatch, H.K. (2002a) *Policy*, Buckingham: OUP.

Colebatch, H.K. (2002b) 'Government and governmentality: using multiple approaches to the analysis of government', *Australian Journal of Political Science*, 37(3): 417–35.

Colebatch, H.K. (2014) 'Making sense of governance', *Policy and Society*, 33(4): 307–16.

Coles, R. (2016) *Visionary Pragmatism*, Durham, NC: Duke University Press.

Collier, D. (2011) 'Understanding process tracing', *PS: Political Science and Politics*, 44(4): 823–30.

Collingridge, J. (2019) 'Heathrow ordered by CAA to rein in third runway costs', *The Sunday Times*, 1 December, Available from: https://www.thetimes.co.uk/article/heathrow-ordered-by-caa-to-rein-in-third-runway-costs-fprgvf32m [Accessed 7 February, 2023].

Commission on the Third London Airport (1971) *Report. Chairman Hon. Mr Justice Roskill*, London: HMSO.

Connolly, W.E. (1995) *The Ethos of Pluralization*, Minneapolis: University of Minnesota Press.

Connolly, W.E. (2019) *Climate Machines, Fascist Drives and Truth*, Durham, NC: Duke University Press.

Convention Citoyenne pour le Climat (2021) *Les Propositions de la Convention Citoyenne pour le Climat*, version 29 January 2021, Available from: https://propositions.conventioncitoyennepourleclimat.fr/le-rapport-final/ [Accessed 7 August, 2022].

Córdoba Azcárate, M. (2020) *Stuck With Tourism*, Oakland, California: University of California Press.

Corr, S. (2021) 'New defeat and extra £60,000 bill for Uttlesford District Council over Stansted Airport expansion', *Bishop's Stortford Independent*, 5 October, Available from: https://www.bishopsstortfordindependent.co.uk/news/r4u-under-fire-as-judge-backs-stansted-airport-9219169/ [Accessed 5 February, 2023].

Court of Appeal (2020) *Judgment*, Case Nos: C1/2019/1053, C1/2019/1056 and C1/2019/1145, [2020] EWCA Civ 214, 27 February, Available from: https://www.judiciary.uk/wp-content/uploads/2020/02/Heathrow-judgment-on-planning-issues-27-February-2020.pdf [Accessed 5 November, 2021].

Cumber, R. (2015) 'Conservative MPs get early wake-up call from Heathrow Airport protesters', *MyLondon*, 6 October, Available from: https://www.mylondon.news/news/west-london-news/conservative-mps-early-wake-up-10203904 [Accessed 6 February, 2023].

Cwerner, S., Kesselring, S. and Urry, J. (eds) (2009) *Aeromobilities*, Abingdon: Routledge.

Date, W. (2016) 'ClientEarth wants clarity over Heathrow air quality plans', *Air Quality News*, 12 May, Available from: http://airqualitynews.com/2016/05/12/clientearth-wants-clarity-heathrow-air-quality-plans/ [Accessed 31 December, 2022].

Davies, H. (2013) 'Aviation Capacity in the UK: Emerging Thinking', 7 October, Available from: https://www.gov.uk/government/speeches/aviation-capacity-in-the-uk [Accessed 20 August, 2020].

Davies, H. (2015a) 'Government's response to the Airports Commission final report', Available from: www.youtube.com/watch?v=neUSOIvdij0 [Accessed 20 December, 2021].

Davies, H. (2015b) 'Independence of Airports Commission questioned over chair's Prudential role', *The Guardian*, 5 August, Available from: https://www.theguardian.com/uk-news/2015/aug/05/independence-airports-commission-chair-prudential-howard-davies-properties-heathrow-report [Accessed 9 August, 2022].

de la Plaza, C. (2021) 'Aviation, carbon offsets and tourism', *Forest Cover*, 64: 18–19.

Dean, M. (1994) *Critical and Effective Histories*, London: Routledge.

Dean, M. (1996) 'Putting the technological into government', *History of the Human Sciences*, 9(3): 47–68.

Dearden, L. (2015) 'Heathrow Airport expansion protest delays international flights after activists lie on runway', *The Independent*, 13 July, Available from: https://www.independent.co.uk/travel/news-and-advice/heathrow-airport-expansion-protest-delays-international-flights-after-activists-lie-on-runway-10384589.html [Accessed 7 August, 2022].

Dearlove, J. and Saunders, P. (1991) *Introduction to British politics: Analysing a Capitalist Democracy*, Oxford: Polity Press.

Deben, Lord (2016) 'Department for Transport's assessment of the case for a third runway at Heathrow', Public letter to Secretary of State for Business, Energy and Industrial Strategy, 22 November, Available from: https://www.theccc.org.uk/wp-content/uploads/2016/11/CCC-letter-to-Rt-Hon-Greg-Clark-on-UK-airport-expansion-November-2016.pdf [Accessed 14 June, 2022].

Department of the Environment, Transport and the Regions (DETR) (1998) *A New Deal for Transport – Better for Everyone*, London: DETR.

DETR (2000a) 'Air traffic forecasts for the United Kingdom 2000', London: DETR, Available from: https://www.open.edu/openlearn/pluginfile.php/630968/mod_resource/content/1/air_traffic_forecasts.pdf [Accessed 8 August, 2022].

DETR (2000b) *The Future of Air Transport: Consultation on Air Transport Policy*, London: HMSO, Available from: https://www.open.edu/openlearn/pluginfile.php/630971/mod_resource/content/1/dft_aviation_pdf_503446.pdf [Accessed 8 August, 2022].

Department for Transport (DfT) (2002a) *The Future Development of Air Transport in the UK: South East Consultation Document*, London: DfT.

DfT (2002b) *The Future of Air Transport: Consultation on Air Transport Policy (Response)*, London: DfT.

DfT (2002c) *The Future Development of Air Transport in The United Kingdom. South East Consultation Document*, 2nd edn, London: DfT.

DfT (2003) *The Future of Air Transport*, Cm 6046, London: DfT.

DfT (2011) *Developing a Sustainable Framework for UK Aviation: Scoping Document*, March, London: DfT.

DfT (2012a) *Draft Aviation Policy Framework*, July, London: DfT.

DfT (2012b) 'Terms of reference. The purpose and objectives of the Airport Commission', Available from: https://www.gov.uk/government/organi sations/airports-commission/about/terms-of-reference [Accessed 21 November, 2021].

DfT (2012c) 'Airports Commission membership', Press release, 2 November, Available from: https://www.gov.uk/government/news/airports-commiss ion-membership [Accessed 21 August, 2020].

DfT (2016) *Further Review and Sensitivities Report: Airport Capacity in The South East*, October, London: DfT.

DfT (2017a) *Consultation on Draft Airports National Policy Statement: New Runway Capacity and Infrastructure at Airports in the South East of England*, February, London: DfT.

DfT (2017b) *Night Flight Restrictions at Heathrow, Gatwick and Stansted, Consultation Document*, January, London: DfT.

DfT (2017c) *UK Airspace Policy Consultation*, Executive summary, January, London: DfT.

DfT (2017d) *Beyond the Horizon: The Future of UK Aviation*, Call for evidence, July, London: DfT.

DfT (2017e) *Revised Draft Airports National Policy Statement: New Runway Capacity and Infrastructure at Airports in the South East of England*, October, London: DfT.

DfT (2018a) *Airports National Policy Statement: New Runway Capacity and Infrastructure at Airports in the South East of England*, June, London: DfT.

DfT (2018b) *Aviation 2050. The Future of UK Aviation*, Cm 9714, December, London: DfT.

DfT (2021a) *Jet Zero Consultation: A Consultation on our Strategy for Net Zero Aviation*, London: DfT.

DfT (2021b) 'Decision on requests to review the Airports National Policy Statement under the Planning Act 2008', Public letter 6 September, Available from: https://assets.publishing.service.gov.uk/government/uplo ads/system/uploads/attachment_data/file/1015207/decision-on-reque sts-to-review-the-anps.pdf [Accessed 13 September, 2021].

DfT and C. Grayling MP (2016) 'Government decides on a new runway at Heathrow', 25 October, Available from: https://www.gov.uk/governm ent/news/government-decides-on-new-runway-at-heathrow [Accessed 13 December, 2021].

Doganis, R. (2006) *The Airline Business*, London: Routledge.

Doherty, B. and Hayes, G. (2015) 'The courts: criminal trials as strategic arenas', in J. W. Duyvendak and J.M. Jasper (eds), *Breaking Down the State*, Amsterdam: Amsterdam University Press.

Drapkin, D. (1974) 'Development, electricity and power stations', *Public Law*, Autumn, 220–53.

Dreyfus, H. and Rabinow, P. (1982) *Michel Foucault: Beyond Structuralism and Hermeneutics*, Brighton: Harvester.

Dudley, G. and Richardson, J. (1998) 'Arenas without rules and the policy change process', *Political Studies*, 46(4): 727–47.

Duit, A., Feindt, P. and Meadowcroft, J. (2016) 'Greening leviathan: the rise of the environmental state?', *Environmental Politics*, 25(1): 1–23.

Dyer, L. (2015) 'Mayoral candidates among heavyweights at anti-Heathrow expansion rally', *Richmond and Twickenham Times*, 9 October, Available at: https://www.richmondandtwickenham Times.co.uk/news/13835637. mayoral-candidates-among-heavyweights-at-anti-Heathrow-expansion-rally [Accessed 9 February, 2023].

Eckersley, R. (2004) *The Green State*, Cambridge, MA: MIT Press.

Eckersley, R. (2021) 'Greening states and societies: from transitions to great transformations', *Environmental Politics*, 30(1): 245–65.

Edgerton, D. (2018) *The Rise and Fall of the British Nation: A Twentieth-Century History*, London: Allen Lane.

Engel, J.A. (2007) *Cold War at 30,000 Feet: The Anglo-American Fight for Aviation Supremacy*, Cambridge: Cambridge University Press.

Environmental Audit Committee (EAC) (2015) *Airports Commission Report: Carbon Emissions, Air Quality and Noise Inquiry Launched*, 23 July, https://committees.parliament.uk/committee/62/environmental-audit-committee/news/100377/airports-commission-report-carbon-emissions-air-quality-and-noise-inquiry-launched/ [Accessed 14 November, 2021].

EAC (2015b) *The Airports Commission Report: Carbon Emissions, Air Quality and Noise*, HC 389, London: TSO.

EAC (2017) *The Airports Commission Report Follow-Up: Carbon Emissions, Air Quality and Noise*, HC 840, London: HoC.

Espeland, W.N. and Stevens, M.L. (2008) 'A sociology of quantification', *European Journal of Sociology*, 49(3): 401–36.

Eurocontrol (2021) 'Forecast update 2021–2027', October, Available from: https://www.eurocontrol.int/sites/default/files/2021-10/eurocont rol-7-year-forecast-2021-2027.pdf [Accessed 15 December, 2021].

Everingham, P. and Chassagne, N. (2020) 'Post Covid-19 ecological and social reset', *Tourism Geographies*, 22(3): 555–66.

Fawcett, P. and Marsh, D. (2014) 'Depoliticisation, governance and political participation', *Policy & Politics*, 42(2): 171–88.

Feldman, E.J. (1985) *Concorde and Dissent: Explaining High Technology Failures in Great Britain and France*, Cambridge: Cambridge University Press.

Feldman, E.J. and Milch, J. (1982) *Technocracy versus Democracy: The Comparative Politics of International Airports*, Boston, Mass: Auburn House Publishing.

Feldman, E.J. and Milch, J. (1983) *The Politics of Canadian Airport Development: Lessons for Federalism*, Duke University Press, Durham, North Carolina.

Finance Monthly (2021) 'Heathrow's pandemic losses near £3 billion', 26 July, Available from: https://www.finance-monthly.com/2021/07/heathrows-pandemic-losses-near-3-billion/ [Accessed 16 December 2021].

Flinders M. and Buller J. (2006a) 'Depoliticization: principles, tactics and tools', *British Politics*, 1(3): 293–318.

Flinders M. and Buller J. (2006b) 'Depoliticization, democracy and arena shifting', in T. Christensen and P. Lagraeid (eds) *Autonomy and |Regulation: Coping With Agencies in the Modern State*, Cheltenham: Edward Elgar, pp 53–80.

Flinders, M. and Wood, M. (2014) 'Depoliticisation, governance and the state', *Policy & Politics*, 42(2): 135–49.

Flowerdew, A. (1972) 'The cost of airport noise', *The Statistician*, 21(1): 31–46.

Flyvbjerg, B., Bruzelius, N. and Rothengatter, W. (2003) *Megaprojects and Risk: An Anatomy of Ambition*, Cambridge: Cambridge University Press.

Fordham, R. (1970) 'Airport planning in the context of the third London airport', *Economic Journal*, 80(318): 307–22.

Foster, C.D. (2001) 'Michael Beesley and cost benefit analysis', *Journal of Transport Economics and Policy*, 35(1): 3–30.

Foucault, M. (1972) *The Archaeology of Knowledge*, London: Tavistock.

Foucault, M. (1977) *Discipline and Punish*, Harmondsworth: Penguin Books.

Foucault, M. (1980) *Power/Knowledge: Selected Interviews and Other Writings 1972–1977*, New York: Pantheon Books.

Foucault, M. (1982) 'The subject and power', in H.L. Dreyfus and P. Rabinow (eds) *Michel Foucault: Beyond Structuralism and Hermeneutics*, London: Harvester Press, pp 208–26.

Foucault, M. (1984) 'Nietzsche, genealogy, history' in P. Rabinow (ed) *The Foucault Reader*, Harmondsworth: Penguin Books, pp 76–100.

Foucault, M. (1988) 'The concern for truth', in L. Kritzman (ed), *Michel Foucault: Politics, Philosophy, Culture*, New York: Routledge, pp 255–67.

Foucault, M. (1991) 'Governmentality', in G. Burchell, C. Gordon and P.H. Miller (eds) *The Foucault Effect: Studies in Governmentality*, London: Harvester Wheatsheaf, pp 87–104.

Foucault, M. (2008) *Birth of Biopolitics*, London: Palgrave.

Fouilleux, E. and Jobert, B. (2017) 'Le cheminement des controverses dans la globalisation néo-libérale', *Gouvernement et Action Publique*, 6(3): 9–36.

Fox, L. (2021) 'Time to get flying again!', *Mail on Sunday*, 20 June, Available from: https://www.dailymail.co.uk/debate/article-9704319/Former-Minister-DR-LIAM-FOX-says-Britain-nation-Covid-neurotics-forever.html [Accessed 10 January, 2023).

Freeden, M. (1996) *Ideologies and Political Theory: A Conceptual Approach*, Oxford: Oxford University Press.

Freeman, R. (2019) 'Meeting, talk and text: policy and politics in practice', *Policy & Politics*, 47(1): 37–56.

Freeman, R. and Maybin, J. (2011) 'Documents, practices and policy', *Evidence & Policy*, 7(2): 155–70.

Frey, B., Oberholzer-Gee, F. and Eichenberger, R. (1996) 'The old lady visits your backyard: a tale of morals and markets', *Journal of Political Economy*, 104(6): 1297–313.

Friedrich, C. (1958) 'Authority, reason and discretion', in C. Friedrich (ed) *Authority*, Cambridge, MA: Harvard University Press, pp 28–48.

Friends of the Earth (FoE) (2013) *Airports Commission Discussion Paper 01: Aviation Demand Forecasting. Response by Friends of the Earth*, London: FoE.

FoE (2020) *Public Inquiries: A Campaigner's Guide*, London: FoE.

Fukuyama, F. (1992) *The End of History and the Last Man*, London: Hamish Hamilton.

Garner-Purkis, Z. (2019) 'Investigation: The human cost of building the world's biggest airport', *Architects' Journal*, 10 October, Available from: https://www.architectsjournal.co.uk/news/investigation-the-human-cost-of-building-the-worlds-biggest-airport [Accessed 12 December, 2021].

Gatwick Airport (2015a) *A Second Runway for Gatwick*, Available from: https://www.gatwickairport.com/globalassets/publicationfiles/business_and_community/all_public_publications/second_runway/airports_commission/airports-commission-final-report-areas-of-concern.pdf [Accessed 21 December, 2021].

Gatwick Airport (2015b) 'Airports Commission's findings simply don't add up', Press release, 17 August, Available from: https://www.mediacentre.gatwickairport.com/press-releases/2015/15-08-17-airports-commission-findings-simply-do-not-add-up.aspx [Accessed 9 November, 2021].

Gatwick Airport (2015c) 'Gatwick expansion remains only deliverable option', Press release, 1 July, Available from: https://www.mediacentre.gatwickairport.com/press-releases/2015/15-07-01gatwick-expansion-remains-only-deliverable-option.aspx [Accessed 9 November, 2021].

Gatwick Area Conservation Committee (GACC) (2014) 'Open letter to the Department for Transport, 3 February', Available from: https://www.airportwatch.org.uk/2014/03/concerns-about-the-effectiveness-of-a-new-airport-noise-authority-and-the-publics-trust-in-it/ [Accessed 12 December, 2021].

Gazzard, J. (2014) 'Comment: response to P. Wintour "Heathrow critics and supporters unite to call for airport noise ombudsman"', *The Guardian*, [online] 10 March, Available from: https://profile.theguardian.com/user/id/3882813?page=3 [Accessed 19 December, 2021].

Georgiadis, P. and Ralph, O. (2021) 'Gatwick in talk with lenders as losses mount', *Financial Times*, 13 August, Available from: https://www.ft.com/content/ccbe4745-fef0-4599-bfa9-c9470cb51f0e [Accessed 7 February, 2023].

Ghosh, P. (2020) 'Climate change boosted Australia bushfire risk by at least 30%', BBC News, 4 March, Available from: https://www.bbc.co.uk/news/science-environment-51742646 [Accessed 4 November, 2021].

Gill, O. (2021) 'British Airways revives plans to abandon Gatwick', *The Daily Telegraph*, 19 June, Available from: https://www.telegraph.co.uk/business/2021/06/19/british-airways-revives-plans-abandon-gatwick/ [Accessed 15 August, 2022].

Glancey, J. (2014) 'What should we do with disused airports?', BBC Culture, 21 October, Available from: https://www.bbc.com/culture/article/20140811-inside-abandoned-airports [Accessed 14 October, 2021].

Glynos, J. (2021) 'Critical fantasy studies', *Journal of Language and Politics*, 20(1): 95–111.

Glynos, J. and Howarth, D. (2007) *Logics of Critical Explanation in Social and Political Theory*, Abingdon: Routledge.

Gordon, A. (2020) 'British Airways could pull out of Gatwick and cut a quarter of its pilots, leaked memo reveals', *The Daily Mail*, 30 April, Available from: https://www.dailymail.co.uk/news/article-8273921/British-Airways-warns-abandon-Gatwick.html [Accessed 3 March, 2023].

Gössling, S. and Humpe, A. (2020) 'The global scale, distribution and growth of aviation: implications for climate change', *Global Environmental Change*, 65: 102194.

Gössling, S., Fichert, F. and Forsyth, P. (2017) 'Subsidies in aviation', *Sustainability*, 9, 1295, DOI:10.3390/su9081295.

Gössling, S., Hanna, P., Higham, J., Cohen, S. and Hopkins, D. (2019) 'Can we fly less? Evaluating the "necessity" of air travel', *Journal of Air Transport Management*, 81: 101722.

Graham, J.R. (2018) 'Heathrow third runway: a horrible mistake', The Myth Breaker [Blog] 30 July, Available from: https://mythbreaker.co.uk/transport/heathrow-third-runway-horrible-mistake/ [Accessed 9 December, 2021].

Gramsci, A. (1971) *Selections From the Prison Notebooks*, London: Lawrence and Wishart.

Greenpeace (2015) 'Davies fails to make the case for a 3rd runway', Climate Crocodile [Blog], 1 July, Available from: https://storage.googleapis.com/gpuk-archive/node/371768.html [Accessed 11 December, 2021].

Grice, A. (2015) 'Jeremy Corbyn's election as leader of the Labour party could scupper plans for third runway at Heathrow', *The Independent*, 1 August, Available from: https://www.independent.co.uk/news/uk/politics/jeremy-corbyn-s-election-as-leader-of-labour-party-could-scupper-plans-for-third-runway-at-heathrow-10431575.html [Accessed 21 August, 2020].

Griggs, S. and Howarth, D. (2002) 'An alliance of interest and identity? Explaining the campaign against Manchester Airport's second runway', *Mobilization*, 7(1): 43–58.

Griggs, S. and Howarth, D. (2013) *The Politics of Airport Expansion in the United Kingdom,* Manchester: Manchester University Press.

Griggs, S. and Howarth, D. (2019a) 'The Airports Commission, depoliticisation and the third runway at Heathrow Airport', in J. Buller, P. Dönmez, A. Standring and M. Wood (eds) *Comparing Strategies of (De) Politicisation in Europe*, London: Palgrave Macmillan, pp 79–102.

Griggs, S. and Howarth, D. (2019b) 'Discourse, policy and the environment: hegemony, statements and the analysis of UK airport expansion', *Journal of Environmental Policy & Planning*, 21(5): 464–78.

Griggs, S. and Howarth, D. (2020) 'Two images of Nantes as a "green model" of urban planning and democratic governance: the "collaborative city" versus the "slow city"', *Town Planning Review*, 91(4): 415–36.

Griggs, S., Howarth, D. and Jacobs, B (1998) 'The second runway at Manchester', *Parliamentary Affairs*, 51(3): 358–69.

Griggs, S., Howarth, D. and Feandeiro, A. (2020) 'The logics and limits of "collaborative governance" in Nantes: myth, ideology and the politics of new urban regimes', *Journal of Urban Affairs*, 42(1): 91–108.

Grimme, W., Maertens, S. and Bingemer, S. (2021) 'The role of very large passenger aircraft in global air transport', *Transportation Research Procedia*, 59: 76–84.

Gudeman, S. (ed) (1998) *Economic Anthropology*, Cheltenham: Edward Elgar.

Gusfield, J.R. (1981) *The Culture of Public Problems*, Chicago: Chicago University Press.

HACAN (2015) 'HACAN backs cross-party campaign against 3rd runway launched today', Press release, 2 September, Available from: https://hacan.org.uk/?p=3320 [Accessed 9 February, 2023].

HACAN (2017) *The Economic Benefits of a Third Runway Officially Downgraded*, Available from: https://hacan.org.uk/wp-content/uploads/2017/02/The-Economic-Benefits-of-a-Third-Runway-Reassessed.pdf [Accessed 15 November, 2021].

Hacking, I. (1981) 'How should we do the history of statistics?', *I&C*, 8: 15–26.

Hajer, M. (1995) *The Politics of Environmental Discourse*, Oxford: Clarendon Press.

Hajer, M. (2005) 'Setting the stage: a dramaturgy of policy deliberation', *Administration & Society*, 36(6): 624–47.

Hajer, M. (2009) *Authoritative Governance*, Oxford: Oxford University Press.

Hall, C., Scott, D. and Gössling, S. (2020) 'Pandemics, transformation and tourism', *Tourism Geographies*, 22(3): 577–98.

Hall, P. (1968) 'Roskill's airport: the first days', *New Society*, 26 December, pp 939–42.

Hall, P. (1971) 'The Roskill argument: an analysis', *New Society*, 28 January, pp 145–8.

Hall, P. (1982) *Great Planning Disasters*, Berkeley, CA: University of California Press.

Hall, S. (1988) *The Hard Road to Renewal: Thatcherism and the Crisis of The Left*, London: Verso.

Hansard (2016) 'Airport capacity, volume 616: debated on Tuesday 25 October 2016', Available from: https://hansard.parliament.uk/Commons/2016-10-25/debates/4D74A7CB-8921-48BD-9960-FD15D5D1EEDF/AirportCapacity#contribution-2EC69836-495B-46B5-B7ED-6033E6EE7940 [Accessed 12 December, 2021].

Hansard (2021a) 'Aviation, travel and tourism industries', Vol. 696. 10 June, Available from: https://hansard.parliament.uk/commons/2021-06-10/debates/0922563F-114D-4D63-86F5-707A8DC2B434/AviationTravelAndTourismIndustries [Accessed 3 January 2023].

Hansard (2021b) 'Prime Minister: Engagements', Vol. 702, Col. 905, 3 November, Available from: https://hansard.parliament.uk/Commons/2021-11-03/debates/DA26E685-87E2-430D-AD81-919688AE9400/Engagements [Accessed 6 February, 2023].

Hansell, A., Blangiardo, M., Fortunato, L., Floud, S., de Hoogh, K., Fecht, D. et al (2013) 'Aircraft noise and cardiovascular disease near Heathrow airport in London: Small area study', *British Medical Journal*, 347: f5432.

Harvey, F. (2015) 'Supreme court orders UK to draw up air pollution cleanup plan', *The Guardian*, 29 April, Available from: https://www.theguardian.com/environment/2015/apr/29/supreme-court-orders-uk-to-draw-up-air-pollution-cleanup-plan [Accessed 21 December, 2021].

Hay, C. (2007) *Why We Hate Politics*, Cambridge: Polity Press.

Hay C. (2014) 'Depoliticisation as process, governance as practice: what did the "first wave" get wrong and do we need a "second wave" to put it right?', *Policy & Politics*, 42(2): 293–311.

Heathrow Airport (2018a) *Airport Expansion Consultation Document*, January, London: Heathrow Airport Limited.

Heathrow Airport (2018b) *Heathrow 2.0. 2018 Sustainability Progress Report*, London: Heathrow Airport Limited.

Heidegger, M. (1962) *Being and Time*, Oxford: Blackwell.

Heidegger, M. (1977) *Basic Writings: From Being and Time (1927) to the Task of Thinking (1964)*, London: Harper and Row.

Helm, T. (2015) 'Why Zac Goldsmith's views on Heathrow and Europe are a problem for Cameron', *The Observer*, 5 July, Available from: https://www.theguardian.com/politics/2015/jul/05/zac-goldsmith-views-heathrow-europe-problem-david-cameron [Accessed 15 February, 2023].

Henderson, C. (2021) 'The hydrogen revolution in the skies', *BBC Future*, 8 April, Available from: https://www.bbc.com/future/article/20210401-the-worlds-first-commercial-hydrogen-plane [Accessed 24 October, 2021].

Hicks, C. (2022) *Expansion Rebellion: Using the Law to Fight a Runway and Save the Planet*, Manchester: Manchester University Press.

High Court (2019) *Approved Judgment*, R (Spurrier and Others) v Secretary of State for Transport, [2019] EWHC 1070 (Admin), Available from: https://www.judiciary.uk/wp-content/uploads/2019/05/Heathrow-main-judgment-1.5.19.pdf [Accessed 7 December, 2021].

High Court (2020) *Transcripts 13 March 2019*, R (Spurrier and Others) v Secretary of State for Transport, Available from: https://www.judiciary.uk/wp-content/uploads/2019/03/130319.txt [Accessed 7 December, 2021].

Hinks, E.K. (2021) 'Downscaling the aviation industry', *Climate Matters* [Blog] 30 June, Available from: https://climatematters.blogs.uni-hamburg.de/2021/06/downscaling-the-aviation-industry/ [Accessed 18 October, 2021].

Hirschl, R. (2011) 'The judicialization of politics' in R. Goodin (ed) *The Oxford Handbook of Political Science*, Oxford: Oxford University Press, pp 253–74.

Hirschman, A.O. (1970) *A Bias for Hope: Essays on Development and Latin America*, New Haven, CT: Yale University Press.

Hirschman, A.O. (1977) *The Passions and the Interests*, Princeton, NJ: Princeton University Press.

Hirschman, A.O. (1982) *Shifting Involvements: Private Interest and Public Action*, Princeton, NJ: Princeton University Press.

HM Treasury (HMT) and Department for Transport (DfT) (2003) *Aviation and the Environment: Using Economic Instruments*, London: DfT.

Hogwood, B. and Gunn, L. (1984) *Policy Analysis for the Real World*, Oxford: Oxford University Press.

Horkheimer, M. and Adorno, T. (2002) *Dialectic of Enlightenment*, Stanford: Stanford University Press.

House of Commons Library (HoCL) (2021) *The UK Emissions Trading Scheme*, Briefing paper 9212, 4 May, Available from: https://researchbriefings.files.parliament.uk/documents/CBP-9212/CBP-9212.pdf [Accessed 10 December, 2021].

Howard, E. (2016) 'Heathrow: Theresa May once opposed expansion on climate grounds', *Unearthed*, 25 October, Available from: https://unearthed.greenpeace.org/2016/10/25/heathrow-theresa-may-opposed-airport-expansion-climate-grounds/ [Accessed 19 August, 2021].

Howarth, D. (2000) *Discourse*, Buckingham: Open University Press.

Howarth, D. (2013) *Poststructuralism and After*, London: Palgrave Macmillan.

Howarth, D. and Roussos, K. (2022) 'Radical democracy, the commons and everyday struggles during the Greek crisis', *British Journal of Politics and International Relations*, DOI: 10.1177/13691481211067147.

Institute for Government (2021) *HS2: Lessons for Future Infrastructure Projects*, G. Tetlow and E. Shearer (eds), London: IfG.

Intergovernmental Panel on Climate Change (IPCC) (2018) *Global Warming of 1.5 °C*, V. Masson-Delmotte, P. Zhai, H.-O. Pörtner, D. Roberts, J. Skea, P.R. Shukla, et al (eds), Available from: https://www.ipcc.ch/site/assets/uploads/sites/2/2019/06/SR15_Full_Report_High_Res.pdf, [Accessed 4 September, 2021].

IPCC (2021) *Climate Change 2021: The Physical Science Basis. Summary for Policymakers*, Geneva: IPCC.

International Air Transport Association (IATA) (2019) *Fact Sheet 7: Liquid Hydrogen as a Potential Low-Carbon Fuel for Aviation*, Montreal: IATA.

IATA (2021) '20 year passenger forecast', Available from: https://www.iata.org/contentassets/fe5b20e8aae147c290fc4880f120c969/4679_passenger-forecast-infographic-update_v2.pdf [Accessed 7 November, 2021].

International Airport Review (2021) 'Chief executive of AOA calls for comprehensive UK aviation support package', 5 January, Available from: https://www.internationalairportreview.com/news/148099/aoa-comprehensive-uk-aviation-support/ [Accessed 24 October, 2021].

International Aviation Climate Ambition Coalition (2021) *COP-26 Declaration*, 10 November, Available from: https://ukcop26.org/cop-26-declaration-international-aviation-climate-ambition-coalition/ [Accessed 21 November, 2021].

International Civil Aviation Organisation (ICAO) (2016) 'Historic agreement reached to mitigate international aviation emissions', ICAO Press release, 6 October, Available from: https://www.icao.int/newsroom/pages/historic-agreement-reached-to-mitigate-international-aviation-emissions.aspx [Accessed 3 January 2023].

ICAO (2019a) *The World of Air Transport in 2019*, Available from: https://www.icao.int/annual-report-2019/Pages/the-world-of-air-transport-in-2019.aspx [Accessed 8 November, 2021].

ICAO (2019b) *Aviation Benefits Report 2019*, Available from: file:///C:/Users/User/AppData/Local/Temp/AVIATION-BENEFITS-2019-web.pdf [Accessed 10 December, 2021].

ICAO (2021a) 'Economic impacts of Covid-19 on civil aviation', Available from: https://www.icao.int/sustainability/Pages/Economic-Impacts-of-COVID-19.aspx [Accessed 12 December, 2021].

ICAO (2021b) *Post-Covid-19 Forecast Scenarios*, Available from: https://www.icao.int/sustainability/Pages/Post-Covid-Forecasts-Scenarios.aspx [Accessed 29 November, 2021].

International Council on Clean Transportation (ICCT) (2019) *CO₂ Emissions from Commercial Aviation, 2018*, Working paper 2019–16, B. Graver, K. Zhang and D. Rutherford, Washington: ICCT.

ICCT (2020) *CO₂ Emissions from Commercial Aviation, 2013, 2018, and 2019*, B. Graver, D. Rutherford and S. Zheng, Washington DC: ICCT.

ICCT (2021) *Estimating Sustainable Aviation Fuel Feedstock Availability to Meet Growing European Union Demand*, Working paper 2021–13, J. O'Malley, N. Pavlenko and S. Searle, Washington DC: ICCT.

IPSOS (2020) 'Two thirds of citizens around the world agree climate change is as serious a crisis as coronavirus', Press release, 22 April, Available from: https://www.ipsos.com/en/two-thirds-citizens-around-world-agree-climate-change-serious-crisis-coronavirus [Accessed 16 September, 2021].

Jenkins, S. (2016) ' "No ifs, no buts": don't forget your Heathrow pledge, Mr Cameron', *Evening Standard*, 7 June, Available from: https://www.standard.co.uk/comment/comment/simon-jenkins-no-ifs-no-buts-don-t-forget-your-heathrow-pledge-mr-cameron-a3265646.html [Accessed 29 December 2022].

Jessop, B. (2014) 'Repoliticising depoliticisation: theoretical preliminaries on some responses to the American fiscal and Eurozone debt crises', *Policy & Politics*, 42(2): 207–23.

Johnson, P. (2018) 'The Heathrow saga shows we need far greater ambition after Brexit', *The Daily Telegraph*, 26 June, Available from: https://www.telegraph.co.uk/news/2018/06/26/heathrow-saga-shows-need-far-greater-ambition-brexit/ [Accessed 20 August, 2022].

Jolly, J. (2020) 'Heathrow overtaken as Europe's busiest airport by Charles de Gaulle', *The Guardian*, 28 October, Available from: https://www.theguardian.com/uk-news/2020/oct/28/heathrow-overtaken-as-europe-largest-airport-by-charles-de-gaulle-london-covid-paris [Accessed 8 January, 2023].

Jones, M. (2019) *Cities and Regions in Crisis*, Cheltenham: Edward Elgar.

Jordan, G. and Richardson, J. (1982) 'The British policy style or the logic of negotiation?', in J. Richardson (ed) *Policy styles in Western Europe*, London: George Allen & Unwin, pp 80–110.

Keate, G. (2016) 'Ministers free to oppose Heathrow decision, says May', *The Times*, 18 October, Available from: https://www.thetimes.co.uk/article/ministers-free-to-oppose-heathrow-decision-says-may-27t5wzfkm [Accessed 27 January, 2023].

Keller, R. (2013) *Doing Discourse Research*, London: Sage.

Kemp, R. (1985) 'Planning, public hearings and the politics of discourse' in J. Forester (ed) *Critical Theory and Public Life*, Cambridge, MA: MIT Press, pp 177–201.

Kennedy, C. (2021) 'COP 26 aviation commitment fails to limit further airport expansions', *New Civil Engineer*, 11 November, Available from: https://www.newcivilengineer.com/latest/cop26-aviation-com mitment-fails-to-limit-further-airport-expansions-11-11-2021/ [Accessed 27 November, 2021].

Kettell, S. and Kerr, P. (2022) '"Guided by the science": (de)politicising the UK government's response to the coronavirus crisis', *British Journal of Politics and International Relations*, 24(1): 11–30.

King, T. and Crewe, I. (2013) *The Blunders of our Governments*, London: Oneworld Publications.

Klein, N. (2014) *This Changes Everything*, London: Allen Lane.

KPMG (2016) *Brexit: Implications for Airlines*, November, London: KPMG.

Krippner, G. (2011) *Capitalizing on Crisis*, Cambridge, Mass.: Harvard University Press.

Laclau, E. (1990) *New Reflections on the Revolution of Our Time*, London: Verso.

Laclau, E. (1996) *Emancipation(s)*, London: Verso.

Laclau, E. (2005) *On Populist Reason*, London: Verso.

Laclau, E. and Mouffe, C. (2014) *Hegemony and Socialist Strategy: Towards a Radical Democratic Politics*, 2nd edn, London: Verso.

Larkin, B. (2013) 'The politics and poetics of infrastructure', *The Annual Review of Anthropology*, 42: 327–43.

Latour, B. (2018) *Down to Earth*, Cambridge: Polity Press.

Latour, B. (2022) *After Lockdown*, Cambridge: Polity Press.

Laville, S. (2019) 'Fight against Heathrow expansion on verge of victory, says McDonnell', *The Guardian*, 17 October, Available from: https://www.theguardian.com/environment/2019/oct/17/heathrow-expansion-protest-on-verge-of-victory-says-shadow-chancellor [Accessed 2 February, 2023].

Le Blond, P. (2018) 'Government decision on Heathrow third runway: an opinion', *Logistics & Transport Focus*, July, 20(7): 13.

Le Blond, P. (2019) *Inside London's Airports Policy*, London: ICE Publishing.

Lee, D. and Forster, P. (2020) 'Calculating the true climate impact of aviation emissions', *Carbon Brief*, 21 September, Available from: https://www.carb onbrief.org/guest-post-calculating-the-true-climate-impact-of-aviation-emissions [Accessed 9 November, 2021].

Lee, D., Fahey, D., Skowron, A., Allen, M., Burkhardt, U., Chen, Q. et al (2021) 'The contribution of global aviation to anthropogenic climate forcing for 2000 to 2018', *Atmospheric Environment*, 224: 117834.

Lees, J. (2015) 'The Heathrow noise sweeteners that act as a smokescreen for Third Runway pollution', *The Huffington Post*, [online] 2 July, Available from: https://www.huffingtonpost.co.uk/james-lees/heathrow-third-runway_b_7711456.html [Accessed 9 December, 2021].

Levin, P. (1979) 'Highways inquiries: a study in government responsiveness', *Public Administration*, 57(1): 21–53.

Liberal Democrat Voice (2021) 'Lib Dems lead cross-party call for urgent support for airlines in return for climate action', 27 April, Available from: https://www.libdemvoice.org/lib-dems-lead-crossparty-call-for-urgent-support-for-airlines-in-return-for-climate-action-64283.html [Accessed 12 December, 2021].

Lichfield, N. (1971) 'Cost-benefit analysis in planning: a critique of the Roskill Commission', *Regional Studies*, 5(3): 157–83.

Little, D. (2013) 'Hirschman on the passions', Blog, available from: https://understandingsociety.blogspot.com/2013/05/hirschman-on-passions.html [Accessed 20 October, 2021].

Lockwood, M. (2013) 'The political sustainability of climate policy: the case of the UK Climate Change Act', *Global Environmental Change*, 23(5): 1339–48.

London Borough of Richmond-upon-Thames (2018) 'Councils set for court challenge on Heathrow decision', Press release, 19 July, Available from: https://www.richmond.gov.uk/heathrow/council_news_on_heathrow/councils_set_for_court_challenge_on_heathrow_decision [Accessed 19 January, 2022].

Lukes, S. (2005) *Power: A Radical View*, 2nd edn, Basingstoke: Palgrave Macmillan.

Lynge, A. (2007) 'Don't melt way our future, Inuit leader tells airlines', *Evening Standard*, 27 July, Available from: https://www.standard.co.uk/hp/front/don-t-melt-away-our-future-inuit-leader-tells-airlines-6601384.html# [Accessed 1 February, 2023].

Mackie, P. and Pearce, B. (2015) *A Note From Expert Advisors, Prof. Peter Mackie and Mr Brian Pearce, on Key Issues Considering the Airports Commission Economic Case*, May, Airports Commission expert advisor note, Available from: https://assets.publishing.service.gov.uk/government/uploads/system/uploads/attachment_data/file/438981/economy-expert-panelist-wider-economic-impacts-review.pdf [Accessed 11 December, 2021].

Mair, P. (2013) *Ruling the Void*, London: Verso.

Manthiou, A., Klaus, P. and Ha Luong, V. (2022) 'Slow tourism', *Tourism Management*, 93: 104570.

Marshall, T. (2011) 'Reforming the process for infrastructure planning in the UK/England 1990–2010', *Town Planning Review*, 82(4): 441–67.

Marshall, T. (2012) *Planning Major Infrastructure*, London: Routledge.

Marshall, T. (2021) *The Politics and Ideology of Planning*, Bristol: Policy Press.

Marshall, T. and Cowell, R. (2016) 'Infrastructure, planning and the command of time', *Environment and Planning C*, 34(8): 1843–66.

Marx, K. (1973) *Grundrisse*, London: Allen Lane.

Marx, K. (1976) *Capital Volume 1*, Harmondsworth: Penguin Books.

Mason, R. and Watt, N. (2015) 'Boris Johnson dismisses Heathrow third runway report: "it won't happen"', *The Guardian*, 1 July, Available from: https://www.theguardian.com/uk-news/2015/jul/01/boris-johnson-heathrow-third-runway-davies-report [Accessed 15 February, 2023].

Matthews, C. (2013) 'A fresh look at UK airport capacity: time for a 3rd runway at Heathrow?', Westminster Energy, Environment & Transport Forum, 31 January, Transcripts, London: Westminster Energy, Environment & Transport, pp 10–11.

May, T. (2017) 'The shared society', Prime Minister's speech at the Charity Commission annual meeting, 9 January, Available from: https://www.gov.uk/government/speeches/the-shared-society-prime-ministers-speech-at-the-charity-commission-annual-meeting [Accessed 15 December, 2021].

May, T. (2018) 'PM speech on our future economic partnership with the EU', 2 March, Available from: https://www.gov.uk/government/speeches/pm-speech-on-our-future-economic-partnership-with-the-european-union [Accessed 15 December, 2021].

McBride, D. (2013) *Power Trip: A Decade of Policy, Plots and Spin*, Hull: Biteback.

McCarthy, D. (2021) 'How can Manchester United defend their 10-minute flight to Leicester?', *The Independent*, 18 October, Available from: https://www.independent.co.uk/climate-change/opinion/manchester-united-fly-to-leicester-climate-crisis-b1940551.html [Accessed 4 November, 2021].

McConnell, A. (2018) 'Rethinking wicked problems as political problems and policy problems', *Policy & Politics*, 46(1): 165–80.

McConnell, A. and 't Hart, P. (2019) 'Inaction and public policy: understanding why policymakers do "nothing"', *Policy Sciences*, 52: 645–61.

McGregor, G. (2020) '"Flights to nowhere" are popular', *Fortune*, 11 October, Available from: https://fortune.com/2020/10/11/covid-travel-flights-to-nowhere-psychology/ [Accessed 4 November, 2021].

McGregor, P., Swales, J. and Winning, M. (2012) 'A review of the role and remit of the Committee on Climate Change', *Energy Policy*, 41: 466–73.

McKennell, A. (1969) 'Methodological problems in a survey of aircraft noise annoyance', *The Statistician*, 19(1): 1–29.

McKie, D. (1973) *The Sadly Mismanaged Affair: Politics of the Third London Airport*, London: Croom Helm.

McLoughlin, P. (2012) 'Independent Airports Commission – increasing the competitiveness of UK airlines and airports', Written statement, 7 September, Available from: https://www.gov.uk/government/speeches/increasing-international-competitiveness-of-uk-airlines-and-airports [Accessed 19 December, 2021].

McLoughlin, P. (2015a) 'Airports Commission final report' Oral statement, 1 July, Available from: https://www.gov.uk/government/speeches/airports-commission-final-report-oral-statement [Accessed 12 November, 2021].

McLoughlin, P. (2015b) 'Oral statement to parliament: aviation capacity', 14 December, Available from: www.gov.uk/government/speeches/aviation-capacity [Accessed 19 November, 2021].

McVeigh, K. (2016) 'Heathrow 13: climate change protesters avoid jail', *The Guardian*, 25 February, Available from: https://www.theguardian.com/environment/2016/feb/24/heathrow-13-climate-change-protesters-avoid-jail [Accessed 2 January, 2022].

Meriluoto, T. (2021) 'Struggles over expertise', *Democratic Theory*, 8(1): 1–22.

Milch, J. (1976) 'Inverted pyramids: the use and mis-use of aviation forecasting', *Social Studies of Science*, 6: 5–31.

Miliband, E. (2021) 'Our biggest enemy is no longer climate denial but climate delay', *The Guardian*, 30 July, Available from: https://www.theguardian.com/commentisfree/2021/jul/30/climate-denial-delay-inaction-british-government [Accessed 6 January, 2023].

Miller, P. and Rose, N. (1990) 'Governing economic life', *Economy and Society*, 19(1): 1–31.

Mishan, E. (1970) 'What is wrong with Roskill?', *Journal of Transport Economics and Policy*, 4(3): 221–34.

Mitchell, T. (1991) *Colonising Egypt*, Cambridge: Cambridge University Press.

Mitchell, T. (2002) *Rule of Experts: Egypt, Techno-Politics, Modernity*, Berkeley: University of California Press.

Mitchell, T. (2011) *Carbon Democracy*, London: Verso.

Mitchell, T. (2014) 'Introduction: life of infrastructure', *Comparative Studies of South Asia, Africa and the Middle East*, 34(3): 437–9.

Mitchell, T. (2020) 'Infrastructures work on time', *e-flux Architecture*, Available from: https://www.e-flux.com/architecture/new-silk-roads/312596/infrastructures-work-on-time/ [Accessed 22 October, 2021].

Monbiot, G. (2020) 'Airlines and oil giants are on the brink: no government should offer them a lifeline', *The Guardian*, 29 April, Available from: https://www.theguardian.com/commentisfree/2020/apr/29/airlines-oil-giants-government-economy [Accessed 3 January 2023].

Moran, M. (1986) *The Politics of Banking*, London: Palgrave Macmillan.

Moran, M. (2003) *The British Regulatory State: High Modernism and Hyper-innovation*, Oxford: Oxford University Press.

Moreton, C. (2015) 'Zac Goldsmith: "I'll trigger a by-election over Heathrow"', *The Independent*, 18 April, Available from: https://www.independent.co.uk/news/uk/politics/generalelection/zac-goldsmith-i-ll-trigger-a-byelection-over-heathrow-10187292.html [Accessed 15 February, 2023].

Morris, S. (2021) '"Decarbonising aviation": the Electric Eel could be the future of flying', *The Guardian*, 24 August, Available from: https://www.theguardian.com/environment/2021/aug/24/decarbonising-aviation-the-electric-eel-could-be-the-future-of-flying [Accessed 7 February, 2023].

Mouffe, C. (1993) *The Return of the Political*, London: Verso.

Mouffe, C. (2005) *On the Political*, London: Routledge.

Mouffe, C. (2013) *Agonistics: Thinking the World Politically*, London: Verso.

Mulholland, H. (2009) 'Boris Johnson appoints Sir David King to examine Thames estuary airport plan', *The Guardian*, 19 October, Available from: https://www.theguardian.com/politics/2009/oct/19/boris-david-king-thames-estuary-airport [Accessed: 31 December, 2022].

Murphy, J. (2014) 'Ed Balls: no more "dither and delay" over Heathrow airport expansion', *London Evening Standard*, 22 September, Available from: https://www.standard.co.uk/news/politics/labour-conference-Ed Balls-promises-no-more-dither-and-delay-over-Heathrow-airport-expansion-9748432.html [Accessed 31 December, 2022].

Murray, J. (2014) 'Osborne promises new wave of high and low carbon infrastructure,' *Business Green*, 29 September, Available from: https://www.businessgreen.com/news/2372747/osborne-promises-new-wave-of-high-and-low-carbon-infrastructure [Accessed 31 December, 2022].

Neate, R. (2020a) 'Nearly 200 airports in UK and Europe could go bust due to collapse in air travel', *The Guardian*, 27 Ocotber, Available from: https://www.theguardian.com/world/2020/oct/27/nearly-200-airports-in-uk-and-europe-could-go-bust-due-to-collapse-in-air-travel [Accessed 6 February, 2023].

Neate, R. (2020b) 'Private jet bookings soar as wealthy flee second England lockdown', *The Guardian*, 3 November, Available from: https://www.theguardian.com/business/2020/nov/03/private-jet-bookings-soar-as-wealthy-flee-second-england-lockdown [Accessed 7 February, 2023].

Needham, D. (2014) 'Maplin: the Treasury and London's Third Airport in the 1970s', *History & Policy*, 27 October, Available from: www.historyandpolicy.org/policy-papers/papers/maplin-the-treasury-and-londons-third-airport-in-the-1970s [Accessed 29 April, 2021].

Nelkin, D. (1974) *Jetport: The Boston Airport Controversy*, New Brunswick, NJ: Transaction Books.

New Economics Foundation (NEF) (2018) *Flying Low: The True Cost of Heathrow's Third Runway*, A. Pendleton and E. Smythe, London: NEF.

NEF (2020) *Crisis Support to Aviation and The Right to Retrain*, A. Chapman and H. Wheatley (eds), London: NEF.

Newell. P. and Simms, A. (2020) 'Towards a fossil fuel non-proliferation treaty', *Climate Policy*, 20(8): 1043–54.

Newman, P. (2009) 'Markets, experts and depoliticizing decisions on major infrastructure', *Urban Research & Practice*, 2(2): 158–68.

Nietzsche, F. (1994) *On the Genealogy of Morality*, Cambridge: Cambridge University Press.

No Third Runway Coalition (2020) 'Heathrow chief executive questions whether third runway will be needed', Press release, 6 May, Available from: https://533d67b8-cd8c-4b9c-be04-d9f1956466a9.filesusr.com/ugd/6eef7a_099710dbacec4983a7fcfe32d4b27384.pdf [Accessed 21 November, 2021].

NOP (2002) *The Future Development of Air Transport in The United Kingdom: Questionnaire*, London: NOP.

Norval, A. (2007) *Aversive Democracy*, Cambridge: Cambridge University Press.

Offe, C. (1984) *Contradictions of the Welfare State*, J. Keane (ed), London: Hutchinson.

O'Riordan, T. and Jordan, A. (1996) 'Social institutions and climate change' in T. O'Riordan and J. Jäger (eds) *Politics of Climate Change*, London: Routledge, pp 65–105.

Orr, J. (2012) 'New Thames Estuary airport "could be built in six years"', *The Daily Telegraph*, 18 January, Available from: https://www.telegraph.co.uk/finance/newsbysector/epic/bba/9022146/New-Thames-Estuary-airport-could-be-built-in-six-years.html [Accessed 29 December, 2022].

Osborne, I. (2014) Speech from Iain Osborne, Director of Regulatory Policy at the Civil Aviation Authority, conference presentation, Summit on Tackling Aviation Noise, 11 March, London.

Owens, S. (2002) 'Commentaries', *Environment and Planning A*, 34: 949–57.

PA Media (2019) 'Extinction Rebellion co-founder arrested at Heathrow protest', *The Guardian*, 14 September, Available from: https://www.theguardian.com/environment/2019/sep/14/extinction-rebellion-co-founder-arrested-at-heathrow-protest [Accessed 19 January, 2023].

Paddison, L. (2021) 'United Airlines promises sustainable flying – but experts aren't convinced', *The Guardian*, 29 December, Available from: https://www.theguardian.com/environment/2021/dec/29/united-airlines-sustainable-green-flying-experts [Accessed 10 March, 2022].

Parker, A. (2013) 'Former airport chief quits commission role', *Financial Times*, 20 September, Available from: https://www.ft.com/content/f192010a-21ec-11e3-bb64-00144feab7de [Accessed 31 December, 2022].

Paton, G. (2020) 'Boris Johnson refuses to back third runway after Supreme Court backs Heathrow', *The Times*, 16 December, Available from: https://www.thetimes.co.uk/article/airport-expansion-heathrow-gets-green-light-for-third-runway-2rg5zlv7x [Accessed 16 August, 2022].

Paton, G. (2021) 'Heathrow expansion thrown off by pandemic', *The Times*, 16 June, Available from: https://www.thetimes.co.uk/article/heathrow-expansion-thrown-off-by-pandemic-058q85j85 [Accessed 21 August, 2022].

Paul, M. (1971) 'Can aircraft noise nuisance be measured in money?', *Oxford Economic Papers*, 22(3): 297–322.

Perman, D. (1973) *Cublington: A Blueprint for Resistance*, London: Bodley Head.

Pickard, C. and Pasqualino, R. (2022) 'Long-term strategies for the compatibility of the aviation industry with climate targets', *Systems*, 10(4), DOI: 10.3390/systems10040090.

Pierce, D. (1971) *Cost-Benefit Analysis*, Basingstoke: Macmillan.

Piggot, G., Erickson, P., van Asselt, H. and Lazarus, M. (2018) 'Swimming upstream: addressing fossil fuel supply under the UNFCCC', *Climate Policy*, 18(9): 1189–202.

Plan B Earth (2018) 'Plan B begins legal action against Heathrow expansion', Press release, 6 August, Available from: https://planb.earth/plan-b-begins-legal-action-against-heathrow-expansion/ [Accessed 15 January, 2022].

Plane Stupid (2015) 'Plane Stupid activists on Heathrow runway in climate protest', [online] 13 July, Available from: https://planestupid.com.archived. website/blogc575.html?page=6 [Accessed 11 December, 2021].

Plimmer, G. and Ford, J. (2018) 'Who will pay for Heathrow airport's £14bn third runway?', *Financial Times*, Available from: https://www. ft.com/content/98e6b128-7533-11e8-aa31-31da4279a601 [Accessed 7 February, 2023].

Plimmer, G. and Georgiadis, P. (2021) 'UK airport expansion plans grounded by Covid and climate change', *Financial Times*, 20 June, Available from: https://www.ft.com/content/40cf97e5-4222-4220-ad10-0704cb37b680 [Accessed 24 August, 2022].

Pollitt, C. and Talbot, C. (eds) (2004) *Unbundled Government*, London: Routledge.

Porter, T.M. (1995) *Trust in Numbers*, Princeton, NJ: Princeton University Press.

Powley, T., Pickard, J. and Beloley, K. (2020) 'Government will not appeal as court blocks third runway at Heathrow', *Financial Times*, 27 February, Available from: https://www.ft.com/content/b0f89152-594b-11ea-a528-dd0f971febbc [Accessed 3 February, 2023].

Pretty, J. (2013) 'The consumption of a finite planet', *Environmental and Resource Economics*, 55: 475–99.

Princen, T. (2003) 'Principles for sustainability: from cooperation and efficiency to sufficiency', *Global Environmental Politics*, 3(1): 33–50.

Princen, T. (2005) *The Logic of Sufficiency*, Cambridge, MA: MIT Press.

Public Accounts Committee (2021) *Lessons from Major Projects and Programmes,* HC694, London: HoC.

Public and Commercial Services Union (PCS), Green House and Green New Deal (2020) *A Green New Deal for Gatwick*, Available from: https:// www.greennewdealuk.org/wp-content/uploads/2020/11/A-Green-New-Deal-for-Gatwick.pdf [Accessed 21 March, 2021].

Rainforest Foundation Norway and Cerulogy (2019) *Destination Deforestation: Aviation Biofuels, Vegetable Oil and Land Use Change*, Oslo: Rainforest Foundation.

Riddington, G. (2006) 'Long range air traffic forecasts for the UK: A critique', *Journal of Transport Economics and Policy*, 40(2): 297–314.

Riker, W.H. (1986) *The Art of Political Manipulation*, New Haven, CT: Yale University Press.

Riker, W.H. (1996) *The Strategy of Rhetoric: Campaigning for the American Constitution*, New Haven, CT: Yale University Press.

Riley-Smith, B. (2016) 'Tory revolt over Heathrow third runway as 60 MPs oppose plans and warn of "catastrophe" for party', *The Daily Telegraph*, 15 October, Available from: https://www.telegraph.co.uk/news/2016/10/15/ tory-revolt-over-heathrow-third-runway-as-60-mps-oppose-plans-an/ [Accessed 29 January, 2023].

Roberts, A. (2010) *The Logic of Discipline*, Oxford: Oxford University Press.

Roffrey, L. (2012) *Privileged Actors in Environmental Policymaking: The Historical Development of the Aviaiton Industry in the UK*, PhD Thesis, School of Environmental Sciences, University of East Anglia.

Rose, N. (1991) 'Governing by numbers: figuring out democracy', *Accounting, Organizations and Society*, 16(7): 673–92.

Rose, N. and Miller, P. (1992) 'Political power beyond the state: problematics of government', *British Journal of Sociology*, 43(2): 173–205.

Ross, G. and Young, M. (2007) *Proof of Evidence on Behalf of Stop Stansted Expansion: Economics Impact*, Doc. No. SSE/8/a, 30 April, Available from: https://stanstedairportwatch.com/wp-content/uploads/2020/07/ 8.-Economic-Impacts.pdf [Accessed 19 July, 2021].

Rough, E. (2011) 'Policy learning through public inquiries?', *Environment & Planning C*, 29(1): 24–45.

Royal Society (2023) Net zero aviation fuels: resource requirements and environmental impacts policy briefing, Available from: https://royalsociety. org/topics-policy/projects/low-carbon-energy-programme/net-zero- aviation-fuels/ [Accessed 2 March, 2023].

Runways UK (2014a) *Event guide, 16.01.14*, London: Runways UK.

Runways UK (2014b) 'Runways UK: A neutral platform for scheme debate', Available from: http://www.runwaysuk.com/ruk/about-runw ays-uk [Accessed 18 November, 2014].

Safe Landing (2020) 'FAQs: Economy', Available from: https://safe-land ing.org/faqs/, [Accessed 20 December, 2021].

Sauven, J. (2016) 'The decision to back a third runway at Heathrow is a grotesque folly', *The Guardian*, [online] 25 October, Available from: https:// www.theguardian.com/commentisfree/2016/oct/25/heathrow-third-run way-davies-commission [Accessed 25 November, 2021].

Schattschneider E.E. (1960) *The Semi-Sovereign People: A Realist's View of Democracy in America*, Chicago: Holt, Rinehart and Winston.

Schmitt, C. (2007) *The Concept of the Political: Expanded Edition*, Chicago: University of Chicago Press.

Schön, D.A. and Rein, M. (1994) *Frame Reflection: Toward the Resolution of Intractable Policy Controversies*, New York: Basic Books.

Scott, J.C. (1998) *Seeing Like a State*, New Haven, CT: Yale University Press.

Self, P. (1970) 'Nonsense on stilts: the futility of the Roskill Commission', *New Society*, 2 July, pp 8–11.

Self, P. (1975) *Econocrats and the Policy Process*, Macmillan: London.

Setzer, J. and Higham, C. (2021) *Global Trends in Climate Change Litigation: 2021 Snapshot*, London: Grantham Research Institute on Climate Change and the Environment and Centre for Climate Change Economics and Policy, London School of Economics and Political Science.

Sharman, F. (1975) 'A United Kingdom's view' in OECD (ed) *Airports and the Environment*, Paris: OECD, pp 43–50.

Shepsle, K.A. (2003) 'Losers in politics (and how they sometimes become winners): William Riker's heresthetic', *Perspectives on Politics*, 1(2): 307–15.

Siddique, H. (2022) 'Dramatic fall in successful High Court challenges to government policy', *The Guardian*, 23 June, Available from: https://www.theguardian.com/law/2022/jun/23/dramatic-fall-in-successful-high-court-challenges-to-government-policy [Accessed 28 August, 2022].

Siddique, H. and Phipps, C. (2016) 'Heathrow expansion: Zac Goldsmith to resign over third runway decision', *The Guardian*, 25 October, Available from: https://www.theguardian.com/politics/live/2016/oct/25/heathrow-gatwick-airport-expansion-decision-day-politics-live [Accessed 26 January, 2023].

Simpson, F. (2017) 'Heathrow airport expansion: campaigners fail in High Court runway battle', *Evening Standard*, 30 January, Available from: https://www.standard.co.uk/news/london/heathrow-airport-expansion-campaigners-fail-to-bring-high-court-challenge-against-third-runway-plans-a3453446.html [Accessed 6 February, 2023].

Skinner, Q. (2002) *Visions of Politics: Volume 1*, Cambridge: Cambridge University Press.

Slingo, J. (2021a) 'Heathrow protest barrister gears up for Supreme Court appeal', *Law Society Gazette*, [online] 15 October, Available from: https://www.lawgazette.co.uk/news/heathrow-protest-barrister-gears-up-for-supreme-court-appeal-/5110180 [Accessed 20 December, 2021].

Slingo, J. (2021b) 'Eco-barrister denies "publicity stunt" in Supreme Court appeal', *Law Society Gazette*, [online] 18 October, Available from: https://www.lawgazette.co.uk/news/eco-barrister-denies-publicity-stunt-in-supreme-court-appeal/5110201.article [Accessed 22 December, 2021].

Sohn-Rethel, A. (1970) *Intellectual and Manual Labour*, Atlantic Highlands, NJ: Hamanities Press.

Somerville, E. (2019) 'Extinction Rebellion Heathrow protest: activists stage "lie in" in front of pink "bulldozer"', *Evening Standard*, 8 December, Available from: https://www.standard.co.uk/news/uk/heathrow-extinction-rebellion-protest-latest-bulldozer-third-runway-a4308041.html [Accessed 4 February, 2023].

Soper, K. (2020) *Post-Growth Living*, London: Verso.

Stavrakakis, Y. (1999) *Lacan and the Political*, London: Routledge.

Stavrakakis, Y. (2007) *The Lacanian Left*, Edinburgh: Edinburgh University Press.

Stay Grounded (2019a) *Progressive Ticket Tax: Frequent Flyer Levy*, Available from: https://stay-grounded.org/wp-content/uploads/2019/04/progressive-ticket-tax-frequent-flyer-levy.pdf [Accessed 4 December, 2022].

Stay Grounded (2019b) *Degrowth of Aviation: Reducing Air Travel in a Just Way*, Available from: https://stay-grounded.org/report-degrowth-of-aviation/ [Accessed 10 September, 2021].

Stay Grounded (2021a) *A Rapid and Just Transition of Aviation: Shifting Towards Climate-Just Mobility*, Discussion paper, February, Available from: https://stay-grounded.org/wp-content/uploads/2021/01/SG_Just-Transition-Paper_2021.pdf [Accessed 21 October, 2021].

Stay Grounded (2021b) 'Frequent flyer programmes incentivise climate destruction', 11 August, Available from: https://stay-grounded.org/frequent-flyer-programmes-incentivise-climate-destruction/ [Accessed 24 October, 2021].

Stevenson, G.M. (1972) *The Politics of Airport Noise*, Belmont, CA: Duxbury Press.

Stewart, J. (2008) 'Royal opening of Terminal 5 "A sad day for residents"', HACAN [Blog], 13 March, Available from: hacan.org.uk/?p=1055 [Accessed 21 July, 2021].

Stewart, J. (2021) *Heathrow: From Pariah to Pioneer*, Available from: http://www.ukna.org.uk/uploads/4/1/4/5/41458009/heathrow_publication_august_2021.pdf [Accessed 12 December, 2021].

Stone, D. (2012) *Policy Paradox: The Art of Political Decision-Making*, 3rd edn, New York: W.W. Norton and Company.

Stone, D. (2020) *Counting*, New York: Liveright Publishing.

Stop Stansted Expansion (SSE) (2002a) 'Government fails to comply with its own code in air transport consultation', Press release, 23 September, Available from: https://stanstedairportwatch.com/press-releases/government-fails-to-comply-with-its-own-code-in-air-transport-consultation/ [Accessed 23 May, 2021].

SSE (2002b) 'Judicial review on airport consultation sought by Stansted' Press release, 24 October, Available from: https://stopstanstedexpansion.com/press-releases/judicial-review-on-airports-consultation-sought-by-stansted/ [Accessed 24 May, 2021].

SSE (2002c) 'Government withholding airport expansion documents', Press release, 29 October, Available from: https://stopstanstedexpansion.com/press-releases/government-withholding-airport-expansion-documents/ [Accessed 23 May 2021].

SSE (2007) *Opening Submission on Behalf of Stop Stansted Expansion, SSE/34*, Available from: https://stanstedairportwatch.com/wp-content/uploads/2020/07/SSE-Opening-Submission.pdf [Accessed 21 July, 2021].

SSE (2021) *Opening Submissions, 12 January 2021*, Available from: http://www.hwa.uk.com/site/wp-content/uploads/2020/10/SSE-Opening-Statement-Stansted-Inquiry-12.01.2021.pdf [Accessed 28 July, 2021].

Stratford, A. (1974) *Airports and the Environment*, New York: St. Martin's Press.

Sturge, D. and Day, G. (2021) 'How could the UK ETS be adapted and aligned with a market framework for zero carbon power?', *Catapult Energy Systems*, Available from: https://es.catapult.org.uk/comment/ukets-zero-carbon-power-part-2/ [Accessed 4 September, 2021].

Sun, X., Wandelt, S., Zheng, C. and Zhang, A. (2021) 'Covid-19 pandemic and air transportation', *Journal of Air Transport Management*, 94: 102062.

Supreme Court (2020a) *Judgment*, R (on the application of Friends of the Earth Ltd and others) (Respondents) v Heathrow Airport Ltd (Appellant) [2020] UKSC 52. On Appeal from: [2020] EWCA Civ 214, Press summary, 16 December, Available from: https://www.supremecourt.uk/cases/docs/uksc-2020-0042-press-summary.pdf [Accessed 26 November, 2021].

Supreme Court (2020b) *Judgment*, R (on the application of Friends of the Earth Ltd and others) (Respondents) v Heathrow Airport Ltd (Appellant), 16 December, Available from: https://www.supremecourt.uk/cases/docs/uksc-2020-0042-judgment.pdf [Accessed 26 November, 2021].

Sustainable Aviation (2020) *Decarbonisation Road-Map: A Path to Net Zero*, London: Sustainable Aviation.

Swyngedouw, E. (2014) 'Where is the political?', *Space and Polity*, 18(2): 122–36.

SYSTRA (2015) *Analysis of the Airports Commission's Consultation Responses*, Available from: https://assets.publishing.service.gov.uk/government/uploads/system/uploads/attachment_data/file/438143/analysis-of-the-airports-commission_s-consultation-responses.pdf [Accessed 11 December, 2021].

Taylor, M. and Gayle, D. (2019) 'Thousands block roads in Extinction Rebellion protests across London', *The Guardian*, 15 April, Available from: https://www.theguardian.com/environment/2019/apr/15/thousands-expected-in-london-for-extinction-rebellion-protest [Accessed 4 February, 2023].

Thomas, N. (2013) 'Airports Commission member faces calls for resignation', *The Daily Telegraph*, 27 July, Available from: https://www.telegraph.co.uk/finance/newsbysector/transport/10206662/Airports-Commission-member-faces-calls-for-resignation.html [Accessed 28 December, 2022].

Topham, G. (2015) 'Heathrow and Gatwick expansion: residents campaign, parties stay silent', *The Guardian*, 5 May, Available from: https://www.theguardian.com/politics/2015/may/05/heathrow-and-gatwick-expansion-election-decision-transport-environment [Accessed 1 January, 2023].

Topham, G. (2016) 'Heathrow promises immediate boost after runway go-ahead', *The Guardian*, 25 October, Available from: https://www.theguardian.com/environment/2016/oct/25/heathrow-promises-immediate-boost-expansion-contracts-imminent [Accessed 2 January, 2022].

Topham, G. (2021a) 'UK airlines warn of job losses as they lose business to Brexit', *The Guardian*, 14 February, Available from: https://www.theguardian.com/business/2021/feb/14/uk-airlines-warn-of-job-losses-as-they-lose-business-to-brexit [Accessed 4 February, 2023].

Topham, G. (2021b) 'BA owner IAG to increase flights but losses hit €2bn', *The Guardian*, 30 July, Available from: https://www.theguardian.com/business/2021/jul/30/ba-owner-iag-to-increase-flights-but-losses-hit-2bn [Accessed 25 August, 2022].

Transport Committee (2014) 'Sir Howard Davies giving evidence to the Transport Committee', 20 January, Available from: https://www.parliamentlive.tv/Event/Index/83bf7f78-abdd-4ed5-a0d0-29403c8b2d5f [Accessed 11 December, 2021].

Transport Committee (2018) *Airports National Policy Statement*, HC 548, London: HoC.

Transport Committee (2020) *The Impact of the Coronavirus Pandemic on the Aviation Sector*, HC 268, London: HoC.

Transport Committee (2021) 'Airlines and airports: supporting the recovery of the UK aviation sector', Oral evidence session, 21 September, Available from: http://committees.parliament.uk/oralevidence/2776/html/ [Accessed 16 December, 2021].

Transport & Environment (2021a) *Corsia: Worst Option for the Climate*, March, Available from: https://www.transportenvironment.org/sites/te/files/publications/2021_03_Briefing_Corsia_EU_assessement_2021.pdf [Accessed 4 September, 2021].

Transport & Environment (2021b) 'Aviation tax consultation: Transport & Environment response', Available from: https://www.transportenvironment.org/sites/te/files/publications/2021_06_Aviation_tax_consultation_TE_response.pdf [Accessed 17 December, 2021].

Transport & Environment (2021c) 'Private jets: can the super-rich supercharge zero-emissions aviation', Available from: https://www.trans portenvironment.org/discover/private-jets-can-the-super-rich-supercha rge-zero-emission-aviation/ [Accessed 8 August, 2022].

Transport & Environment (2022) *UK ETS: Broken But Fixable*, Available from: https://www.transportenvironment.org/wp-content/uploads/2022/06/UK-ETS-Briefing.pdf [Accessed 8 August, 2022].

Transport for London (2013) *Airports Commission Discussion Paper 01: Aviation Demand Forecasting. The Mayor of London's Response*, Available from: http://content.tfl.gov.uk/airport-commission-discussion-paper-01-demand.pdf [Accessed 22 May, 2021].

Triantafillou, P. (2012) *New Forms of Governing*, London: Palgrave Macmillan.

Tyers, R. (2020) 'People want to avoid flight shame without actually avoiding flights', *The Independent*, 13 February.

Tyers, R. (2022) *Regional Airports: Research Briefing*, 5 April, London: House of Commons Library.

UK FIRES (2019) *Absolute Zero 2050*, Cambridge: Cambridge University.

Upham, P. (2003) 'Climate change and planning and consultation for the UK aviation white paper', *Journal of Environmental Planning and Management*, 46(6): 911–18.

Valentine, J. (2013) 'Opening remarks' in Westminster Energy, Environment & Transport Forum. A Fresh Look at UK Airport Capacity: Time for a 3rd Runway at Heathrow? 31 January, transcripts, London: Westminster Energy, Environment & Transport, p 6.

Vernon, J. (2021) 'Heathrow and the making of neoliberal Britain', *Past & Present*, 252(1): 213–47.

Wallis, J. and Brodtkorb, T. (2020) 'The leadership legacy of commission chairs', *Canadian Public Policy*, 46(2): 290–303.

Walls, H. (2018) 'Wicked problems and a "wicked" solution', *Globalization and Health*, 14(34), DOI: 10.1186/s12992-018-0353-x

Ward, J. (2021) 'Reasserting the centre: the Brexit doctrine and the imperative mandate in British politics', *Parliamentary Affairs*, 74(4): 890–910.

Waters, B. (1971) 'Planning by commission', *Official Architecture and Planning*, 34(3): 202–5.

Watt, N. and Wintour, P. (2014) 'Blow to Nick Clegg as Lib Dems defy leadership over airport expansion', *The Guardian*, 7 October, Available from: https://www.theguardian.com/politics/2014/oct/07/liberal-democrats-airport-runways-pledge [Accessed 31 December, 2022].

Watts, J. (2021) 'Head of Independent Sage to launch international climate change group', *The Guardian*, 20 June, Available from: https://www.theguardian.com/science/2021/jun/20/head-of-independent-sage-to-launch-international-climate-change-group [Accessed 25 August, 2022].

Widdicombe QC, D. (1978) 'Foreword' in J. Tyme, *Motorways versus Democracy*, London and Basingstoke: Macmillan Press, pp vii–vii.

Williams, C. and McKenna, C. (1998) 'The Heathrow Terminal 5 Inquiry', *CMS Law-Now*, 17 April, Available from: www.cms-lawnow.com/eale rts/1998/04/the-heathrow-terminal-5-inquiry-why-it-has-taken-so-long-and-the-importance-of-a-fifth-terminal?sc_lang=en [Accessed 19 July, 2021].

Wilson, J. (1980) 'The politics of regulation', in J. Wilson (ed) *The Politics of Regulation*, New York: Basic Books, pp 357–95.

Winnett, R. (2012) 'Nich Clegg threatens to veto "unviable" vision of a new airportin the Thames Estuary', *The Daily Telegraph*, 19 January, Available from: https://www.telegraph.co.uk/travel/news/Nick-Clegg-threatens-to-veto-unviable-vision-of-a-new-airport-in-the-Thames-Estuary [Accessed 29 December, 2022].

Wintour, P. (2014) 'Heathrow critics and supporters unite to call for airport noise ombudsman', *The Guardian*, 10 March, Available from: https://www.theguardian.com/world/2014/mar/10/heathrow-critics-supporters-independent-ombudsman-airport-noise [Accessed 1 January, 2023].

Wood, F. (2021) 'The cult of the quantifiable', *Prometheus*, 37(1): 8–26.

Wood, M. and Flinders, M. (2014) 'Rethinking depoliticisation: beyond the governmental', *Policy & Politics*, 42(2): 151–70.

World Bank (2020) 'Air transport, passengers carried', Available from: https://data.worldbank.org/indicator/IS.AIR.PSGR [Accessed 22 December, 2022].

Wraith, R. (1966) 'The public inquiry into Stansted Airport', *The Political Quarterly*, 37(5): 265–80.

Wurzel, R. (2002) *Environmental Policy-Making in Britain, Germany and the European Union*, Manchester: Manchester University Press.

Xie, Q. and Baynes, C. (2020) 'Heathrow expansion blocked by Court of Appeal in a victory for climate campaigners', *The Independent*, 27 February, Available from: https://www.independent.co.uk/climate-change/news/heathrow-expansion-court-of-appeal-ruling-boris-johnson-third-runway-a9362581.html [Accessed 29 December, 2022].

Young, M. (2020) 'Capital, class and the social necessity of passenger air transport', *Progress in Human Geography*, 44(5): 938–58.

Žižek, S. (1989) *The Sublime Object of Ideology*, London: Verso.

Žižek, S. (1990) 'Eastern Europe's Republics of Gilead', *New Left Review*, 183: 50–62.

Žižek, S. (1994) 'The spectre of ideology', in S. Žižek (ed), *Mapping Ideology*, London: Verso pp 1–33.

Žižek, S. (1997) *Plague of Fantasies*, London: Verso.

Žižek, S. (2006) 'Against the populist temptation', *Critical Inquiry*, 32(3): 551–74.

Index

References to figures appear in *italic* type;
those in **bold** type refer to tables. References to endnotes show
page number, note number and (where appropriate) chapter number (204n1[c1]).

G

H